Full Tables, Closed Doors, Open Fields

# Full Tables, Closed Doors, Open Fields

The Changing Shape of Grace as American Methodists Move from Immigrant Society to Indigenous Church

by STEVEN DAVID BRUNS

◥PICKWICK *Publications* • Eugene, Oregon

FULL TABLES, CLOSED DOORS, OPEN FIELDS
The Changing Shape of Grace as American Methodists Move from Immigrant Society to Indigenous Church

Copyright © 2018 Steven David Bruns. All rights reserved. Except for brief quotations in critical publications or reviews, no part of this book may be reproduced in any manner without prior written permission from the publisher. Write: Permissions, Wipf and Stock Publishers, 199 W. 8th Ave., Suite 3, Eugene, OR 97401.

Pickwick Publications
An Imprint of Wipf and Stock Publishers
199 W. 8th Ave., Suite 3
Eugene, OR 97401

www.wipfandstock.com

PAPERBACK ISBN: 978-1-5326-1474-3
HARDCOVER ISBN: 978-1-5326-1476-7
EBOOK ISBN: 978-1-5326-1475-0

*Cataloguing-in-Publication data:*

Names: Bruns, Steven David, author.

Title: Full tables, closed doors, open fields : the changing shape of grace as American Methodists move from immigrant society to indigenous church / Steven David Bruns.

Description: Eugene, OR : Pickwick Publications, 2018 | **Includes bibliographical references.**

Identifiers: ISBN 978-1-5326-1474-3 (paperback) | ISBN 978-1-5326-1476-7 (hardcover) | ISBN 978-1-5326-1475-0 (ebook)

Subjects: LCSH: Methodist Church—History—18th century. | Methodist Church—United States—History—18th century. | Methodist Church—United States—Liturgy. | Lord's Supper—History of doctrines. | United States—Church history—18th century.

Classification: BX8236 .B78 2018 (paperback) | BX8236 .B78 (ebook)

Manufactured in the U.S.A.  05/09/18

For my wife, Pamela, who always knew.

# Contents

*Abbreviations* | ix
*Introduction* | xi

## Section I—Background

Chapter 1
Survey of English Eucharistic Theology | 3

Chapter 2
Survey of American Colonial Eucharistic Theology | 13

## Section II—Wesley's Methodism

Chapter 3
Wesley's Eucharistic Theology through Aldersgate | 23

Chapter 4
Wesley's Eucharistic Theology after Aldersgate | 35

Chapter 5
Full Tables of Methodism | 52

## Section III—American Methodism: Immigrant Society

Chapter 6
Eucharistic Tensions Prior to 1784 | 67

Chapter 7
American Methodist Leadership | 78

Chapter 8
Sacramental Schism: Flauvanna 1779 | 90

Chapter 9
Healing the Schism | 108

**Section IV—American Methodism: Indigenous Church**

Chapter 10
1784 and the Indigenous Church | 125

Chapter 11
1784 and the Sacraments | 136

Chapter 12
On the Defensive | 150

Chapter 13
Closed Doors | 165

Chapter 14
Open Fields | 176

*Conclusion* | 191

Appendix A
Eucharistic References in John Wesley's Works (Jackson) | 197

Appendix B
American Methodist Membership by Circuit | 199

Appendix C
Francis Asbury's Eucharistic Celebrations 1785–1800: As Recorded in His Journal | 201

*Bibliography* | 209

# Abbreviations

*1798 Discipline*  *The Doctrines and Disciplines of the Methodist Episcopal Church in America with Explanatory Notes by Thomas Coke and Francis Asbury*. Philadelphia: Henry Tuckniss, 1798. Reprint ed., Frederick A. Norwood, Garrett-Evangelical Theological Seminary, 1979.

*Disciplines*  *Methodist Disciplines 1785–1789*. Library of Methodist Classics. Nashville: United Methodist Publishing House, 1992.

*HLS*  Charles Wesley, *Hymns on the Lord's Supper*. Bristol: Felix Farley, 1745. Facsimile. Madison, NJ: Charles Wesley Society, 1995.

*JLFA*  *The Journal and Letters of Francis Asbury*. Edited by Elmer T. Clark. Nashville: Abingdon, 1958.

*Minutes*  *Minutes of the Methodist Conferences Annually Held in America from 1773 to 1813 Inclusive*. New York: Daniel Hitt and Thomas Ware, Publishers, 1813. Reprint ed., Swainsboro, GA: Magnolia, 1983.

*Works*  *The Bicentennial Edition of the Works of John Wesley*. General eds., Frank Baker and Richard P. Heitzenrater. Nashville: Abingdon, 1976–.

*Works* (Jackson)  *The Works of John Wesley*. Edited by Thomas Jackson. 14 vols. 3rd ed. London: Wesleyan Methodist Book Room, 1872. Reprinted, Grand Rapids: Baker, 2002.

# Introduction

As the Church progresses further into the twenty-first century, many groups within it from across the liturgical spectrum have been seeking out what has commonly been referred to as the "smells and bells" of liturgical worship and its co-equal emphasis upon the sacraments. Robert Webber coined the term "Ancient-Future worship" to describe this movement decades ago. It is a form of worship that seeks to fuse liturgy with contemporary worship passion and energy, and it has been extremely sacramental in nature, wanting to transcend the mundane events of everyday of life in an attempt to touch the Divine. Webber wrote

> In almost every evangelical college and seminary in North America, students who have been put off by culturally driven, programmed worship are experimenting with ancient worship . . . This recovery of ancient practices is not the mere restoration of ritual but a deep, profound, and passionate engagement with truth—truth that forms and shapes the spiritual life into a Christlikeness that issues forth in the call to a godly and holy life and into a deep commitment to justice and to the needs of the poor.[1]

This interest in sacramental worship for the Wesleyan Methodist tradition is not simply a fad of the postmodern mindset. Rather, the sacraments were central to the piety and theology of Methodism's founder, John Wesley. Wesley's revival in eighteenth-century England held together a high value of the sacraments with a personal experience of salvation. As this revival movement spread, Wesley's synthesis of sacraments and experience was introduced to countless numbers of souls yearning for something more in Europe, America, and beyond. It created a movement that resulted *full tables* for the Lord's Supper as people experienced the presence of Christ in a more complete and real way. It was precisely over the issue of the sacraments that

1. Webber, *Ancient-Future Worship*, 109.

Methodism in America became an indigenous Church—The Methodist Episcopal Church. And yet, even though the sacraments were a part of the legacy of John Wesley to his Methodists, unfortunately so too was the infrequency of receiving the sacraments a part of the legacy of the Methodist Episcopal Church to the various denominational descendants of the MEC today.

The question with which one is left, however, is this: If the Methodist Episcopal Church was created to provide for the reception of the sacraments to its members in the newly created United States of America, how did this denomination pass on a legacy of infrequent reception of the Lord's Supper? How is it that a Church's *raison d'être* can be to provide for the sacraments, and then their provision be apparently so neglected to the point where, two hundred years later, the heirs of that Church feel the need to recapture a sacramental form of worship within its respective congregations? How did American Methodists lose the full tables for which Methodism was famous?

From a cursory reading of the history of the Methodists in America, it becomes obvious that this convoluted position of the sacraments significantly predates the formation of any of the current Wesleyan denominations, and even the formation of the Methodist Episcopal Church in 1784. In fact, one must go back to the beginning of the Methodist movement in America to see how this problem arose prior to the formation of any Methodist related denomination in the United States. By all accounts, John Wesley, the principal founder of the Methodist movement, authorized the creation of an independent Methodist Episcopal Church in America in 1784 because of a dearth of ordained Anglican priests sympathetic to Methodism by which the American Methodists could receive the sacraments. While being a strict supporter of the Church of England and never advocating a separation from that national Church, the issue of the sacraments and their unavailability in America took Mr. Wesley into a new direction. "Here, therefore, my scruples are at an end,"[2] wrote Wesley to the American Methodists in explaining his decision to break with "the established order of the national Church to which I belong."[3] In breaking with that order, Wesley ordained two of his lay preachers, Richard Whatcoat and Thomas Vasey. He also set apart Dr. Thomas Coke, already ordained within the Church of England, as a superintendent (later to be renamed a bishop) with the authority to ordain even more of the lay preachers in America, for ordination in Wesley's understanding meant access to the sacraments. Wesley also sent instructions with these three men that, among other things pertinent to the creation of

---

2. Wesley, *Works* (Jackson), 13.252.
3. Ibid.

a new Church, Francis Asbury was to be ordained to the position of joint superintendent with Dr. Coke.

Wesley had to convince himself that he was perfectly within his right to ordain, even though he was not a bishop. The reason a bit of self-convincing was necessary was because Wesley believed, according to the "established order" of the Anglican Church, that only one who is properly ordained can be authorized to administer the sacraments. Robert Tuttle stated that "Wesley had reached an impasse. He was still determined that lay preachers should not serve the sacraments. If Methodism was to survive, therefore, he felt compelled to ordain one who could then ordain others in America."[4] Through his studies on the issue Wesley came to see himself in the line of bishops in the New Testament and early Church. He saw his actions in leading the Methodist societies in England, Scotland, Ireland, and America as having an Episcopal nature to it, save only the action of ordination. Being convinced that his position was, in practice, Episcopal, he only needed the extreme situation of the almost total lack of ordained clergy in America to take his thoughts to their logical conclusion and convince himself that it was the right course of action to ordain lay preachers for the Methodists in America. While he may have convinced himself of that fact, he was not able to convince many others within the Anglican Church including his own brother, Charles.[5]

In America, the issue of the sacraments had been one of contention for years. Robert Strawbridge, one of the first active Methodists in America, began his ministry administering the sacraments even though he was a lay preacher. Quarterly conferences and annual conferences repeatedly addressed the issue of whether or not Methodist preachers ought to have the right to administer the sacraments. One annual conference even allowed its preachers to administer the sacraments, but then that decision was rescinded one year later. Time and again, the Methodists in America were talking about, debating, or administering the sacraments from the 1760s to the Christmas Conference of 1784, which created the Methodist Episcopal Church. The frustration was, as Kenneth Kinghorn stated, "These preachers believed that God had called them to a full ministry that included the proclamation of God's word *and* the administration of the sacraments."[6]

While Wesley took a monumental, and much debated, step in seeking to provide the American Methodists access to the sacraments, and amidst all the debates surrounding the sacraments in America, it would nevertheless

---

4. Tuttle, *On Giant Shoulders*, 43.
5. Norwood, *American Methodism*, 97.
6. Kinghorn, *Heritage of American Methodism*, 42, emphasis included.

seem that the American Methodists did not attach the same weight to the sacraments as Wesley did. The American Methodists in 1784 had the opportunity to ordain as many elders as they thought would be necessary to carry on the work of this newly created Methodist Episcopal Church. If ordination were a necessary step towards making an independent Church, and if ordination were necessary to administer the sacraments, it would be logical to conclude that these American Methodists would have thought about the frequency of reception of the sacraments in considering how many men to ordain at the founding of this new ecclesial body. The reason frequency of reception would have been a logical factor in the number of ordinations is precisely because those who were ordained were itinerant, and therefore not always present with a particular congregation. The more ordained itinerants there were, the more frequently an ordained itinerant could be with any given congregation to celebrate the sacraments and have those full tables.

Across the Atlantic, Wesley's ideal for frequency of reception of the Lord's Supper was weekly. There are numerous instances within the Wesley corpus that attest to his view. One prominent instance is found in the *Directions Given to the Band-Societies* in which Wesley states that one of the duties of a Methodist is "To be at church and at the Lord's table every week."[7] Wesley's *The Duty of Constant Communion* (Sermon 101)[8] is another prime example of Wesley's piety and theology pressing the Methodists for more frequent Communion. Wesley's own instructions within his *Letter to Dr. Coke, Mr. Asbury, and Our Brethren in North America* also highlights this increased desire for access to the Lord's Supper, for in it he writes, "I also advise the Elders to administer the supper of the Lord on every Lord's day."[9] These instances are a few among many that will be investigated as this study progresses, and all definitely lead one to the conclusion that for John Wesley, the ideal frequency of reception of the sacrament of the Lord's Supper for his Methodists was, in fact, weekly. There has been just as much recent work pointing to the fact that, while Wesley may have desired weekly reception of the Lord's Supper, it simply was not a reality in eighteenth-century England.[10] What these scholars seem to neglect, however, is the impact Wesley's piety and theology had on the average Methodist. While Anglican clergy may have been reluctant to serve the Lord's Supper frequently, those that did serve it saw an increase in their congregational attendance, in large part

---

7. Wesley, *Works*, 9.79.
8. Ibid., 3.427–39.
9. Wesley, *Works* (Jackson), 13.252.
10. Lester Ruth, Karen Westerfield Tucker, and Russell Ritchie are among the most prominent of this line of reasoning.

due to Methodists crossing parish boundaries in order to receive the sacrament, and, ironically, creating one more opportunity for the establishment to complain that the Methodists were somehow abrogating the Church's established canons and procedures by crossing those parish boundaries.[11] In addition to these instances, there is still the example of the Bristol Society which, after much cajoling of John and Charles, finally got the Wesleys to concede to administering the Lord's Supper every other week at the society meeting,[12] which according to Methodism of the day (straight from John Wesley's leadership and direction) should not have happened since the Methodists in Bristol were members of a society *within* the Established Church, and it was to that Church that they ought to have gone for the sacrament. Whatever the situation in eighteenth century Anglicanism in regards to opportunities to receive the Lord's Supper, the Methodists wanted more.

It is at this point, then, on the eve of the Christmas Conference of 1784 that created the Methodist Episcopal Church that the American Methodists found themselves with a unique opportunity for ordination and administration of the sacraments clear of the Anglican patterns and frequency. Yes, they had been functioning for nearly twenty years on the North American continent, but they had never had the privilege of being "properly" ordained or having the authority to administer the sacraments.[13] Finally, this was the opportunity for one section of the Methodist movement to institute, if not Wesley's ideal for weekly reception of the Lord's Supper among its members, at least the obvious Methodist longing for more frequent reception of the Lord's Supper than three to four times per year, as was the average opportunity of reception in an average congregation of the Church of England.

The ecclesial framework the Methodist Episcopal Church created in December of 1784, however, led to the situation in which, by 1800 (just fifteen years after the founding of the new Church) it provided for the reception of the sacrament of the Lord's Supper quarterly at best. Only twelve men were ordained at the Christmas Conference, two of whom were designated to minister in Canada. That left ten men ordained at the Christmas Conference, plus Richard Whatcoat and Thomas Vasey (who were the two elders ordained by Wesley before they left England for America), Francis Asbury, and Thomas Coke (for a total of fourteen) who were authorized

11. Wesley, *Works*, 11.78–89, 11.185.
12. Ibid., 22.254–5.
13. As alluded to above, the American Methodists in the South had already tried a Presbyterian style of ordination in 1779, but became convinced by their Northern brethren that this form of polity was not compatible with Methodism. This will be investigated thoroughly in this study.

to administer the sacraments for the newly independent thirteen United States of America. These fourteen men were given the awesome responsibility of seeing that the entire Methodist Episcopal Church in America was adequately provided with the sacraments, a charge that included the entire Eastern seaboard of the United States of America over which nearly 15,000 members resided. In actuality, the number of available ordained men was thirteen since Dr. Coke spent most of his time commuting between England, the Bahamas and America. There was no discrepancy in this fact, though, because the American Methodists had experienced God's grace and Christ's presence in their meetings behind *closed doors*, their itinerant-led meetings. These instances highlighted the Love Feast and testimonials, along with the accountability of the Band meeting.

This change in emphasis has not gone unnoticed by pastors and scholars alike. Retired Bishop Timothy Whitaker stated

> Here in America Methodism is not renown [sic] as a Christian community that has a strong sacramental piety. Somehow the sacramental emphasis in the original British Methodism became muted in American Methodism. This loss of emphasis upon the sacraments in American Methodism is one of the ironies of American Methodist history. One of the primary reasons that American Methodists separated from the Episcopal Church and formed their own church was so that Methodists could have their own ordained ministers who would administer Holy Communion. (After the American Revolution there were few priests left in America, and therefore the Episcopalians, including the Methodists, were not able to receive the sacrament very often.) Yet the church that was established partly for the purpose of enabling the American Methodists to receive the sacraments evolved into a church that did not place as much emphasis upon the sacraments as Mr. Wesley had![14]

In order to analyze successfully how this shift occurred among the American Methodists in the early days of the movement, it will be necessary to place certain time limits on the research area. Since no one knows for certain when the first Methodists arrived to take up permanent residence in the New World (only that it was sometime in the decade between 1760 and 1770) the starting date will be set generally at 1760. The late-date limit of 1800 will be set for several reasons. In 1801 the first sizable camp meeting occurred in the Cumberland area of Kentucky. This event ushered in the era of camp meeting revivalism that spread through the Methodist Episcopal

---

14. Whitaker, "A Sacramental Piety."

Church during the nineteenth century. In short order, the camp meeting took over in importance from the quarterly meeting within American Methodism and the Methodist Episcopal Church adapted its ecclesiology, including its sacramental practice, to accommodate this new mode of worship, as now the *open fields* of the camp meeting became one of the central opportunities to encounter Christ. Also, beginning in the nineteenth century the American Methodists began looking to English theologians such as Adam Clarke and Richard Watson to guide them in interpreting the Wesleyan faith they inherited.[15] By limiting the study to the eighteenth century, it allows the investigation to focus on American piety, that piety's resultant theological decisions, and an ecclesiology that predated the commencement of camp meeting revivalism.

In order to trace the changing shape of the grace-filled experience in American Methodism from full tables to closed doors to open fields, it will be necessary to understand John Wesley's views of the Lord's Supper, he being the founder of the Methodist movement and having considerable influence over his spiritual children through his own theology and piety. Because Wesley was a man of his era, in order to understand John Wesley, a survey of the Anglican understanding of the sacrament in John Wesley's day will be necessary. From there it must be seen how Wesley accepted or adapted that Anglican understanding in his own Eucharistic theology and in the theology he passed on to his Methodist societies. Then it will be essential to witness and investigate the foundation of Methodist societies in America and how they interpreted and applied John Wesley's Eucharistic theology to their own particular situation and how it was lived out in their own Eucharistic piety. This part of the investigation will need to be divided into two main time periods: prior to the Christmas Conference of 1784 when Methodism was still an immigrant society and was forbidden to administer the sacraments due to its being a lay movement, and subsequent to the Christmas Conference when Methodism was an indigenous church. After analyzing these time periods in the life of the Methodist Episcopal Church, it will be possible to see the changes as they took place.

---

15. Chiles, *Transition*, 32–33.

# Section I
# Background

Chapter 1

# Survey of English Eucharistic Theology

THE CHURCH UNIVERSAL EXISTED for nearly 1700 years prior to John Wesley's birth, and the Eucharist had a central place in its life, spirituality, practice, thought, piety, theology and debates for that entire time. There are numerous references in the historical record, going back to the Book of Acts, detailing how the Sacrament of the Lord's Supper was celebrated as a central and frequent event in the life of the Church. This history and heritage was carried down through the ages in various forms, interpretations and practices within the sacramental life of the Church. Within the Church of England, due to its unique position regarding the Reformation (trying to balance a *via media* between Catholicism and Protestantism), there were representatives of differing theologies regarding the Eucharist. John Wesley, being a faithful Anglican priest, was shaped by these views and tried to pass on his own understanding to his theological children, the Methodists. Therefore, since John Wesley was the founder of the Methodist movement, and being a product of his day, it is necessary to have a working knowledge of differing Eucharistic theologies that were present in John Wesley's day and how the Church of England adopted or adapted them in its own theology before we can successfully analyze Methodism's particular understanding of the Eucharist.

The Church of England did not begin with so many theological disputes as those of Reformation bodies in continental Europe did. Instead, the Church found itself separated from Rome over an issue that would continue to resurface time and again: who is ultimately in control of a country and the Church within that country? At the Church of England's genesis, the debate was whether a political entity, Henry VIII, had authority over ecclesial matters within his dominions, or whether an ecclesial authority,

Pope Clement VII, had authority over civil matters within any dominion that was Christian.[1] There had been Protestant ideas and vernacular Bibles making their way into England prior to its separation from Rome in 1534, and there was a rise in national sentiment and consciousness, but the main point of contention was whether or not Henry could do as he wished to secure his own dynasty in the manner he chose. This was the primary cause of the separation of the English Church from Rome, but it was not without grumblings for reformation of the Church prior to the dissolution.

> When Henry VIII began his reign, the church in England was beset by many evident weaknesses, both in structure and in personnel. The prelates were, on the whole, royal servants, appointed for their dedication and usefulness to the crown . . . the "careerism" of the bishops and higher clergy—their search for advancement and enrichment through royal patronage and civil service—naturally fostered the abuses of pluralism, absenteeism, and simony, and, more dangerously still, left the parishes in the hands of poorly educated and usually impecunious curates.[2]

The issue of the Eucharist was a primary subject for debate in England during its reformation period. As Horton Davies stated, "one's Eucharistic beliefs were in many of the Tudor years literally a matter of life and death."[3] There seemed to be no one element of Christian worship as the Eucharist and Christ's presence or lack thereof that was so hotly debated in this entire period. And it was in this theological milieu that four differing understandings of the Eucharist existed in England. "These may be labeled in the most general fashion as: Transubstantiation; the Real Presence (sometimes affirmed as Consubstantiation, but occasionally without any theory, merely affirming the mystery of Christ's corporal presence as an inexplicable mystery); Virtualism; and Memorialism."[4] Each of these Eucharistic theologies (which are described below) are ultimately defined in their concurrence or divergence from the Roman Catholic Church's doctrine of transubstantiation. Timothy Ware, in his *The Orthodox Church*, quotes a letter written by Alexis Khomiakov in 1846 to one of his English friends illustrating this point by writing, "All Protestants are Crypto-Papists . . . To

---

1. This is a very simple statement regarding complicated political and ecclesial interests and motives during the sixteenth century between Rome, England, France, and the German States (Holy Roman Empire). A decent overview of this situation can be found in Grimm's *The Reformation Era 1500–1650*, 289–98.
2. Walker, *History*, 481.
3. Davies, *Worship*, 1.77.
4. Ibid., 1.80.

use the concise language of algebra, all the West knows but one datum $a$; whether it be preceded by the positive sign +, as with the Romanists, or with the negative -, as with the Protestants, the $a$ remains the same."[5] The doctrine of transubstantiation that was present in England was the complete, Tridintine formulation that

> [B]y the consecration of the bread and wine there takes place a change of the whole substance of bread into the substance of the body of Christ our Lord and of the whole substance of wine into the substance of his blood. This change the holy Catholic Church has fittingly and properly named transubstantiation.[6]

In addition to the concept of transubstantiation was the Roman Catholic understanding of concomitance, the doctrine that the whole of Christ's body and blood are found in either of the consecrated Eucharistic elements. In other words, the body and blood of Christ are present in the bread, and likewise both are present in the cup. It was this understanding of the Eucharistic elements that justified the development of withholding the cup from the laity. This led to the practice of receiving the Eucharist in "one kind" that was so prevalent, and such a source of contention for the Reformers.[7]

Real Presence as a theological concept could be most fully identified with Martin Luther's understanding of the sacrament. Luther did not reject Christ's presence in the elements because God is omnipresent, so by definition, Christ (being God) necessarily had to be present in the communion elements. This was Luther's appeal to the ubiquity of Christ, not only in a spiritual sense as God, but also in his physical and ascended body by virtue

---

5. Ware, *Orthodox Church*, 1.

6. O'Collins and Farrugia, *Catholicism*, 262–63. This concept had grown out of statements from Patristic sources. Among them are Justin Martyr, "So likewise have we been taught that the food which is blessed by the prayer of His word, and from which our blood and flesh by transmutation are nourished, is the flesh and blood of that Jesus who was made flesh" (Justin Martyr, *First Apology* in Coxe, Roberts, and Donaldson, *Apostolic Fathers*, 1.85). As well there is Irenaeus of Lyon, "For as the bread, which is produced from the earth, when it receives the invocation of God, is no longer common bread, but the Eucharist, consisting of two realities, earthly and heavenly" (Irenaeus, *Against Heresies*, in ibid., 1.486). Statements such as these were then mediated through the debate between Paschaius Radbertus and Ratramnus of Corbie in the ninth century (See Louth, *Greek East and Latin West*, 147). Then this was further explicated by Thomas Aquinas' statement that "the words of consecration bring a change in the 'substance' of the bread and wine, while the 'accidents' (the secondary characteristics that do not belong essentially to the substance) remain." O'Collins and Farrugia, *Catholicism*, 262. This position led to the conclusion that each Mass was a re-sacrifice of Christ on behalf of the people.

7. Walker, *History*, 345.

of the two natures (God and man) joined together. It was this point that he made so forcefully when recounting his debates with Huldrych Zwingli concerning the nature of the sacrament. Luther wrote in *Confession Concerning Christ's Supper* (1528):

> Again, since they [Zwinglians] do not prove that the right hand of God is a particular place in heaven, the mode of existence of which I have spoken also stands firm, that Christ's body is everywhere because it is at the right hand of God which is everywhere, although we do not know how that occurs. For we also do not know how it occurs that the right hand of God is everywhere. It is certainly not the mode by which we see with our eyes that an object is somewhere, as the fanatics regard the sacrament. But God no doubt has a mode by which it can be somewhere and that's the way it is until the fanatics prove the contrary.[8]

Virtualism is equated with John Calvin's assertion that Christ is spiritually present in the Eucharist even as his body is enthroned in heaven. This is not to be understood, however, in the sense of "virtual reality" in which Christ is present in some imaginary sense. Rather virtualism is the understanding that all the virtues of Christ's presence are to be had within the sacrament itself. Thus, Daniel Stevick noted in *The Altar's Fire*, "Rejecting scholastic terms of 'substance,' and using biblical categories, Calvin taught that in the sacrament, Christ, by the Holy Spirit, is immediately present to the believer."[9] This position is then corroborated by a statement from Calvin himself. "The virtue of the Holy Spirit is joined to the sacraments when they are duly received."[10] Calvin walked a fine line between both Zwinglian understanding and Lutheran understanding on this point. To counter Zwingli he wrote, "For unless a man means to call God a deceiver, he would never dare assert that an empty symbol is set forth by him."[11] And to counter Luther and his argument that because of the ubiquity of Christ's body Christ is necessarily present in the Eucharist, Calvin wrote, "They [Lutherans] would therefore like to have the body of Christ considered invisible and immeasurable, so as to lie hidden under bread."[12] Instead, Calvin promoted the concept of Christ being spiritually present in communion, actually being present in spirit but physically remaining at the right hand of God

---

8. Luther, *Theological Writings*, 382–83.
9. Stevick, *The Altar's Fire*, 10.
10. Calvin, "Holy Supper," 149.
11. Calvin, *Institutes*, 21.1371.
12. Ibid., 21.1379.

the Father enthroned in heaven. It is through the sacrament, then, that the believer is spiritually elevated to Christ's presence in heaven. Calvin's own words to this effect are thus

> But if we are lifted up to heaven with our eyes and minds, to seek Christ there in the glory of his Kingdom, as the symbols invite us to him in his wholeness, so under the symbol of bread we shall be fed by his body, under the symbol of wine we shall separately drink his blood, to enjoy him at last in his wholeness ... In short, he feeds his people with his own body, the communion of which he bestows upon them by the power of his Spirit. In this manner, the body and blood of Christ are shown to us in the Sacrament.[13]

Memorialism is Zwingli's assertion that the Lord's Supper is a memorial act only and there is neither the presence of Christ nor grace conferred in the sacrament. Zwingli, ever logical and the product of his humanist studies, believed that it was impossible for Christ to be ascended into heaven in body and be physically present in every instance of communion from the dawn of the Church until his present day. In commenting upon this aspect of Zwingli's theology, Potter pointed out that, in Zwingli's introduction to Bible Study in 1523, Zwingli made clear "Immortality was assumed; therefore, all people desire salvation, which means an eternal life with God for the soul, which is so much more than the body with which it is fused in this earthly life."[14] It was with this understanding, then, of the material world acting as an obstacle of the spiritual reality of God, Zwingli concluded the Eucharist was a memorial, merely a remembrance of Christ's sacrifice and death and that Christ could not be present in the material elements.

As these views ebbed and flowed in the theological development of the Church of England, the official position advocated by the Church was one of latitude. Bainton defines this as *comprehension* and explains it thus:

> Only one religion is recognized in a given territory but in order to reduce emigration the attempt is made to satisfy as many as possible by making only minimal demands. The doctrinal and liturgical requirements are whittled down to such slenderness that only the ultra-scrupulous will decline conformity and the way of assent is further facilitated because the necessary tenets

---

13. Ibid., 21.1381.

14. Potter, *Zwingli*, 87. This position was further upheld by Zwingli in having the debate upon the matter of the Eucharist revolve around the definition of "is." As Potter noted, "There [in the Eucharist] Zwingli now insisted, the operative word was the verb, *is*; and *is* was used in the sense of signifies" (157).

are so clothed in a garment of ambiguity that each can place upon them his own construction in a spirit of latitude.[15]

It is in this spirit of comprehension that Thomas Cranmer left the language of the Lord's Supper as vague as possible so it could be interpreted to support or deny transubstantiation. He did so when he compiled the *Book of Common Prayer* during Edward VI's reign (1547–1553) in an effort to avoid much of the fighting that had occurred on the continent over this very issue, and as a result of his own transformation and development of theological understanding of the Eucharist.[16]

After the break with Rome, Protestant theology entered more explicitly into England, created new movements, and caused great debates, many times resorting to violence, concerning the nature of the Church, the sacraments, worship, and the relationship of the Church and the state. Part of the confusion during this time and following was the policy of Henry's that the Church change virtually nothing in its functions or theology save the identity of its head: "Catholic in its theology, yet autonomous from Rome."[17] After this, reformation and continental reformation ideals under the reign of Edward VI went forward and induced changes in key aspects of Church life such as imagery in worship, the place of the saints, clerical celibacy, and the Eucharist. Soon, though, Catholicism was restored under Queen Mary (1553–1558), and Protestantism was then reasserted under Queen Elizabeth (1558–1603). Nevertheless, the spirit of comprehension was firmly in place by the end of Elizabeth's reign and up to this point, although Protestants and Catholics had been executed under opposing monarchs, England had been spared the outright religious warfare that had been seen on the continent. This was about to change.

Among the most influential of these new movements were a disjointed group of clergy "called 'Precisionists' because they determined to be 'precise' in following the mandates of the Bible, but the label that stuck lastingly was 'Puritans.'"[18] Puritans were "determined to rid religion in England of all its 'popish remnants, thereby making it 'pure.'"[19] It should not be implied, though, that the Puritans were a cohesive group with identical ideals, goals and theology. At their beginning, in the 1560s, they were an amorphous grouping of different movements who all agreed that the influence of Rome and traditional worship must end. As Hillerbrand has stated

15. Bainton, *Reformation*, 143.
16. Davies, *Worship*, 1.111–20
17. Hillerbrand, *Division*, 232.
18. Ibid., 256.
19. Ibid.

> "Puritanism" as it emerged in the second half of the sixteenth century and "Puritanism" as it characterized the English scene in the seventeenth century differed significantly. The former ... was devoid of the sectarian propensity (most sixteenth-century Puritans wanted only to reform the established church and did not consider leaving the established church). At issue were issues of biblical interpretation and worship ... Nor did sixteenth-century Puritanism have the political involvement it was to have in the seventeenth century.[20]

Later, at the start of the reign of James I (1603–1625), the Puritans objected and debated peacefully, if vociferously with the king and the Established Church. Following the early years of James' reign, many ecclesial canons were enacted that defended and supported the Episcopal form of church governance, to the extent of even declaring that "episcopal hierarchy was an institution of divine origin, and that without it there could be no true church," much to the disappointment of the Puritans who saw this as a rejection of the congregational polity of several Protestant churches on the European Continent, and therefore a potential method for reintroducing Catholicism in England.[21] Yet within the Puritan disappointment revolt was not a foregone conclusion. The peace of the English Church with respect to the Puritans endured to the extent that James continued his "conscious policy not to force conformity or conscientious issues."[22]

With the advent of the reign of Charles I (1625–1649), the Puritans had reached their limit of verbal objections. From the onset of his reign Charles had problems with the Puritans. He was much more formal in his approach to worship than James had been, which looked too familiar to Catholicism to many.[23] As well, Charles seems to have feared Puritanism from the beginning of his reign. "The royal fear of Puritanism was at its heart a dread of disorder, disunity, and the contamination of 'popularity.'"[24] Then the measures put in place by William Laud, also a supporter of high liturgy and a proponent of uniformity of worship, further enraged the Puritans. Laud was a student of the Patristics and the Eastern Church. As such, he had an "emphasis on the sacraments and the institutional Church" that did not accommodate the Puritans' more Zwinglian or Calvinistic theology.[25] Since

20. Ibid.
21. Davies, *Worship*, 2.152.
22. Davies, *Caroline Captivity*, 10.
23. Ibid., 20.
24. Ibid., 13.
25. Ibid., 54.

many, if not most, of the English loved what had become traditional Church of England worship over the previous nearly seventy years with ministers instead of priests, communion tables instead of altars fixed against the wall, and the liberty to omit sections of the Book of Common Prayer's worship service, when Laud attempted to "correct" these problems, as his theology and ecclesiology prompted him to do, ecclesial peace was jeopardized. This is because Laud believed that there must be unity within the Church. "The emphasis which Laud placed on the visibility of the Church meant in effect that he could conceive of such a 'unity of communion' only through the uniformity of outward expression."[26] As the situation deteriorated, it plunged England into a civil war (actually three "separate" wars that raged from 1642–1651 with a few respites throughout) that pitted Puritans and their allies against Charles and his allies (mostly those who supported a high church view). This also pitted the Puritans' predominantly Zwinglian understanding of the Lord's Supper against the more Calvinistic (or Lutheran or even Catholic in some circles) understanding of the Eucharist as having a real presence of Christ within it. While the Puritans began their Eucharistic theology more in line with the high church Anglican view, their resultant theology was Zwinglian. Horton Davies explains thus

> There is a perpetual danger in Reformed churchmanship for a high Genevan evaluation of the Lord's Supper to deteriorate into a low Zurich diminishing of its value, as Calvin's theory and practice is replaced by Zwingli's. The Zwinglian interpretation is much less complex, therefore easier to understand than Calvin's, and to defend. This is to regard Communion as a sign of the Christian community's loyalty, and as a vivid illustration of Christ's love for His people; in a word it is a powerful mnemonic. Puritanism allowing its ministers with freedom to be inspired by the Holy Spirit in interpreting the Word of God, or equally to be inspired by the *Zeitgeist*, was unprotected in it Communion doctrine.[27]

The Puritans and their allies were temporarily successful in the English Civil War, which led to the creation of a Commonwealth and later a Protectorate under the leadership of Oliver Cromwell and, after his death in 1658, his son, Richard. Eventually the monarchy was restored in 1660, as was Anglican worship and the episcopacy. Along with this restoration was an understanding that the Church of England was to be united in worship according to the *Book of Common Prayer*. Many of the Puritans could not

26. Ibid., 61.
27. Davies, *Worship*, 2.323.

abide by the BCP and joined the ranks of Dissenters within England. Despite continued persecution by the Established Church, Dissenters were tolerated to exist (eventually) provided they did not interfere with the established Church. Dissent was given a legal status in 1689, but the prevailing view was the official Prayer Book version of Church and Church theology. This had the net effect, however, of preserving a High Church and Low Church division within the country. High Church worship, typified by Laud prior to the Commonwealth and Protectorate, retained much of the ceremonies and theology of the Roman Church, including its emphasis upon the sacraments as a part of ecclesial life. Low Church worship, typified by the Puritans (now transformed into Presbyterian and Congregational Churches as Dissenters or Nonconformists), dropped much of the ceremonies and liturgy of the Established Church, including its emphasis upon the sacraments as a part of ecclesial life.

It will be seen that, for much of John Wesley's life, the temptation against which he continually cautions his Methodists is to become Dissenters and leave the Church of England. One reason for this temptation is because the early Methodists were not constituted of a uniform group; there were both Church of England members and Dissenters. In America, the diversity was even greater as there was a much greater pool of Christian bodies from which the Methodists drew their members. This issue will be analyzed in depth; however, it is important here to note that the main reason Wesley had against separating was that his movement was a movement. The Methodists were to be agents of renewal within the Established Church, and as such, much of the Methodist life presupposed a context within that Church. Henry Knight, in his analysis of this dynamic, has noted

> To separate from the church was to either become a new church, thus losing the disciplined fellowship of a voluntary society, or to invite sectarian narrowness and experiential enthusiasm. To remain in the church was to retain the discipline and community necessary for faith in a present God without losing that which provides narrative and descriptive identity of the God who is present. The experience of God's identity forms and shapes the conversation in the class meeting, the language of extemporaneous prayer, and the practice of general means of grace. *The practices of the [Methodist] societies not only presuppose those of the church, they are pervaded by those of the church.*[28]

As the Methodists debated their place within the Established Church (or apart from it) in the later years of Wesley's life (and beyond), this interplay

---

28. Knight, *Presence of God*, 95, emphasis added.

between the two entities, an interplay that was not always recognized by those in the debate, would lead the English Methodists and the American Methodists down different paths in an attempt to find a resolution.

Chapter 2

# Survey of American Colonial Eucharistic Theology

THE SITUATION IN NORTH America from the beginning of European and English settlement to the time of the American Revolution was decidedly different from the Old World. In the first place, there was no one nation that was colonizing the New World, so there could be no one national Church. Second, even though England came to dominate the colonization of the North American eastern coast, significant populations of radical dissenters and radical Puritans settled in places like New England and Pennsylvania prior to the established Church having a strong presence on the continent, which made it impossible to impose religious uniformity on the colonists who settled there. Third, many of the colonists who came to the New World did so to escape religious hegemony across the Atlantic Ocean, the ones being in the majority in the Old World having no religious need to emigrate. These factors contributed to a much more diffuse religious climate in North America.

This is not to say that religion was unimportant in the New World—quite the contrary. Radical Puritans settled in Massachusetts and tried to establish a pure Christian community. Baptists settled in Rhode Island as a haven from Congregationalist persecution, and Roman Catholics settled Maryland for similar reasons. Quakers settled in Pennsylvania in an attempt to exercise their religion without fear of persecution. The reality of all these religious parties necessarily coexisting together was that most realized that it would be impossible to force participation or conformity to one particular sect. William Warren Sweet has noted

> In nine of the thirteen colonies there were established churches; the Congregational Church being established by law in Massachusetts, Connecticut and New Hampshire; while in Maryland, Virginia, North and South Carolina, Georgia and in a section of New York around New York City the English Church was established. Only in Rhode Island and the Quaker colonies— New Jersey, Pennsylvania, and Delaware—were there no state churches . . . But it must not be supposed that there was anything like complete uniformity in religion even in those colonies where there were established churches.[1]

To adequately understand the religious climate of the colonies, it will be necessary to examine the regions in question.

## THE NEW ENGLAND COLONIES

It was in the northern colonies of New England (Massachusetts, Connecticut, New Hampshire, and Rhode Island) that the Puritans and other Congregationalists had the most influence. Radical Puritans, finding life in England intolerable prior to the civil war and subsequent Commonwealth, left Old England for the New in the 1620s and 1630s. It was in this New World that those Puritan faithful could construct their holy society without any interference from the established State Church of England. They were free to form their governments and churches as they saw fit, and they did so modeled after Calvin's Geneva, thereby becoming the established Church for their new settlement.

To be a citizen in Massachusetts (of which the Plymouth colony, which had heretofore been independent, became a part in 1691) or Connecticut (of which New Haven became a part in 1662) or a member in one of its official churches, one had to be a Christian, one of the elect. To prove such a state, one had to have a conversion experience and live a regenerate lifestyle. Mark Noll, in his *A History of Christianity in the United States and Canada*, stated

> Almost as soon as they arrived, the Massachusetts ministers and magistrates agreed on a more visible measure of conversion than they had practiced in England. Now a new stress was placed on relating an experience of conversion as a prerequisite for full church membership. In the Old World, merely choosing to associate with the Puritans had set people apart; in the New World, it seemed necessary to encourage a higher standard.

---

1. Sweet, *Methodism*, 9.

Prospective members were expected to accept Puritan doctrines and live moral lives, but they were also expected to confess before their fellows that they had experienced God's saving grace.[2]

The sacraments were to be administered only to those who were members of the church already, or in the case of baptism of their children, as a seal and confirmation of the parents' conversion experience.

This plan did well for the first generation of Puritans, but created a conundrum for the next generation, "for the zeal of the founders was often not matched by their children and grandchildren."[3] As children who were baptized grew, married, and had children, they failed to have the most important milestone in Puritan life: the conversion experience. The problem became whether or not these adults who did not have a conversion experience or did not live the regenerate lifestyle could have their children baptized. Could their children be members of the church? Should they, parents and children, be allowed to participate in the Lord's Supper? The solution to this problem came to be called the Half-Way Covenant, which was placed in effect in 1662.[4] This new approach allowed the children of church members who did not have a conversion experience to become baptized members of the church, but not full members. As subsequent generations grew up under this plan, fewer and fewer people had those conversion experiences necessary for full membership in the church and, consequently, fewer and fewer people were allowed to receive the Lord's Supper, further reinforcing the distinction between the elect and everyone else.

Rhode Island became a different sort of colony than its neighbors, due to the work and ideas of Roger Williams. Williams saw absolutely no value for the Christian or the Church in attempting to combine religion and state. As a result, and because he would not keep his opinions quiet in Massachusetts where Church and State were intimately intertwined, he was expelled from the colony. Williams made his way to Rhode Island and founded the city of Providence. It was here that he made his most lasting contribution to American history. Noll recorded, "Roger Williams is known as America's greatest early 'democrat,' and that reputation is not entirely unjustified. Under his direction, Rhode Island became the first place in the North American colonies where freedom of religious worship was defined as a human right for all groups . . . It was also the first American colony to attempt a separation between the institutions of religion and the institutions

---

2. Noll, *History*, 42.
3. Walker, *History*, 575.
4. Noll, *History*, 48.

of the state."⁵ As a result of these developments in New England, Sweet has concluded, "New England presented the nearest approximation to uniformity [of religion in the colonies], but by the middle of the eighteenth century, Baptist, Anglican, Quaker, and Presbyterian congregations were to be found here and there in New England communities."⁶

## THE MIDDLE COLONIES

The situation in the Middle Colonies (New Jersey, New York, Delaware and Pennsylvania) was markedly different from New England. There was a large population of Dutch Reformed churches that were not independent and Congregationalist like New England, but Presbyterian in their governance. This is because much of this area was originally colonial holdings of the Dutch, and "for many years [after the Dutch surrender to the English in 1664] the Dutch Reformed Church continued to be the strongest religions body in the colony of New York."⁷ There was also a large population of Scots-Irish, who were likewise Presbyterian. These churches were Calvinistic in their theology as well as in their sacramental understanding. In addition to these groups, there was an Anglican presence, most notably in New York City, and a very large Quaker presence.

The Middle Colonies became a haven for the Quakers. Because of their leniency with respect to other sects, these colonies attracted other Christian groups precisely because the Quakers were present there. "In Pennsylvania, for instance, were to be found English Quakers, Welsh Baptists, and Scotch-Irish Presbyterians, besides Mennonites, Dunkers, German Reformed and German Lutherans."⁸ In Pennsylvania as well, there was also a presence of Moravians, whose primary concern was missions to the Native Americans.

With so many differing expressions of the Christian faith, it was nearly impossible for any one group or interpretation of the sacraments to gain ascendancy, if they even had an interpretation of the sacraments. Most of the Anglicans were located in the urban areas and were more high church in their approach to the sacraments, tending towards a more solid doctrine of Christ's real presence in the Eucharist. The Presbyterians who descended from the Dutch held to Christ's spiritual presence in the Eucharist, while it would seem that those from the Scots-Irish tended towards a

---

5. Ibid., 60.
6. Sweet, *Methodism*, 9.
7. Ibid., 23.
8. Ibid., 15.

more Zwinglian approach, and the Quakers did not have sacraments among themselves at all.

## THE SOUTHERN COLONIES

By far, the majority position of the southern colonies (Maryland, Virginia, North Carolina, South Carolina, and Georgia) was that of Anglicanism. The Church of England was the official Church of those colonies, either from their formation or through legislation during the colonial period. However, that is not to say there was a uniformity of Christian expression in these colonies, either. Sweet has noted, "In none of the Church of England colonies were the members of that church in the majority, with the possible exception of Virginia, and in all the middle and southern colonies the dissenting churches were making rapid progress from the middle of the century to the outbreak of the Revolution."[9] These Anglicans had a high view of the sacrament, but ironically, they should not have availed themselves of it. The major Eucharistic problem in these colonies was, as in New England, official church membership. Unlike the Congregational churches of New England, whose criteria for full membership and Eucharistic privilege included a conversion experience, the Church of England congregations of the South officially required something that most Anglicans born and raised in the New World could not have: confirmation.

Confirmation as a rite could only be administered by a bishop, and there were no English bishops in America. The Bishop of London had jurisdiction over the colonies, and this resulted in extremely few ordained clergy (since only a bishop can perform ordinations) and even fewer confirmations. Thus, while citizens of the southern colonies may have been nominally members of the Church of England, according to its own canon laws, they ought not to have received the Eucharist since they had never been confirmed. It was this sort of situation that led many colonists to see the Church of England as containing unnecessary ritual and an elite clergy that held power over the masses of its members.[10] This attitude made fertile ground for the religious awakening that would sweep through all the colonies during the 1740s and 1750s. Additionally, the Church of England suffered from another problem, as it was the church of the ruling governors. Because of this fact, "it therefore had little popular appeal, and as the

---

9. Ibid., 9–10.
10. Noll, *History*, 99, 112.

eighteenth century wore on, it became increasingly easy for Presbyterians, Baptists, and Methodists to make converts from among its members."[11]

## THE GREAT AWAKENING

Important for the understanding of the development of religion in the New World is the First Great Awakening and its effects upon the colonists. Thomas Kidd has noted that the term *First* Great Awakening is most probably a misnomer. Kidd wrote, "The standard framework of the 'First' and 'Second' Great Awakenings may obscure the fact that the evangelical movement continued to develop after 1743 and before 1800. There were important, widespread revivals that happened before the First, and between the First and Second, Great Awakenings."[12] The beginnings of revival occurred prior to Jonathan Edwards and George Whitefield, two of the most prominent preachers of this period, and continued throughout the advent of Wesleyan Methodism in the 1760s. Nevertheless, for the purposes of this brief survey, the conventional understanding of the First Great Awakening as occurring in the 1740s will be retained. It was during this period that both Whitefield and Edwards preached, and both called their hearers to a new or renewed experience of God in their lives. Whitefield especially traveled up and down the eastern seaboard preaching in all the English colonies to enormous crowds of people, many of whom responded positively to his messages, and it was Edwards who interpreted the results of the revival theologically.[13]

The net effect of this Awakening was that while Church membership and adherence declined during the 1700s, more people were awakened to God's grace in their lives.[14] It was impossible for those who were members of the Church of England to become full members simply because of a conversion experience; confirmation was necessary and there were still no bishops in the colonies to perform such a rite. In addition to this, most of those awakened during this period experienced something they did not wish to integrate with the Church of England. As Noll stated, "the most important effect of the revivals was to create an alternative to the Church of England" in the southern colonies where "this alternative involved the popularization of emotional personal faith as opposed to formal ceremonial worship."[15] And likewise, for those Congregationalist churches in New England, the

---

11. Sweet, *Methodism*, 20.
12. Kidd, *The Great Awakening*, xix.
13. Noll, *History*, 97.
14. Ibid.
15. Ibid., 99.

congregations were divided. "The revival left four distinct ecclesiastical parties, each of which looked upon itself as the proper heir or worthy successor of the English dissenting tradition."[16] There were those who accepted the revival and Great Awakening outright, and these became Baptists. There were those who followed Edwards and his explanation of the revival and saw conversion as God shining "afresh into the sinner's soul," and were termed "New Lights" for this view.[17] There were those who rejected the conversion experiences during the revival for the inherent instability introduced by the methods used (which will be discussed in detail in Chapter 14) and were referred to as "Old Lights" or Old Calvinists.[18] And there were those who viewed with suspicion the method of revivalist practice that preached for an emotional response instead of a well-reasoned conversion. These eventually became New England's Unitarians because of many of their presuppositions concerning reason as being able to explain much of faith and experience.[19] As a result, many of the newly awakened Christians who could have been decent members of these churches were denied membership because of the method of their conversion in such a setting. Essentially, the result was that colonists responded in faith to a working of God's grace in their lives, but they did it quite apart from any ecclesial structure and devoid of any sacramental understanding, and the churches to which they could turn to receive that sacramental understanding kept them out of membership and fellowship, if they even wanted to join those congregations at all.

To summarize, then, the variety of Christian expression in the colonies prior to the American Revolutionary War, Sweet recorded

> The total number of congregations of all denominations is given as 3,105, with about one thousand each for New England, the Middle colonies and the Southern colonies. Ranking first in number of congregations were the Congregationalists with 658; Presbyterians came next with 543; ranking third were the Baptists with 498; Anglicans came fourth with 480; the Quakers or Friends had 295; German and Dutch Reformed together had 251; Lutherans, 151; and Catholics, 50.[20]

It is among these varied groups that John Wesley's Methodists would begin their work, drawing to themselves disenchanted members of the denominations and those individuals neglected or rejected by them.

16. Ibid., 98.
17. Ibid.
18. Ibid.
19. Ibid.
20. Sweet, *Methodism*, 26.

# Section II

# Wesley's Methodism

Chapter 3

# Wesley's Eucharistic Theology through Aldersgate

WHEN INVOLVED IN THE study of Methodism in general or John Wesley (1703–1791) one must inevitably come to the date of May 24, 1738—John Wesley's Aldersgate experience. There are many scholars who see this as a conversion experience in Wesley and see all their research through pre-conversion and post-conversion filters. This vision of Wesley allows scholars to postulate a dichotomy in Wesley's life and theology. For example, Robert Coleman, in *Nothing to Do But to Save Souls,* tries to draw the comparison of Methodist evangelism's success (or failure) to Aldersgate, just as Wesley had supposed failure prior to this experience and success after it. Coleman stated, "Only in the same way [as Wesley's experience at Aldersgate], can evangelism be sustained today . . . Too often we have tried to work it up by well-intentioned exhortations or expertly designed programs. But there is no action of love because there is no 'strangely warmed' heart."[1] Consciously or unconsciously, this effort divorces God's working in John Wesley's life from the means of grace of which he partook during his entire life up to that point; it separates the life of the Christian in the Church from the life of God in the Christian. This is something that Wesley himself would never have done. And yet so many Wesleyan and Methodist historians have adopted this view of the Aldersgate experience. Abel Stevens, referring to the event, stated, "such is 'regeneration,' according to Methodism."[2] William Warren Sweet referred to Aldersgate in this same manner when, leading into a sec-

---

1. Coleman, *Save Souls,* 28–29.
2. Stevens, *History of the Methodist Episcopal Church,* 1.36.

tion on Wesley's ministry, he described it as "his conversion experience."[3] W. H. Daniels simply introduced the section of Aldersgate with the subtitle "The Conversion of Rev. John Wesley."[4] All of these instances implicitly or explicitly direct the reader of Methodist history to assume there was a radical difference in the man, John Wesley, and his approach to the Christian faith and life after this date.

There are other scholars who do not see a radical difference between these two time periods in Wesley's life, but rather see Aldersgate as merely a stepping-stone in Wesley's life and see their data as having an internal continuity before and after the event. Charles Yrigoyen Jr., when writing about this period of Wesley's life, stated that

> Aldersgate did convince him [Wesley] that the holiness he sought does not begin with human striving but by trusting the pardoning and empowering grace of God in Christ... Upon his return to England in the fall of 1738 [from his visit to Herrnhut in Germany], Wesley became engrossed in religious activity. Reading, studying, praying, visiting prisoners, celebrating Holy Communion, and preaching the evangelical message of God's unmerited love in Christ occupied his time.[5]

This tries to show that there may have been a difference of understanding, but there was no difference of substance between the Wesley of May 23, 1738 and the Wesley after the Aldersgate experience. Frederick Norwood actually dismisses the event almost entirely when he wrote, "For all the significance of that evening meeting his journey toward abiding faith was not complete."[6] Horton Davies tried to dismiss the event as well by marking off the word *conversion* with quotation marks.[7] What these views tend not to do is consider the radical shift in direction and results of Wesley's ministry after the event.

Robert Tuttle, in his *John Wesley: His Life and Theology* put forth a third option, namely that the Aldersgate experience was a continuation of Wesley's desire to give himself wholly to God in 1725 when he was ordained, and a transformation of Wesley's faith to something more than was previously. Tuttle wrote thus

---

3. Sweet, *Methodism*, 37.
4. Daniels, *Illustrated History*, 134.
5. Yrigoyen, *John Wesley*, 16.
6. Norwood, *American Methodism*, 27.
7. Davies, *Worship*, 3.187.

> I am personally convinced that the nature of Wesley's religious conversion in 1725 and the relentless consistency of his religious pursuits beyond, made an Aldersgate (in one form or another) inevitable. Wesley, between 1725 and 1738, was more than the Pharisee with a façade of religious duty disguising a deceitful heart. He was a determined seeker, through and through. God would not have denied grace to a man in dead earnest about being altogether a Christian. To be sure, the strength of Wesley's ability to reason and the passion of his pilgrimage through the various stages of development made it difficult for him to trust Christ *utterly* by faith alone (a doctrine thought robbery by most men of "religious" worth), but it had to happen . . . After 1767, Aldersgate would no longer be interpreted [by Wesley himself] as a conversion from condemnation to saving faith, but as a "conversion" from the faith of a servant (clearly acceptable to God) to the faith of a son. One should not, however, allow this amended interpretation . . . to detract from the importance of Aldersgate. Again, Wesley, prior to Aldersgate, had no power, no peace, no joy, no heart, no expectation to see God at work among his people. He did not preach faith (as he did consistently for the rest of his life) and there was no revival. Now, all this was to change![8]

Tuttle holds both the transformation that took place and the continuation of Wesley's life in tension. This allows the scholar to look throughout the entirety of Wesley's life, both before and after Aldersgate with unity and treat Wesley's theology as a whole, moving like most individuals do throughout life, building on one aspect from another, instead of divorcing Wesley from his thirty-five years prior to Aldersgate and the theological insights and experiences he had during those years. It also restricts the scholar from choosing which references in Wesley to use and ignoring the others and justifying the decision by appealing to a disconnected version of his theology and life.

Nevertheless, it is beyond the scope of this study to make any determination about the "true" nature of what happened in John Wesley's life on that night. Whether it was a radical break with the past, a continuation of what came before, or the logical progression of a conversion that began thirteen years earlier, Aldersgate will continue to be debated by Wesleyan scholars in every generation with one view gaining temporary ascendancy over another. What is obvious is that from May 24, 1738 forward, John Wesley and his Methodist movement began to grow, expand spheres of influence,

---

8. Tuttle, *John Wesley*, 216, 229.

and demonstrate a drive that connected with more people than prior to the experience. Whether there was a radical change in the man, a change in the methods of the man, or a continuing change and transformation of the man is not of concern here. However, as so much scholarship has used Aldersgate as a delineation point for periods in Wesley's life and ministry, this study will retain that division and look at his Eucharistic understanding and theology both prior to and after May 24, 1738.

## EMPHASES PRIOR TO ALDERSGATE

John Wesley was born on June 28, 1703 and grew up in an Established Church home, his father being an ordained priest. This is not to say that there was no exposure to dissenting theology within the household. Both of John's parents, Samuel and Susanna, grew up in dissenting households and both decided independently of one another to become a part of the Anglican Church. John Wesley's paternal grandfather, also named John, was a Nonconformist, sided with the Parliament during the Civil War, and was ejected from his parish following the passage of the Act of Uniformity in 1662.[9] This elder John arranged for his son, Samuel, to become a Dissenting minister and sent him to school for such an end. "While he resided there [at one of their Academies], his sentiments were so entirely changed, that he left the Academy without consulting any of his relations, and entered as a student of Exeter College, Oxford."[10] Following his education at Oxford, Samuel was ordained within the Church of England, became a chaplain on a Man of War, and then "he was presented to the Living of Epworth, and also to that of Wroote, both in the county of Lincoln."[11]

Susanna Wesley was the daughter of Samuel Annesley. Annesley was also a Nonconformist and, as Whitehead recorded, "He was turned out of his lecture because he would not comply with some things which he deemed extravagant and wrong; he thought conformity in him would be a sin, and he chose to quit a full maintenance rather than injure his conscience."[12] He was very well respected by the various groups within the Dissenting community, and even assisted in the first public ordination of a Dissenter in 1694.[13] Susanna, growing up in such a religious household, had a keen mind for matters of faith. She began to examine the claims that were made

---

9. Coke and Moore, *Life of John Wesley*, 18–19.
10. Ibid., 24.
11. Ibid.
12. Whitehead, *Life of John Wesley*, 23.
13. Ibid., 25.

by Dissenters and decided for herself. "Before she was thirteen years old, she had examined the whole controversy between the Dissenters and the Established Church, and from that time became a member of the Church of England."[14] It is most likely this combination of serious education, pious upbringing in a Dissenting household, and determined acceptance of the Established Church that led to Susanna's remarkable way of raising and educating her children.[15]

During his formative years at Epworth under the tutelage of his mother (1703–1714), his time at the Charter-house (1714–1719), and at Oxford (1719–1735), all the way up to and including his missionary journey to Georgia Colony (1735–1738), John struggled with how best to live the Christian life. In fact, Wesley's general approach to Christianity and the faithful life can be summed up in a conversation he had with a slave girl when he was in Georgia. On April 23, 1737, Wesley made one of his excursions outside of Savannah and had an encounter with the slave of a man in whose home he was staying. She had been a child in a minister's household in Barbados prior to arriving in Georgia and entered into conversation with Wesley on Christianity, of which she knew practically nothing. Wesley took the opportunity to teach her, "He [God] made you to live with himself above the sky. And so you will, in a little time, —if you are good. If you are good, when your body dies, your soul will go up, and want nothing, and have whatever you can desire . . . The next day she remembered all, readily answered every question; and said, she would ask Him that made her, to show her how to be good."[16]

Wesley came to this understanding based upon what he had been studying and trying to implement in his own life prior to his Georgia mission, among those works being Thomas á Kempis' *The Imitation of Christ* and Jeremy Taylor's *Rules for Holy Living and Dying*. In January of 1731, six years before this conversation, Wesley wrote to his father, Samuel, concerning Archbishop King's *Origin of Evil*. In his summary and analysis, Wesley stated that "Happiness rises from a due use of our faculties: If, therefore, this be the noblest of all our faculties, then our chief happiness lies in the due use of this; that is, in our elections."[17] This seems to tend in a semi-Pelagian direction, equating happiness with holiness and basing them upon his own volitional choices, but it is a direction in which Wesley traveled for some time. In November of the same year Wesley wrote to his brother, Samuel, Jr.

---

14. Ibid., 36.
15. Watson, *Life of John Wesley*, 9.
16. Wesley, *Works*, 18.180.
17. Ibid., 25.266.

> First. As to the end of my being, I lay it down for a rule, that I cannot be too happy, or, therefore, too holy; and thence infer, that the more steadily I keep my eye upon the prize of our high calling, the better, and the more of my thoughts, and words, and actions are directly pointed at the attainment of it. Secondly. As to the instituted means of attaining it, I likewise lay it down for a rule, that I am to use them every time I may. Thirdly. As to prudential means, I believe this rule holds of things indifferent in themselves: Whatever I know to do me hurt, that to me is not indifferent, but resolutely to be abstained from; whatever I know to do me good, that to me is not indifferent, but resolutely to be embraced.[18]

Here it is seen that Wesley applied what he wrote to his father by way of commentary to the way of life for himself, namely that happiness, equated with holiness, is found through our conscious choices to avail ourselves of those means of grace that will draw us closer to Christ. Just as Wesley would instruct the slave girl years later, if one does good, one goes to heaven. And in his understanding, partaking of the sacrament, one of the instituted means of grace, is a major part of doing good. And Wesley apparently yearned not just for an experience of happiness and holiness, but an assurance of salvation that he expected would precede such a state. Later in the same letter he responded to a criticism his brother leveled at him for being continually serious. "You are glad, because you are 'passed from death to life:' Well, but let him be afraid, who knows not whether he is to live or die. Whether this be my condition or no, who can tell better than myself?"[19]

Wesley evidently found his way of living, being happy and holy, easier to communicate than to experience. This can be clearly seen in a letter to his mother two months after the letter to Samuel, Jr. In this letter, dated February 28, 1732, Wesley stated his understanding of the presence of Christ in the Eucharist, the benefits of such a presence, and his lamentation that he has not received those benefits:

> One consideration is enough to make me assent to his and your judgment concerning the holy sacrament; which is, that we cannot allow Christ's human nature to be present in it, without allowing either con- or trans-substantiation. But that his divinity is so united to us then, as he never is but to worthy receivers, I firmly believe, though the manner of that union is utterly a mystery to me. That none but worthy receivers should find this

---

18. Ibid., 25.321.
19. Ibid., 25.322.

effect, is not strange to me, when I observe how small effect many means of improvement have upon an unprepared mind. Mr. Morgan and my brother were affected, as they ought, by the observations you made on that glorious subject; but though my understanding approved what was excellent, yet my heart did not feel it. Why was this, but because it was pre-engaged by those affections with which wisdom will not dwell? because the animal mind cannot relish those truths which are spiritually discerned? Yet I have those writings which the Good Spirit gave to that end! I have many of those which he hath since assisted his servants to give us; I have retirement to apply these to my own soul daily; I have means both of public and private prayer; and, above all, of partaking in that sacrament once a week. What shall I do to make all these blessings effectual, to gain from them that mind which was also in Christ Jesus?...You say you 'have renounced the world.' And what have I been doing all this time? What have I done every since I was born? Why, I have been plunging myself into it more and more.[20]

Here it is evident that Wesley was in perfect continuity with the reformers of previous generations in his theological understanding of rejecting Christ's physical presence and promoting Christ's spiritual presence in the Eucharist, leaning heavily toward Calvin's specific interpretation. It is also evident that Wesley, for all his religious pursuits, attention to and participation in the sacrament, did not experience what he thought he ought to have experienced, namely the mind of Christ. For all the good he was doing, he had not received the benefits. He was reading the appropriate books, taking the appropriate time for prayer, worshiping, receiving the sacrament weekly, and still did not experience the happiness or holiness of which he wrote to his brother.

Nevertheless, it would appear that Wesley continued his practice of weekly reception of the sacrament, as can be seen in the details of the Introductory Letter of his *Journal*, which concerned the rise of Methodists at Oxford.[21] In this letter, Wesley stated several times that the little group of men at the University endeavored to pursue the holy life, and to that end, employed all the means of which they knew to grow in that manner. Wesley stated, "Upon this encouragement [from his own father] we still continued to meet together as usual; and to confirm one another, as well as we could,

---

20. Ibid., 25.329.

21. This was a letter written to Mr. Morgan's father in order to explain that it was not the self-imposed asceticism of the Methodists that ultimately killed his son while he was at school.

in our resolutions, to communicate as often as we had opportunity; (which is here once a week;) and to do what service we could to our acquaintance, the prisoners, and two or three poor families in town."[22] Wesley also, within this letter, explicitly linked the notion of doing good with receiving the sacrament. He writes, "The two points whereunto, but the blessing of God and your son's help, we had before attained, we endeavoured to hold fast: I mean, the doing what good we can; and, in order thereto, communicating as often as we have opportunity."[23]

Within one of Wesley's sermons from the era, one of the few existent from prior to Aldersgate, there may be a subtle autobiographical note pertaining to his own state at this time. Wesley originally preached *The Duty of Constant Communion* in 1733 at Oxford, just after these aforementioned letters. While this sermon was not published until 1788, Wesley included an introductory note stating that his opinions had not changed in the ensuing years.[24] Wesley stated in this sermon that one of the objections to constantly receiving Communion put forward is, "I have communicated constantly so long, but I have not found the benefit I expected."[25] His resolution of this objection is telling for his own state. As an answer, Wesley stated that for the person who would make such an objection (possibly eyeing himself one year prior), "Was it not his own fault? Either he was not rightly prepared, willing to obey all the commands and to receive all the promises of God, or he did not receive it aright, trusting in God. Only see that you are duly prepared for it, and the oftener you come to the Lord's table, the greater benefit you will find there."[26] In other words, the advice he would give himself is to continue his efforts to do good, and to receive the sacrament even more so that it can become the means to happiness and holiness at some point in the future. Yet for all this action, Wesley still did not experience what he desired. "Yet when, after continuing some years in this course, I apprehended myself to be near death, I could not find that all this gave me any comfort, or any assurance of acceptance with God."[27] Nevertheless, Wesley knew of no other way to experience and know that salvation which he sought. He continued on the same path.

22. Wesley, *Works*, 18.127.
23. Ibid., 18.131.
24. Ibid., 3.428. "The following Discourse was written above five-and-fifty years ago, for the use of my pupils at Oxford. I have added very little, but retrenched much; as I then used more words than I do now. But, I thank God, I have not yet seen cause to alter my sentiments in any point which is therein delivered. J.W. 1788."
25. Ibid., 3.437.
26. Ibid., 3.438.
27. Ibid., 18.245.

Wesley took his own advice for continuing to receive the sacrament, for in his *Journal* it is seen that he and his band of missionaries bound for Georgia administered the sacrament every Sunday while they were at sea. The entry for January 21, 1736 reads: "We had fifteen communicants, which was our usual number on Sundays: On Christmas-day we had nineteen; but on New Year's day fifteen only."[28] And again, Wesley instituted a similar policy once he took up residence in Savannah. The entry for March 14, 1736 states, "Having before given notice of my design to do so, every Sunday and holiday, according to the rules of our Church, I administered the holy communion to eighteen persons."[29]

Of Wesley's sojourn in Georgia and return, as pertains to this study, the most significant outcome was his introduction to the Moravians, and particularly Peter Böhler in London in 1738. Böhler had introduced Wesley to a desire in salvation for "Dominion over sin, and constant Peace from a sense of forgiveness."[30] It is for this, then that Wesley began to strive, not eliminating his former practices of frequently using the means of grace, but rather adding to them "continual prayer for this very thing."[31] It is interesting to note that, on the day of Wesley's heart-warming experience at Aldersgate, May 24, 1738, prior to the Moravian meeting Wesley attended the Church service at St. Paul's and received the Lord's Supper. This may shed light on why Wesley was so reluctant to dispense with the use of the means of grace when the Stillness Controversy arose less than two years later, as he did not give up receiving the ordinances and using all the means of grace available to him and still received assurance of his faith.

## EMPHASES AFTER ALDERSGATE

Within days of Wesley's experience at Aldersgate, he and several others decided to travel to Germany and visit the spiritual home of the Moravians, Herrnhut, which was on Count Zinzendorf's land. On the way, on June 17, several English asked Wesley to administer the Lord's Supper to them, which he readily did.[32] On July 28, Wesley observed a church service in Meissen, Germany. He was offended by the actions and dress of the people. He did not think it proper for the people to be dressed as lavishly as he saw they were dressed, nor did he think they showed proper respect during the

---

28. Ibid., 18.141.
29. Ibid., 18.154.
30. Ibid., 18.248.
31. Ibid.
32. Ibid., 18.256.

service. In addition to dress and lack of respect, Wesley also took affront at the fact that most of the people did not receive the Lord's Supper. "All of them stayed during the holy communion, though but very few received. Alas, alas! What a *Reformed* country is this!"[33]

Once Wesley arrived at Herrnhut, he began to converse with several of the members of the Moravian community in residence. Through them he encountered differing opinions of the Lord's Supper. First, there was the church's theological constitution that was written in 1733. It stated, "If any man among us, having been often admonished, and long forborne, persists in walking unworthy of his holy calling, he is no longer admitted to the Lord's Supper."[34] Second, there was the conversation with Christian David in which he stated that he tried "to persuade them [Moravians] not to insist on the assurance of faith, as a necessary qualification for receiving the Lord's Supper."[35] Finally, there was the testimony of Zacharias Neusser, who stated of his journey in faith, "He [a Lutheran minister] offered to receive me into communion with him, which I gladly accepted of; and in a short time after, I received the Lord's Supper from his hands. While I was receiving, I felt Christ had died for *me*. I knew I was reconciled to God."[36] So, Wesley encountered one who had experienced justifying grace during the Lord's Supper, one who encouraged the Moravians to drop assurance as a prerequisite for receiving the Lord's Supper, and the official teaching of the Moravians at Herrnhut which stated that people could be excluded from the Lord's Supper for unrepentant living. Each of these facets of piety and doctrine would manifest themselves in the coming controversy Wesley had with the Moravians at Fetter Lane.

Before moving to the Stillness Controversy, though, it is necessary to round out the biographical sketch of Wesley's faith at this point, for it has some bearing upon his view of the sacraments. Wesley continued to vacillate concerning his state with reference to God. On October 14, 1738, Wesley received a response from a friend whom he had questioned for advice concerning those weak in faith. The response "threw me into great perplexity."[37] Wesley remained in this state until he cried to God, opened a Bible and read I Chronicles 4.10, the Prayer of Jabez. This, however, forced "me upon considering my own state more deeply."[38] The result of this introspection for

---

33. Ibid., 18.265, italics included.
34. Ibid., 18.297.
35. Ibid., 18.281.
36. Ibid., 18.287.
37. Ibid., 19.16.
38. Ibid.

Wesley was that he lacked the assurance he so completely desired. He wrote of his state

> I cannot find in myself the love of God, or of Christ. Hence my deadness and wanderings in public prayer: Hence it is, that even in the holy communion I have frequently no more than a cold attention . . . I have not yet that joy in the Holy Ghost, nor the full assurance of faith, much less am I, in the full sense of the words, "in Christ a new creature:" I nevertheless trust that I have a measure of faith, and am "accepted in the Beloved:" I trust "the hand-writing that was against me is blotted out;" and that I am "reconciled to God" through his Son.[39]

It would appear that Wesley found himself in a slightly better place in his faith than before his Aldersgate experience, for before then he did not even believe he was "reconciled to God," yet now he holds out belief that he is. Unfortunately, this was not the only time he felt this way. On January 4, 1739, Wesley wrote

> My friends affirm I am mad, because I said I was not a Christian a year ago. I affirm, I am not a Christian now. Indeed, what I might have been I know not, had I been faithful to the grace then given, when, expecting nothing less, I received such a sense of the forgiveness of my sins, as till then I never knew. But that I am not a Christian at this day, I as assuredly know, as that Jesus is the Christ . . . From hence I conclude, (and let all the *saints of the world* hear, that whereinsoever they boast, they may be found even as I,) though I have given, and do give, all my goods to feed the poor, I am not a Christian. Though I have endured hardship, though I have in all things denied myself and taken up my cross, I am not a Christian. My works are nothing, my sufferings are nothing; I have not the fruits of the Spirit of Christ. Though I have constantly used all the means of grace for twenty years, I am not a Christian.[40]

Here is the final time Wesley would revisit the sentiments he had concerning salvation and using the means of grace that he explicated in his letters and sermons noted above, namely that despite using the means of grace and trying his best, he did not have faith. This spiritual and verbal self-flagellation ended for Wesley shortly after this when a woman was converted during his preaching on January 21, 1739.[41] Being the instrument

39. Ibid., 19.18.
40. Ibid., 19.29–31.
41. Ibid., 19.32

of this woman's salvation was apparently the confirmation Wesley needed that he had indeed experienced and been the recipient of salvation himself. Never again does Wesley voice any doubt of the efficacy of the means of grace in a believer's life. Specifically, with respect to the Lord's Supper, this no doubt helped inform Wesley's opinion that this particular sacrament could deliver grace to those who sought it even prior to their experience of and assurance of salvation. Because of this experience, Wesley could not ever concede the point that devoutly using the means of grace was an act of works-righteousness, because those very means evidently did convey God's grace to him, or at least they prepared the way for God's grace to reach him.

# Chapter 4

# Wesley's Eucharistic Theology after Aldersgate

## THE STILLNESS CONTROVERSY

SHORTLY AFTER WESLEY RETURNED from Herrnhut in November of 1739 he became embroiled in what is known as the Stillness Controversy. This was a major theological disagreement between Wesley and the Moravian leadership of the society at Fetter Lane. The question that arose was: if one avails himself or herself of any of the means of grace prior to experiencing salvation, would that be a form of works-righteousness and, therefore, trying to earn a spot in heaven apart from God's gracious work on the part of the person utilizing the means? The Moravians answered this in the affirmative and taught their people to be completely still, not using any of the means of grace at all, including worship, prayer, Bible study, and the sacraments (specifically the Lord's Supper) because to do so, in their estimation, would be trying to work one's way into heaven. Wesley wrote of the situation, "In the evening I met the women of our society at Fetter-Lane; where some of our brethren strongly intimated that none of them had any true faith; and then asserted, in plain terms, 1. That, till they had true faith, they ought to be still; that is, (as they explained themselves,) to abstain from the means of grace, as they are called; the Lord's Supper in particular. 2. That the ordinances are not means of grace, there being no other means than Christ."[1]

---

1. Wesley, *Works*, 19.119–20.

The essential premise on which the Moravians based such a conclusion was that either a person had faith or did not have faith, and that there were no intermediate steps of faith at all. Given this premise, one either was a Christian or was not a Christian, and means of grace would mean very little. This position is very similar to the self-reflection Wesley had in January of 1739 noted above. It is very probable that, because of the similarity of the two understandings of salvation, and the fact that Wesley came to understand that his ideas at that time were wrong, that Wesley argued so staunchly against this Moravian position. Wesley reported a conversation he and his brother Charles had with Philipp Heinrich Molther in which this doctrine of stillness was defined.

> Fri. 25 [April 1740]—My brother and I went to Mr. Molther again, and spent two hours in conversation with him. He now also explicitly affirmed, 1. That there are *no degrees* in faith; that none has any faith who has ever any doubt or fear; and that none is justified till he has a clean heart, with the perpetual indwelling of Christ, and of the Holy Ghost; and 2. That every one who has not this, ought, till he has it, to be *still*: That is, as he explained it, not to use the ordinances, or means of grace, so called. He also expressly asserted, 1. That to those who have a clean heart, the ordinances are not matter of duty. They are not commanded to use them: They are free: They may use them, or they may not. 2. That those who have not a clean heart, ought not to use them; (particularly not to communicate;) because God neither commands nor designs they should; (commanding them to none, designing them only for believers;) and because they are not means of grace; there being no such thing as means of grace, but Christ only.[2]

This problem continued to grow and would ultimately result in a split of the society. Many of the men and women who were members began to question the veracity of their faith and ended up rejecting their past experiences of God's grace, owing to the convincing arguments put forth that if they had any doubt, they were not saved. These Christians "[denied] what God had done for their souls; to own they never had living faith."[3]

Wesley, on the other hand, found this position absolutely revolting. Besides his own experiences in life, for all his striving to work out his own salvation through use of the means of grace prior to Aldersgate, Wesley was still a Church of England man who believed whole-heartedly that the

2. Ibid., 19.147.
3. Ibid., 19.146.

presence of Christ was in the Lord's Supper and it was an instituted way for Christians to encounter Christ. Through his experiences after Aldersgate as well, Wesley had witnessed God bestowing grace through means. In one telling instance, as the genesis of the Methodist societies was underway, Wesley recounted an episode about a group of women and then a group of men agreeing to meet together weekly in the same form of accountability as was done in London. Seeing how this movement spread and how people grew in faith through the groups, Wesley stated, "How dare any man deny this to be (as to the substance of it) a means of grace, ordained by God? Unless he will affirm (with Luther in the fury of his Solifidianism) that St. James' Epistle is an epistle of straw."[4] It was this "fury of Solifidianism" with which Wesley was now engaged, the idea that faith can be divorced from any outward working in a person's life who was actively seeking salvation.

Wesley also had evidence that the Lord's Supper conveyed even a converting grace to people based upon the experience of at least one woman in the Fetter-Lane Society. He recounted

> Till *Saturday*, the 10th, I think I did not meet with one woman of the society who had not been upon the point of casting away her confidence in God. I then indeed found one, who, when many (according to their custom) laboured to persuade her she had no faith, replied, with a spirit they were not able to resist, "I know that the life which I now live, I live by faith in the Son of God, who loved me, and gave himself for me: And He has never left me one moment, since the hour He was made know to me in the breaking of bread." What is to be inferred from this undeniable matter of fact, —one that had not faith received it in the Lord's Supper? Why, 1. That there are means of grace, that is, outward ordinances, whereby the inward grace of God is ordinarily conveyed to man; whereby the faith that brings salvation is conveyed to them who before had it not. 2. That one of these means is the Lord's Supper. And, 3. That he who has not this faith ought to wait for it, in the use both of this, and of the other means which God hath ordained.[5]

It is also quite probable that Wesley had the memory of an exchange with his mother[6] in mind as he defended the Lord's Supper as a means

---

4. Ibid., 19.47.

5. Ibid., 19.120–21.

6. J. Ernest Rattenbury postulates that this quotation by Susanna Wesley and the reference to a woman who was converted at the sacrament in the above *Journal* entry were one and the same occurrence. See *Eucharistic Hymns*, 10. While Susanna was living with John at the Foundry at this time, it is unclear whether or not she was ever

of grace when she told him it was during the Lord's Supper that she first understood Christ to have died for her sins specifically.

> I talked largely with my mother, who told me, that, till a short time since, she had scarce heard such a thing mentioned, as having forgiveness of sins now, or God's Spirit bearing witness with our spirit: Much less did she imagine that this was the common privilege of all true believers. "Therefore," said she, "I never durst ask for it myself. But two or three weeks ago, while my son Hall was pronouncing those words, in delivering the cup to me, 'The blood of our Lord Jesus Christ, which was given for thee;' the words struck through my heart, and I knew God for Christ's sake had forgiven *me* all *my* sins."[7]

Because Wesley saw in this new idea of Stillness a contradiction, as he perceived it, to "the old paths," likewise fearing this position would lead to antinomianism and, thus worried for the salvation of the members of that society, he launched a theological attack against stillness. Unfortunately, the attack was not to be a complete success, as the society did split and the Moravians continued at Fetter-Lane and the Methodists commenced meeting at the Foundry.

There was one bright spot in this controversy, though. This issue forced Wesley to articulate very clearly, and very early, his Eucharistic theology in order to combat such an error on the part of the Moravian leadership, leadership that apparently did not have the same understanding of regeneration and salvation as those Moravians at Herrnhut since there were testimonies of members there being converted while receiving the sacrament. It is in combating this pernicious doctrine within the society that Wesley taught on the nature of the sacrament. First, he showed that the ideal from Scripture was for frequent reception of the sacrament (daily in the early days of the Church). Second, he reminded them that it could be a converting ordinance, as evidenced by some of the members' own testimonies. Third, he used the institution of the Lord's Supper as scriptural proof that it was to be given to those who had not yet been fully saved, as shown by the fact that the disciples themselves had not yet been fully saved when they were told

---

a member of the society at Fetter-Lane. If she was not, these two instances could not be the same account. A perhaps better case can be made for Jane Muncy, who was one of the early women in the Fetter-Lane Society and, who, according to Wesley, "when the controversy concerning the means of grace began, stood in the gap, and contended earnestly for the ordinances once delivered to the saints" (Wesley, *Works*, 19.206–7).

7. Wesley, *Works*, 19.93, emphasis included.

to continue to "Do this in remembrance of me."[8] Then he summarized his teaching on the subject with four points:

> I showed at large, 1. That the Lord's Supper was ordained by God, to be a means of conveying to men either preventing, or justifying, or sanctifying grace, according to their several necessities. 2. That the persons for whom it was ordained, are all those who know and feel that they want the grace of God, either to restrain them from sin, or to show their sins forgiven, or to renew their souls in the image of God. 3. That inasmuch as we come to his table, not to give him any thing, but to receive whatsoever he sees best for us, there is no previous preparation indispensably necessary, but a desire to receive whatsoever he pleases to give. And, 4. That no fitness is required at the time of communicating, but a sense of our state, of our utter sinfulness and helplessness; everyone who knows he is fit for hell, being just fit to come to Christ, in this as well as all other ways of his appointment.[9]

This statement represents one of the cornerstones of Wesley's Eucharistic theology, namely that it is a means of grace, ordained by God, in which God touches all those who approach it in faith, knowing their personal state, in whichever way God needs to touch them. Ole Borgen, in his seminal work *John Wesley on the Sacraments*, summarized this position quite succinctly. He stated, "The believer, therefore, through his regular partaking of the Lord's Supper, is empowered to live the life of holiness and is given strength to remain in God's love and endure to the end."[10]

It is apparent that the Moravians not only believed that being still was the only way to reach salvation, they adamantly argued with those of the Fetter Lane society who disagreed with them and agreed with Wesley concerning the ordinances as means of grace. Wesley recorded an instance on March 26, 1740, in which he had to take aside the Stillness supporters and reprimand them for trying to force their own opinion on the rest of the group. Wesley wrote

> Complaint was made again, (as indeed had been done before, and that not once or twice only,) that many of our brethren, not content with leaving off the ordinances of God themselves, were continually troubling those that did not, and disputing with them, whether they would or no. The same complaint was made the next night also, at the meeting of the society. I then

8. Ibid., 19.158.
9. Ibid., 19.159.
10. Borgen, *Wesley*, 212.

plainly set before them the things they had done, expostulated the case with them, and earnestly besought them to trouble or perplex the minds of their brethren any more; but at least to excuse those who still waited for God in the ways of his own appointment.[11]

This admonition did little, if any good for the whole of the society. By April 25, it was obvious that reconciliation would not be possible. On this date both John and Charles Wesley went to speak with Molther and spent two hours with him. During this time Molther "explicitly affirmed" the doctrines espoused by the Stillness group, mainly that those who do not have faith ought not use the ordinances, and those that have faith are not required to use the ordinances.[12] The situation finally erupted into a schism within the society on July 20, 1740. Wesley read some prepared remarks concerning the history of the disagreement between the Stillness doctrine and Wesley's understanding of grace. Upon the completion of this presentation Wesley stated succinctly, "I then, without saying anything more, withdrew, as did eighteen or nineteen of the society."[13] Three days later this small group (along with a few others totaling twenty-five) began meeting at the Foundry. Not one to squander an opportunity to have the last word in an argument, even if in print years later, Wesley recorded of this group on Sunday, August 1, 1740, "At St. Luke's, our parish church, was such a sight as, I believe, was never seen there before: Several hundred communicants, from whose very faces one might judge, that they indeed sought Him that was crucified."[14]

## HYMNS ON THE LORD'S SUPPER

Five years after the Stillness Controversy resulted in the creation of the society at the Foundry, John and his brother Charles published a volume in 1745 entitled *Hymns on the Lord's Supper*, in which was included an extract John Wesley made of a previous work by Daniel Brevint entitled *The Christian Sacrament and Sacrifice, by way of discourse, meditation, and prayer upon the nature, parts, and blessings of the Holy Communion*. In John's extract, followed in order by Charles' hymns, there are eight sections, five of which concern the nature of the sacrament, and three of which concern the nature

---

11. Wesley, *Works*, 19.139–40.
12. Ibid., 19.147.
13. Ibid., 19.162.
14. Ibid., 19.163.

of the sacrifice in the sacrament. The first five sections are *The Importance of well understanding the Nature of this Sacrament; Concerning the Sacrament, as it is a Memorial of the Suffering and Death of CHRIST; Concerning the Sacrament, as it is a Sign of Present Graces; Concerning the Sacrament, as it is a Means of Grace;* and *Concerning the Sacrament, as it is a Pledge of Future Glory.*[15] The remaining three sections are *Concerning the Sacrament, as it is a Sacrifice. And first, of the Commemorative Sacrifice; Concerning the Sacrifice of Ourselves;* and *Concerning the Sacrifice of our Goods.*[16] It is within the pages of this book that Wesley delineated his own Eucharistic theology.

In the first section, *Understanding the Nature of the Sacrament*, Wesley[17] wrote, "The Lord's Supper is without doubt one of the greatest Mysteries of Godliness, and the most solemn Feast of the Christian Religion. At the Holy Table the People meet to worship God, and God is present, to meet and bless his People."[18] Here is a doctrine of a very real presence of Christ in the Eucharist, much like the letter Wesley sent to his mother in 1732, from which was quoted above. Careful not to fall into an extremism on either the right or the left theologically, this section also contains the injunction that, because the Lord's Supper is a sacrament of such import, "It was on this Account that the Devil from the very beginning, has been so busy about this sacrament, driving Men either to make it a *False God*, or an *Empty Ceremony*."[19] This steered the reader clear of the Eucharistic "Scylla and Charybdis" for a faithful Anglican, namely transubstantiation (or consubstantiation) and memorialism.

In the second section, *Sacrament as a Memorial*, Wesley related that this sacrament, when administered in the Church, reminds Christians of Christ and his death, but does so in a way that goes beyond simply imagining what had happened 1700 years ago. To do this, the Eucharist is linked together with the Old Testament Passover celebration, wherein the Israelites were brought into complete fellowship with the generation that escaped Egypt, "Especially because this Sacrament duly receiv'd, makes the thing

---

15. *HLS*, 3–20.

16. Ibid., 20–32.

17. In dealing with this extract, this study will refer to the work as Wesley's, as he took ownership of the beliefs in the text from Brevint, as Wesley published this work numerous times during his life as a guide for Methodists and all Christians to better understand the sacrament. In instances where the differences between the two, Brevint's original and Wesley's extract, are significant, distinction will be made as to the ownership of the work.

18. *HLS*, 3.

19. Ibid., 4, italics included.

which it represents, as really present for our Use, as if it were newly done."[20] This interpretation approximates how Gregory Dix would define *anamnesis* 200 years later as not simply recalling an event, but re-presenting the event and re-participating in it.[21] To explain this concept further, since, as was referenced by Davies above, it was a slippery theological slope from holding a Calvinistic view of Christ's presence to a Zwinglian memorialism, Wesley further added, "The main Intention of Christ herein, was not, the bare *Remembrance* of his Passion, but over and above, to invite us to his Sacrifice, not as done and gone many Years since, but, as to Grace and Mercy, still lasting, still *new*, still the same as when it was first offer'd for us."[22]

In the third section, *Sign of Present Graces*, Wesley made the statement that could have come almost directly from the Thirty-Nine Articles. He stated, "Christ ordained Outward Visible Signs of his Inward and Spiritual Grace, to assure every one who believes, that he shall be cleansed from his Sins, as certainly as he sees that *Water*, and that he shall be fed with the Grace of God, as certainly as he feeds on this *Bread* and *Wine*."[23] Wesley further explained that "as Bread and Wine keep our *Natural Life*, so doth our Lord Jesus by a continual *Supply* of Strength and Grace, represented by Bread and Wine, sustain that *Spiritual Life* which he hath procured us by his Cross."[24] There can be no doubt as to Wesley's belief that the elements used for the Holy Communion service do, in fact, act in the fullest sense of the Reformation's definition of a sacrament, as a physical sign instituted by Christ to point beyond to the thing signified, the presence and grace of Christ.

The fourth section, *Means of Grace*, summarizes the previous three and draws conclusions from them. To sum up, Wesley stated

> I come then to God's Altar with a full Persuasion, that these Words, *This is my Body*, promise me more than a *Figure*; That this Holy Banquet is not a bare *Memorial* only, but may actually *convey* as many Blessings to me, as it brings Curses on the Profane Receiver. Indeed in what *manner* this is done, I know not; it is enough for me to admire. *One thing I know* (as said the Blind Man of our Lord) *He laid Clay upon mine Eyes and behold I see.* He hath blessed and given me this Bread and my Soul received Comfort.[25]

20. Ibid., 5.
21. Dix, *The Shape of the Liturgy*, 245.
22. *HLS*, 6.
23. Ibid., 9, italics included.
24. Ibid., 10, italics included.
25. Ibid., 13–14, italics included.

These elements convey Christ's real presence in a fuller way than merely recalling a past event, and in so doing, they dispense, to the one who faithfully receives them, God's grace. It is at this point in the extract that Wesley made a statement that is a defining statement of his view on the Lord's Supper as a means of grace, which is an important point considering how prominent the means of grace were to the Methodist movement in general and to John Wesley in particular. Wesley wrote

> Of these Blessings Christ from above is pleased to bestow sometimes more, sometimes less, in the several Ordinances of his Church, which as the Stars of Heaven, differ from each other in Glory. *Fasting, Prayer, Hearing* his Word, are all good Vessels, to draw Water from this Well of Salvation. But they are not all equal. The Holy Communion when well used, exceeds as much in Blessing, as it exceeds in danger of a Curse, when wickedly and irreverently taken.[26]

In light of this passage, Borgen stated, "for John and Charles Wesley the Lord's Supper is, and always remains, the means of grace *par excellence*."[27] This understanding was informed and reinforced, no doubt, from Wesley's exchange with the Moravians over the Stillness Controversy. It was there, it will be remembered, that Wesley first put forth the notion that the Lord's Supper could convey not only confirming grace to a Christian already, but justifying grace in saving one spiritually ready for the experience of salvation, and even prevenient grace for those who are in the early stages of the journey.

Because the above quotation is so pivotal for discerning Wesley's Eucharistic theology, it is important here to compare it to Brevint's original statement. The passage in Brevint is as follows:

> Of these Blessings, Christ from above is pleased to dispense, sometimes more, sometimes less, into these *inferior Courts of the People*, either according to the several Degrees of their Faith, or according to the several Ways and Times which he hath appointed to them, for presenting themselves nearer to him. All Worshipers do not come to him with the same Faith; nor have all Seasons and Ways (though approved and appointed by him) the same or equal Privilege: and his Ordinances in the Church, as well as his Stars in Heaven, differ in Glory one from another. *Fasting, Prayer, Hearing* of the Word, publick [sic] and private *Services*, and all like holy Duties, are all very good Vessels to

---

26. Ibid., 15, italics included.
27. Borgen, *Wesley*, 120.

> draw Water from this Well of Salvation; but yet they are not all equal. The blessed Communion must exceed as much in Blessings, when well used, as it exceeds in Danger of a Curse, when it is not.[28]

Wesley obviously abbreviated this passage. Any reference that could be construed in a Calvinist manner, in supporting the doctrine of predestination, was removed (such as the "Ways and Times" portion) and the sentence structure in what was left was improved for ease of reading. Ultimately, what this shows is that the statement Wesley printed in his extract was not simply Brevint's understanding of the Eucharist, but Wesley's own theological understanding of it. The passage did not escape Wesley's notice nor was it accidentally printed in his extract; Wesley seriously edited it and published it for the edification of believers in his own time. Wesley took ownership of this passage as truth concerning the Eucharist.

The fifth section, *Pledge of Future Glory*, completed the discussion of the Eucharist as a sacrament. In this section, Wesley rounded out the temporal aspects of the Lord's Supper. Having written at length on the way in which it looks back to Christ's sacrifice (yet not merely recall, but re-present), and how it is a present means of receiving God's grace given to us, he then described how it also points forward to the Christian's inheritance in the future. Comparing this aspect of the Eucharist to a king giving an emblem or implement to a person in order to signify the honor given or a parent giving land, but through a piece of paper, to a child, "the Giver cannot put into his Friend's Hands, Houses and Lands, because they are of an immoveable Nature. And therefore this must be supplied by some Forms or Tokens, by which his Design may be sufficiently made known."[29] Wesley then made this connection explicit. "Wherefore as the Kingdom of *Israel* was once made over to *David*, with the Oil that *Samuel* pour'd upon his Head: So the Body and Blood of Jesus, is *in full Value*, and heaven with all its Glory, *in sure Title* made over to True Christians by that Bread and Wine which they receive in the Holy Communion: The Minister of Christ having as much Power from his Master for doing this, as any Prophet ever had for what he did."[30] With this delineated, Wesley now had shown that the Lord's Supper conveyed grace to believers through Christ's presence in the sacrament, pointing them at once back to Calvary and forward to Eternity.

The remaining three sections, detailing how the sacrament is also a sacrifice, essentially countered the concept described by the twentieth

---

28. Brevint, *Christian Sacrament*, 51–52.
29. *HLS*, 19.
30. Ibid., italics included.

century term "cheap grace," as delineated by Dietrich Bonhoeffer.[31] There was for Wesley a very sacrificial nature to the Eucharist, although not in the same way the Roman Catholic Church would describe it with the implications of re-sacrifice inherent in transubstantiation. A few quotations from these sections will suffice to illustrate Wesley's view.

> All comes to this, 1. That the *Sacrifice* in itself, can never be repeated; 2. That nevertheless, this Sacrament, by our Remembrance, becomes a kind of *Sacrifice*, whereby we present before God the Father, that precious Oblation of his Son once offered. And thus do we every Day offer unto God, the meritorious Sufferings of our Lord, as the only sure ground whereon God may give, and we obtain the Blessings we pray for.[32]

> Tho' the Sacrifice of ourselves cannot *procure* Salvation, yet it is altogether needful to our *receiving* it ... Christians are not crucified in the same manner as Christ was, yet because they cast themselves upon his Cross and Sufferings, as the only Means of Atonement for their Sins and Salvation for their Souls, because of the Grief they suffer to think of the Son of God thus dying, dying only for their Sake, which is as a Sword both to pierce their Hearts, and to pierce and crucify their Sins, and because their whole Body of Sin being thus crucified, there remains no Life in them, but what is offered up to God's Service: On all these Grounds, the Saviour thus offering himself, and the Saved so united to Him by Faith, so partaking of his Sufferings, and so given up to his Will, are accounted before God, one and the same Sacrifice.[33]

> In a Word, whensoever we offer ourselves, we offer by the self same Act, all that we *have*, all that we *can*, and do therein engage for all, that it shall be dedicated to the Glory of God, and that it shall be surrender'd [sic] into his Hands, and employed for such Uses as he shall appoint.[34]

These show that, for Wesley, Communion was not only a person coming to receive a blessing from God that occurred in the Lord's Supper, but a person coming to be identified with the sacrifice of Christ, and to likewise make a self-sacrifice, as it were, as he or she received the gifts of God.

31. "Cheap grace means the justification of sin without the justification of the sinner" (Bonhoeffer, *Cost of Discipleship*, 35).
32. *HLS*, 21–22, italics included.
33. Ibid., 23, 25, italics included.
34. Ibid., 29–30, italics included.

These concepts of the Eucharist, found in this extract, would carry on throughout Wesley's teaching and preaching concerning the Lord's Supper. It is echoed in his sermon *The Means of Grace* (Sermon 16) when he asked, "Is not the eating of that bread, and the drinking of that cup, the outward, visible means, whereby God conveys into our souls all that spiritual grace . . . which were purchased by the body of Christ once broken and the blood of Christ once shed for us?"[35] It is also found in numerous places among his *Journal* entries relating how the grace of God was present at the celebration of the Eucharist.

## AN ADDITIONAL UNDERSTANDING: THE ECCLESIOLOGICAL DIMENSION

In addition to the above references to the Lord's Supper and Wesley's theology surrounding the sacrament, there are also instances of the Lord's Supper that do not fit directly into this soteriological understanding as being a means of grace. These references focus on, not the relation of the Eucharist to a believer, but on the relation of the Eucharist to the Church. Wesley had not only a soteriological dimension of the Eucharist, but also an ecclesiological dimension to his Eucharistic theology. In other words, the Lord's Supper was not only a means of grace for an individual believer, conveying the presence of God and God's redeeming work in that person's life, but it also had a communal function in helping define what a true Church is.

Of course, this ecclesiological dimension is perfectly Anglican in understanding as well. Article XIX of the Thirty-Nine Articles of Religion stated plainly that "The visible Church of Christ is a congregation of faithful men, in which the pure Word of God is preached, and the Sacraments be duly ministered according to Christ's ordinance."[36] It was with this understanding of the ecclesial function of the sacrament that Wesley kept the Methodists securely within the fold of the Church during his lifetime. It was also to this one point that Wesley repeatedly referred critics who accused him or his movement from Dissenting and separating from the Established Church. This can be seen in several instances throughout his *Works*. Two instances in Wesley's sermons are in *Attending the Church Service* and *The Ministerial Office* respectively. In *Attending the Church Service* (Sermon 104) Wesley wrote, "Yea, it was one of our original rules, that very member of our society should attend the church and sacrament, unless he had been

---

35. Wesley, *Works*, 1.389–90.
36. *Queen Elizabeth's Prayer Book*.

bred among Christians of any other denomination,"[37] in which the implication was that this person ought to go to the denomination of which he "had been bred" in order to receive the Eucharist. In *The Ministerial Office* (Sermon CXV) he wrote

> I wish all of you who are vulgarly termed Methodists would seriously consider what has been said. And particularly you whom God hath commissioned to call sinners to repentance. It does by no means follow from hence, that ye are commissioned to baptize, or to administer the Lord's Supper. Ye never dreamed of this, for ten or twenty years after ye began to preach . . . Ye were, fifty years ago, those of you that were then Methodist preachers, *extraordinary messengers* of God . . . to "provoke to jealousy," the ordinary messengers. In God's name, stop there . . . Ye yourselves were at first called in the Church of England; and though ye have and will have a thousand temptations to leave it, and set up for yourselves, regard them not; be Church-of-England men still.[38]

The point Wesley made was that for the Methodists to have the Eucharist it would mean a schism from the Church of England, a schism that Wesley never desired to occur. Thus, since the Methodists under Wesley's leadership were not to become a separate Church from the Established Church, they necessarily could not have the sacraments within their worship as this would, per Article XIX above, have meant they were a separate ecclesial body. Ironically, Wesley used this exact Article of Religion to defend his Methodists early in their life from a critic who accused them of separating from the Church. On February 6, 1740, Wesley deftly wrote that it was the vast majority of the members of the Church of England that have separated from it because they were not faithful men, were unholy, denied the veracity of Scripture, and receive the Lord's Supper in an unworthy manner.[39]

In his polemical writings Wesley continued this ecclesiological dimension of his Eucharistic theology. In *An Earnest Appeal to Men of Reason and Religion*, written in 1744, Wesley wrote when dealing with this particular Article of Religion

> The Third thing requisite (if not to the being, at least) to the well-being of a Church, is the due administration of the sacraments, particularly that of the Lord's Supper. And are we, in this respect, underminers or destroyers of the Church? Do we, either

37. Wesley, *Works*, 3.466.
38. Wesley, *Works* (Jackson), 7.279–80.
39. Wesley, *Works*, 19.138.

> by our example or advice, draw men away from the Lord's table? Where we have laboured most, are there the fewest communicants . . . Do we leave the ordinances of the Church? You daily see and know the contrary . . . You know they [Methodists] are more diligent therein than ever; it being one of the fixed rules of our societies, that every member attend the ordinances of God . . . Hence, wherever the power of the Lord spreads, springs outward religion in all its forms. The houses of God are filled; the table of the Lord is thronged on every side.[40]

Wesley further elucidated the ecclesiological dimension in *A Farther Appeal to Men of Reason and Religion*, written between 1744 and 1745, in which he stated, "We continually exhort all who attend on our preaching to attend the offices of the Church. And they do pay a more regular attendance there than ever they did before."[41]

Later in this treatise Wesley brought up another criticism of the Methodists, that they were trying to subvert the Church of England by not adhering to its canons regarding the Lord's Supper. To this Wesley responded, "You object also, that they break through the twenty-eighth Canon, which requires, 'That if strangers come often to any church from other parishes, they should be remitted to their own churches, there to receive the communion with their neighbours.' But what, if there be no communion there? Then this Canon does not touch the case; nor does anyone break it, by coming to another church purely because there is no communion at his own."[42] This particular response is illuminating for two reasons. First, the Methodists obviously understood Wesley's soteriological dimension of Eucharistic theology. They were willing to travel across parish boundaries simply to have the opportunity to receive the Lord's Supper. The desire for this means of grace *par excellence* had indeed been planted within their souls. Second, Wesley reaffirmed his commitment to the ecclesiological dimension of his Eucharistic theology by encouraging the Methodists to go to an Established Church parish, *any* Established Church parish, to receive the Lord's Supper, and then defended them from criticism for so doing.

Finally, Wesley stated one last defense of his lay preachers in the same treatise that would be echoed years later in *The Ministerial Office* above. Of them he wrote, "But they [the lay preachers] no more take upon them to be Priests than to be Kings. They take not upon them to administer the

---

40. Ibid., 11.78, 82, 83, 89.
41. Ibid., 11.122.
42. Ibid., 11.185.

sacraments,—an honour peculiar to the Priests of God."[43] Here again is the understanding that, since Methodism is a society within the Church, its preachers have no right to administer the sacraments. Rather, the Methodists are to attend the Church services in order to receive the sacrament as often as possible. Methodists do not wish to separate from the Church of England (at least as far as Wesley was concerned), and therefore they do not administer the sacraments. This sentiment was then reiterated in *Principles of a Methodist Farther Explained* in 1746 when Wesley stated emphatically, "No. This society does not separate from the communion of the rest of the Church of England. They continue steadfastly with them, both 'in the apostolical [sic] doctrine, and in the breaking of bread, and in prayers.'"[44]

It is also necessary here to explicitly illustrate what has been alluded to in many of the above quoted passages, namely the rules governing the Methodist societies, from the average members to the itinerant lay preachers. The *General Rules of the United Societies*, which were written in 1743, stated that Methodist society members would continue in good standing within the societies (the only condition for membership being a "desire 'to flee from the wrath to come'") "by attending upon all the ordinances of God. Such are, the public worship of God; the ministry of the word, either read or expounded; the supper of the Lord; family and private prayer; searching the Scriptures; and fasting, or abstinence."[45] While this only states that a Methodist society member will receive the Lord's Supper, it does not state how often that reception should occur. However, in the *Directions given to the Band-Societies* in 1744, that issue is clarified. As a member of a Band, a Methodist is "to be at church and at the Lord's table every week."[46] The location, an Established Church, and the frequency, every week, are delineated for the Band member.

In addition to the requirements to receive the Lord's Supper as a faithful Methodist member, there were also instructions and items of clarification for those in Methodist leadership. These are contained within the *Minutes of Some Late Conversations* and *Minutes of Several Conversations* (more commonly known as the *Large Minutes*). These two documents, especially the latter, served as the doctrine and discipline for the Methodist societies while Wesley was alive. They were also the basis for the first official polity book for the Methodist Episcopal Church in America years later. In *Late Conversations*, the following is found:

43. Ibid., 11.300.
44. Ibid., 9.192.
45. Ibid., 9.73
46. Ibid., 9.79.

> Q.7. Do we separate from the Church?
>
> A. We conceive not: We hold communion therewith for conscience' sake, by constantly attending both the word preached and the sacraments administered therein.[47]

Within the *Large Minutes* there are numerous instructions for various leaders within the societies. Advice given to Assistants included, "Exhort all our people to keep close to the Church and sacrament."[48] In addition to this example for the Assistants, in order to watch over the Helpers, the question was asked of them, "Do you constantly attend the church and sacrament?"[49] Each of these quotations shows the value of the soteriological dimension of the Eucharist. There is no other reason why leaders would be so instructed to receive it as often as this. However, there is also the ecclesiological dimension to the advice, namely that the Assistant and Helper attend the Church to receive the sacrament. There is the constant reminder that it is within the context of the Established Church's services that the sacrament is to be received.

This fact cannot be underestimated. When dealing with Wesleyan studies and Methodist understandings of the Eucharist, this ecclesiological dimension of Wesley's teaching and understanding of the sacrament is often overlooked, only to be brought up as a side item in relation to the reception of the Methodists within the Church or with respect to Wesley's ordinations. The unfortunate result of this is that many of the references Wesley made to the Eucharist are left out of the discussion of Wesley's Eucharistic theology. For example, in Borgen's *John Wesley on the Sacraments*, there is no mention of the ecclesiological dimension at all. Wesley had both a Calvinistic understanding of the Eucharist and a Zwinglian understanding of the Eucharist, which ought not be surprising given the atmosphere of "comprehension" within the Church of England. Christ was, indeed, present in the sacrament and it was an effectual means of grace (the supreme means of grace) in the life of a believer (Calvin); but the sacrament was also a marker of what a true Church is, showing the life of the Church and the fellowship of her members to the world (Zwingli). Of course, Wesley did not call himself Calvinist or Zwinglian with respect to the Eucharist; he was a Church of England man—a Church which had both Calvinist and Zwinglian aspects to its theology. And since those theological terms have much wider implications attached to them, both today and in the eighteenth century, implications that have nothing to do with the Eucharist at all, for the purposes of

---

47. Wesley, *Works* (Jackson), 8.280.
48. Ibid., 8.320.
49. Ibid., 8.325.

this study functional labels are used for these two views: soteriological and ecclesiological. For Wesley, the Eucharist was both soteriological, a means of grace, and ecclesiological, a marker of a true Christian Church, and it is to this issue that we will now turn.[50]

---

50. See Appendix A for a chart listing several of Wesley's references categorized in these two terms.

# Chapter 5

# Full Tables of Methodism

## THE STRUCTURE OF METHODISM

To describe adequately and accurately how John Wesley's Eucharistic theology was viewed, accepted, rejected or modified in Methodist piety, we must first have a working knowledge of what Methodism looked like and how it functioned during Wesley's lifetime. With this in mind, it will be necessary to describe Methodist polity briefly in order to facilitate a more comprehensive understanding of Methodist piety, and even though that is a straightforward endeavor, it will be seen that the organizational structure of Methodism moved in anything but a straightforward manner.

Methodism was a renewal movement, and it was reactionary in its logistical and organizational structure. Wesley made a fairly typical account of creating one of the structural innovations during the early years of the movement in which he stated, "While we were thinking of quite another thing, we struck upon a method for which we have cause to bless God ever since."[1] As needs arose, so did structure. In fact, the entire rise of Methodism was a reaction to a need. Several people wanted to receive from Wesley leadership "to direct and quicken us in our way, to give us the advices which you well know we need, and to pray with us, as well as for us."[2] Out of this was born the first Methodist Society. Wesley remarked, "Thus arose, without any previous design on either side, what was afterwards called *a Society*; a very innocent name, and very common in London, for any number of

---

1. Wesley, *Works*, 9.260.
2. Ibid., 9.256.

people associating themselves together."³ As the groundwork was set for this initial group of people seeking guidance, the admission requirement was set; "There is one only condition previously required in those who desire admission into this society,—'a desire to flee from the wrath to come, to be saved from their sins.'"⁴

Having such a broad entry requirement, the Methodist Society quickly had many and varied groups of people within it. Those who were serious about growing in grace were organized into small accountability groups called Bands, while the rest were simply members of the Society. This proved an inadequate design, for it gave no real oversight or guidance to those who (probably) needed it most. As a result, much time was spent reviewing the conduct and growth of every member of the Society by Wesley himself. This can be seen in a *Journal* entry for April 7, 1741.

> In the evening, having desired all the Bands to meet, I read over the names of the United Society; and marked those who were of a doubtful character, that full inquiry might be made concerning them. On *Thursday*, at the meeting of that society, I read over the names of these, and desire to speak with each of them the next day, as soon as they had opportunity. Many of them afterwards gave sufficient proof, that they were seeking Christ in sincerity. The rest I determined to keep on trial, till the doubts concerning them were removed.⁵

The Methodist Society continued in this manner for one more year, and as it continued to grow, this method continued to become untenable. On February 15 of the next year, there was a decision made for the Bristol Society that, not just the serious members, but also the whole Society be grouped together in smaller units, for the purposes of discharging their debt. Each member of the Society was grouped into "little companies, or classes—about twelve in each class"⁶ and a leader was placed over them to collect one penny from each member weekly. As this scheme began, Wesley recounted that "some of [the leaders] informed me, they found such and such an one did not live as he ought. It struck me immediately, 'This is the thing; the very thing we have wanted so long.'"⁷ Once this concept and structure of Classes proved to be a success in watching after members, it was transported to all the Societies, and speaking of the institution of

3. Ibid.
4. Ibid., 9.257.
5. Ibid., 19.190.
6. Ibid., 19.251.
7. Ibid., 9.261.

them in London on April 25, 1742, Wesley stated, "This was the origin of our classes at London, for which I can never sufficiently praise God; the unspeakable usefulness of the institution having ever since been more and more manifest."[8]

It should be noted here that the organizational structure of Methodism occurred backward from the conventional wisdom of its development. In *A Plain Account of the People Called Methodists*, written in 1748, Wesley recounted the beginnings of the United Societies. Then he proceeded to tell of the creation of the class meetings and many of the Methodists' objections to being required to attend a class meeting. Further on in the treatise Wesley explained the creation of the band. He stated that there were some people who desired to watch over their Christian walk more closely. "In compliance with their desire, I divided them into smaller companies," which he called bands.[9] This ordering of the creation of classes and bands has led most Methodist history works to delineate the creation of bands after the creation of the class meeting. However, a simple look at the dates of the entries from Wesley's Journal proves that the bands predated the classes by at least one year. The earliest reference to a band Wesley provided was with respect to several of the women who joined the new meeting at the Foundry after the schism with the Fetter Lane society over the Stillness Controversy on July 23, 1740, one-and-a-half years before the creation of the first class in Bristol and nearly two years before the structure was replicated in London.[10] This is important for one illustrative reason: Methodism created new ways of being and doing as an answer to specific problems in one locale and, when the new method or mode proved successful in one place, it was exported to all others to be replicated and implemented. This is a facet of Methodist life that will be revisited in the future.

Nevertheless, after 1742 and the replication of the classes, the Methodist movement had the discernable structure for which it became well known. A Methodist was a member of the Society, of which all were members of a class. Those who were more serious about growing in their faith continued in their respective Bands, arranged according to marital status and gender. Finally, a new layer was added after this, the Select-Band. It was the smallest of all the sub-groups within Methodism, and was comprised of those individuals who claimed to have experienced entire sanctification or who were sincerely seeking after it. Each layer of organization, from the Bands to

---

8. Ibid., 19.258.
9. Ibid., 9.267.
10. Ibid., 19.163.

the Classes to the Select-Bands, was founded out of necessity to continue to provide the best oversight and care for the people called Methodist.

## METHODIST EUCHARISTIC PIETY

### The Methodist Piety

J. Earnest Rattenbury has stated, "The claim has sometimes been made that the religious revival of the eighteenth century might as truly be called Sacramental as Evangelical."[11] This understanding is due, in large part, to John Wesley's insistence that the Lord's Supper was the means of grace *par excellence*, and his understanding was communicated very clearly to English Methodists. This had the net result of Methodism's spread in a new spiritual understanding among its members and a renewed commitment to receiving the sacrament as often as it was made available. Within the major urban areas of London and Bristol, it was possible for most Methodists to receive the sacrament monthly, if not weekly, either from Established Churches or (much later) within their own chapels; and they availed themselves of this opportunity.[12]

It has already been seen how John Wesley viewed the Lord's Supper, and much of that view did, in fact, transfer to his spiritual children. In correspondences dated to 1751, Rev. Henry Booker, an Anglican priest, wrote to Dr. Maule, the Bishop of Meath,

> Last Christmas Day I had at the Sacrament above fifty whose faces I had scarce seen at the church before, and upon enquiry into their characters, found them mostly to have been persons of very profligate lives. About a fortnight ago one of them told me it was a great trouble to the [Methodist] Society that they had not more frequent opportunities of receiving the Communion . . . Some had come that morning, as I was informed, very near ten miles on foot, though the weather was very severe and had prevented several. I had seventy communicants, true piety and charity sat smiling on their face; and I must say I never saw Divine service heard with so much reverence and attention. I was told there were but three in the congregation that did not profess themselves of that Society . . . I must declare that my church, at least its Communion table, owes almost nine in ten of

11. Rattenbury, *Eucharistic Hymns*, 3.
12. Bowmer, *Sacrament*, 72.

its company to their labours, and I can affirm the same of one or two neighbouring parishes.[13]

This quotation is telling in that it is from one who was not a Methodist and yet saw, firsthand, the effect Methodism had on its members' Eucharistic piety. This same event could have been told in numerous parishes all over England during much of Wesley's life.[14] Wesley lifted up examples like these in generalities (for the instances were profuse) to prove the value of his Methodist movement. One such generality was highlighted in the last chapter; in *An Earnest Appeal to Men of Reason and Religion* Wesley wrote

> The Third thing requisite (if not to the being, at least) to the well-being of a Church, is the due administration of the sacraments, particularly that of the Lord's supper. And are we, in this respect, underminers or destroyers of the Church? Do we, either by our example or advice, draw men away from the Lord's table? Where we have laboured most, are there the fewest communicants? How does the fact stand in London, Bristol, Newcastle? O that you would no longer shut your eyes against the broad light which encompasses you on every side.[15]

And he continued the sentiment throughout the work when he continued, "You know they [Methodists] are more diligent therein than ever; it being one of the fixed rules of our societies, that every member attend the ordinances of God . . . Hence, wherever the power of the Lord spreads, springs outward religion in all its forms. The houses of God are filled; the table of the Lord is thronged on every side."[16] In fact, it was instances such as these that got Wesley and the Methodists into trouble in some locales. Also highlighted above, in his *Farther Appeal to Men of Reason and Religion* Wesley had to defend the piety of his Methodists from verbal attack. It was in that treatise that Wesley defended the conduct of Methodists' breaking the twenty-eighth Canon by jumping parish boundaries to receive the Eucharist where ever and when ever it was celebrated. Rev. Booker's letter above shows this parish-jumping firsthand. Such was the Eucharistic piety among early Methodists.

Many Methodists of the era wrote and spoke of their own experiences surrounding the Lord's Supper. One prime example is an early Methodist

13. Church, *Early Methodist People*, 5.

14. With the exception of the Society at Norwich, this was the case. For the peculiarities in that locale, see Bowmer, *Sacrament*, 73–75.

15. Wesley, *Works*, 11.78.

16. Ibid., 11.83, 89.

convert named Sarah Ryan. Sarah was at Spitalfields Church in April of 1754 when she heard John Wesley preach. She was convicted of sin and went forward to receive the Lord's Supper. Unable to partake on Wesley's first pass by her while he was serving Communion for the enormity of grief she felt, she was given the bread when Wesley came back again. This still did not resolve her inner struggle. She said, "I wanted a clear witness that my sins were forgiven and ardently did I wish for the next Sunday, hoping I should receive it at the table."[17] Finally, on Easter Eve, during Communion, Sarah received that which she sought.

> Just as I came to the rails, God spoke these words to my soul, "Lift your Eyes of Faith, and look / On the signs He did ordain! / Thus the Bread of Life was broke, / Thus the Lamb of God was slain, / Thus was shed on *Calvary* / His last Drop of Blood for me!" Immediately I was filled with light and joy and love, and said with confidence, "Thou art the resurrection and the life" [John 11.25] . . . I fell back in my seat and was quite overwhelmed with the power and love of God.[18]

Another example is Sarah Crosby. This Sarah had a conversion experience, but was doubtful of its reality. She said, "I feared to believe he had done it, but asked a token and prayed he would stamp me with his Spirit's seal and speak to my soul at his table,"[19] which God did and confirmed, through Communion, that she was indeed saved.

Hester Ann Rogers was one more eminent Methodist woman who had a profound Eucharistic piety. A book entitled *The Experience of Mrs. Hester Ann Rogers* was first published in 1796 containing extracts from her journal. In later editions of the book letters, devotionals, and her funeral sermon preached by Thomas Coke were included. This "quickly became one of the most popular devotional publications in early Methodism, on both sides of the Atlantic."[20] In her journal, there are several instances where she was profoundly moved by the Communion service and sacrament. She wrote, "As Mr. Simpson was reading that sentence in the communion service, 'If any man sin, we have an advocate with the Father, Jesus Christ the righteous, and he is the propitiation for our sins,' a ray of divine light and comfort was darted on my soul and I cried, 'Lord Jesus, let me feel thou art

---

17. Chilcote, *Early Methodist Spirituality*, 79.
18. Ibid. The part in verse is from *HLS,* Hymn XVIII, 14.
19. Ibid., 85.
20. Ibid., 104.

the propitiation for my sins.' I was enabled to believe there was mercy for me, and I, even I, should be saved!"[21]

This account was a recurring theme in the Wesleyan revival, people describing their assurance of salvation during Holy Communion. It would seem that, due to this event, Hester carried a deep appreciation of the sacrament throughout her life. Nineteen years later she wrote, "I was very happy at the new church especially while I viewed in the elements of bread and wine my Savior's body broken and his blood shed for me. Never do I partake of this blessed ordinance in vain. Coming in faith I always prove his flesh is meat indeed and his blood is drink indeed, and often do I wonder how any that love the Redeemer can stay away when this table is spread before them."[22] This instance, coupled with an extract from the journal of a Methodist woman from later years, Mary Entwisle, show the depth of Eucharistic piety and the variety of theological understandings within Methodism concerning the "blessed ordinance." Mary wrote in 1795, "O Lord if it be your blessed will grant that liberty of conscience may be granted us with respect to our commemorating your dying love."[23] Here we see Methodists continually pressing for the sacraments, even while holding such varying views of it that tend toward both Zwinglian memorialism and a real, physical presence (trans- or con-substantiation). Whether these Methodists understood Christ to be physically present, spiritually present, or remembered in the past, they had a profound appreciation and draw towards the sacrament of his Supper.

## Wesley's Soteriological Eucharistic Theology Shapes the Methodist Piety

Of course, these instances of Methodism's desire for the sacrament are only natural when one sees how John Wesley's Eucharistic theology informed and shaped Methodist piety on the subject. We have seen above that Methodists continually attended the sacrament in greater numbers than many parish churches had seen in previous years, even to the point of crossing parish boundaries to receive when it was not administered within their home parish. There are examples from Wesley's own works, both when teaching Methodists and when trying to defend Methodism from attacks by its opponents, describing how the average Methodist felt towards and reasoned about the sacrament.

21. Rogers, *Experience of Hester Ann Rogers*, 23.
22. Chilcote, *Early Methodist Spirituality*, 118.
23. Ibid., 129.

First and foremost with respect to the sacrament for Methodists, as it has been previously noted above, there are the *General Rules of the United Societies* (which all Methodists were required to keep), the *Directions Given to the Band-Societies* (which those seeking or professing sanctification were required to keep), and the *Large Minutes* (which the leaders were required to follow) which built into the Methodist system a requirement to participate in and receive the Lord's Supper, which, based upon the extracts from various journal entries above, was not just an empty requirement, but rather one adhered to by the Methodists. In these simple requirements to be a Methodist and qualify for leadership within Methodism, Wesley's understanding of the Eucharist as the means of grace *par excellence* can be seen as an embodied reality to inculcate Eucharistic piety among the Methodists, leaders and people alike.

Beyond these official requirements to be a Methodist lay leader or member in good standing highlighted above, Wesley published or preached upon the Lord's Supper either as a main point or a subsidiary point in several instances. The sermon that is most readily identified with Wesley's understanding of the Lord's Supper is *The Duty of Constant Communion* (Sermon 101) in which Wesley stated, "It is the duty of every Christian to receive the Lord's Supper as often as he can."[24] This was also reiterated in a sermon preached in 1790 entitled *On the Wedding Garment* (Sermon 127) in which Wesley stated, "There needs no more to induce any man of a tender conscience to communicate at all opportunities, than that single commandment of our Lord, 'Do this in remembrance of me.'"[25] Also concerning the Lord's Supper is *The Means of Grace* (Sermon 16) in which Wesley preached, "All who desire the grace of God are to wait for it in partaking of the Lord's supper."[26] One can hear the echo of the Stillness Controversy within the words of this sermon with the emphasis on waiting by receiving the sacrament in opposition to waiting in stillness. In his sermon *On Zeal* (Sermon 92) Wesley preached that, "At the same time they [all that truly fear God] should be more zealous for the *ordinances* of God; for public and private prayer, for hearing and reading the word of God, and for fasting, and the Lord's Supper."[27] In *Working Out our Own Salvation* (Sermon 85) Wesley said, "At every opportunity, be a partaker of the Lord's Supper. 'Do this in remembrance' of him; and he will meet you at his own table."[28] In

---

24. Wesley, *Works*, 3.428.
25. Ibid., 4.141.
26. Ibid., 1.389.
27. Ibid., 3.318–19.
28. Ibid., 3.205–6.

*The Scripture Way of Salvation* (Sermon 43) Wesley, in reference to sanctification, preached, "'But what good works are those, the practice of which you affirm to be necessary to sanctification?' First, all works of piety; such as public prayer, family prayer, and praying in our closet; receiving the supper of the Lord."[29] Finally, there are Wesley's statements in the *Fifth* and *Sixth Discourses Upon the Sermon on the Mount* (Sermons 25 and 26)

> Let not thy righteousness fall short of theirs [Pharisees] with regard to the ordinances of God ... Neglect no occasion of eating that bread and drinking that cup which is the communion of the body and blood of Christ.[30]

> It was the judgment of many of the ancient fathers, that we are here to understand [with reference to "daily bread"] the sacramental bread also; daily received in the beginning by the whole church of Christ, and highly esteemed, till the love of many waxed cold, *as the grand channel whereby the grace of his Spirit was conveyed to the souls of all the children of God*.[31]

These instances within Wesley's writings focus on the soteriological dimension of his Eucharistic theology. It is obvious that this dimension of his theology was transferred to the Methodists within his lifetime. Instances of full communion tables and parishioners crossing parish boundaries to receive the sacrament can only be understood in light of this soteriological dimension. Nevertheless, it is crucial to remember that Wesley also had an ecclesiological dimension to his Eucharistic theology. This ecclesiological aspect to his theology was also transferred to the Methodists, although not as uniformly as his soteriological dimension, and it, too, had an impact upon their whole Eucharistic theology.

## Wesley's Ecclesiological Eucharistic Theology Shapes Methodist Piety

The ecclesiological dimension of Eucharistic theology in Wesley's writings takes on a different attitude towards Methodists and the Lord's Supper than the soteriological dimension. Whereas the latter dimension dealt with the Eucharist as the supreme means of grace, the former dimension dealt with the issue of potentially separating from the Church of England. In these instances, Wesley constantly advocated self-restraint concerning the

---

29. Ibid., 2.166.
30. Ibid., 1.569–70.
31. Ibid., 1.584–5, emphasis added.

sacraments. In Wesley's view, only a true Church could duly administer the sacraments, and since he did not wish for Methodism to become a separate Church, he discouraged Methodists from receiving (or even desiring to receive) the Lord's Supper outside of a regular Church service.

This ecclesiological dimension served a dual role for Wesley during his life. First, he could defend his Methodists against critics who would argue that Wesley and those who followed him were dissenters. Several quotations to this effect were referenced in the preceding chapter, but to these it should be added the following

> *Principles of a Methodist Farther Explained* (1746)—Nothing can prove, I am no member of the Church, till I either am excommunicated, or renounce her communion, and no longer join in her doctrine, and in the breaking of bread, and in prayer.[32]

> *An Answer to an Important Question* (1787)—They [Established clergy] are well pleased, that their parishioners grow more diligent and honest, and are constant attendants on the church and sacrament [because of Methodism].[33]

> *To Certain Persons in Dublin* (1789)—I do not separate from the Church, nor have any intention so to do. Neither do they that meet on Sunday-noon [Methodists] separate from the Church, any more than they did before: Nay, less; for they attend the church and sacrament oftener now than they did two years ago.[34]

> *To the Bishop of—*(1790)—The Methodists, in general, my Lord, are members of the Church of England. They hold all her doctrines, attend her service, and partake of her sacraments.[35]

Second, through this ecclesiological dimension of his Eucharistic theology, Wesley could ensure the continuation of the Methodists within the Church of England by denying the lay preachers the authority of administering the sacrament. This can be best illustrated in *The Ministerial Office* and the *Large Minutes* regarding the question of separation and the duties of the itinerant lay preachers, both detailed in the preceding chapter.

The problem—and it was a problem that continued to grow throughout Wesley's life—was that Methodism was becoming more and more organized along the lines of an independent Church and the Methodists began

---

32. Ibid., 9.195.
33. Wesley, *Works* (Jackson), 13.262.
34. Ibid., 13.267
35. Ibid., 13.144.

thinking of their society meetings more and more in the light of an actual worship service. This, coupled with the heavy emphasis upon the necessity of all the means of grace in one's life, led to an increasing desire to receive the sacraments, the supreme means of grace, at the meetings in which they already experienced God's grace. These Eucharistic tensions could not be easily solved because, quite obviously, they pointed in two separate directions. On the one hand, Wesley encouraged his people to avail themselves of the Lord's Supper every chance they could; but on the other hand, he denied the Methodists the very sacrament they so desired within their own meetings. By October of 1770 this led to a compromise with the society in Bristol in which the Wesleys themselves would administer the Lord's Supper every other Sunday in the society meeting. John Wesley thus recorded

> *Sunday, October 7, 1770*—My brother and I complied with the desire of many of our friends, and agreed to administer the Lord's Supper every other Sunday at Bristol. We judged it best to have the entire Service, and so began at nine o'clock.[36]

This statement sheds light on the two differing dimensions of Eucharistic theology and piety in both Methodism at that time and John Wesley. First, there was an overwhelming desire to have the sacrament on a regular basis by the Methodists in Bristol. This makes perfect sense given the soteriological understanding of the Eucharist that Wesley instilled in them. Second, even though Wesley compromised and administered the sacrament at the Methodist society meeting, he did so by using the full Sunday Service for the Church of England. If the Methodists could not (or would not) receive the sacrament at a Church of England parish, Wesley would bring the Church of England Service to the Methodists in order for them to receive the sacrament. This also makes perfect sense given the ecclesiological understanding of the Eucharist that Wesley had.

This compromise also seems to have been merely an interim step in the evolution of Methodist worship, even during the life of Wesley. As he explicitly encouraged the Methodists to attend the Church of England for the Lord's Supper, then he allowed that either he or his brother Charles could administer it in the Methodist meeting every other week. By 1787 the frequency of reception had changed.[37] In a sermon entitled *On God's Vineyard* (Sermon 107) Wesley recounted, "Their [Methodist] public service is at five in the morning, and six or seven in the evening, that their temporal business

---

36. Wesley, *Works*, 22.254–55.
37. Outler, *John Wesley*, 104.

may not be hindered. Only on Sunday it begins between nine and ten, *and concludes with the Lord's Supper.*"[38]

Evidently, every other week in one location was not enough for the Methodists. There is no mention of location in this sermon, but the implication in the sermon (and from prior Methodist experience in replicating what "works" from one locale to another) is that weekly administration and reception of the Lord's Supper within the context of Methodist worship was widespread throughout the British Isles. The soteriological dimension was beginning to win out over the ecclesiological dimension of Methodist Eucharistic piety in England, as the Methodists were more and more successful in finding ways to celebrate the Lord's Supper within the context of their own society meetings; they were becoming less tied to the Established Church (or Dissenting congregations if the Methodists were dissenters rather than members of the Church of England) for reception of the Eucharist.

Before leaving the influence Wesley and his *Works* had on Methodist piety, it is necessary to point out one caveat that Wesley regularly explicated in his writings. It is best illustrated by a passage from his sermon *The Means of Grace* (Sermon 16): "Settle this in your heart, that the *opus operatum*, the mere *work done*, profiteth nothing; that there is no *power* to save but in the Spirit of God, no *merit*, but in the blood of Christ; that, consequently, even what God ordains, conveys no grace to the soul, if you trust not in Him alone."[39]

Wesley was very clear that the sacraments themselves were not the end, but the means to the end, which was a salvific relationship with God based upon faith. In this he showed his Protestant heritage quite definitively. It is this mistaken concept of the Lord's Supper, and indeed all the means of grace, that Wesley argued against whenever he set up his argument against having a dead, ritualistic faith. In *The Almost Christian* (Sermon 2) Wesley painted a caricature of one who did not have salvific faith, but yet had all the outward appearances of vital religion. One of the aspects of this was that "when he approaches the table of the Lord, it is not with a light or careless behaviour, but with an air, gesture, and deportment, which speak nothing else, but 'God be merciful to me a sinner.'"[40] Wesley stated this even more forcefully earlier in the *Means of Grace* when he stated

> But we allow, that the whole value of the means [of grace] depends on their actual subservience to the end of religion; that, consequently, all these means, when separate from the end, are

---

38. Wesley, *Works*, 3.512.
39. Ibid., 1.396, emphasis included.
40. Ibid., 1.134.

> less than nothing and vanity; that if they do not actually conduce to the knowledge and love of God, they are not acceptable in his sight; yea, rather, they are an abomination before him, a stink in his nostrils; he is weary to bear them. Above all, if they are used as a kinds of *commutation* for the religion they were designed to subserve, it is not easy to find words for the enormous folly and wickedness of thus turning God's arms against himself; of keeping Christianity out of the heart by those very means which were ordained for the bringing it in.[41]

And in the *Fourth Discourse Upon the Sermon on the Mount* (Sermon 24) he restated the issue, but put forth a resolution as well: "I allow that you, and ten thousand more, have thus abused the ordinances of God; mistaking the means for the end; supposing that the doing these, or some other outward works, either was the religion of Jesus Christ, or would be accepted in the place of it. But let the abuse be taken away, and the use remain. Now use all outward things, but use them with a constant eye to the renewal of your soul in righteousness and holiness."[42]

Here is the caveat and the resolution to the problem. Wesley's Eucharistic theology, with both dimensions, can be summarized as follows: Receive the Eucharist as often as possible because it is the grand channel by which God conveys His grace to us, the means of grace *par excellence*, trusting in God alone to provide the grace through the sacrament; and receive it at an Established Church parish, for that is where it is duly administered. This was a message that was readily received and implemented by the Methodists in England, the first half more so than the second. The first section, to receive the Eucharist as often as possible, was so readily received that it would appear even before Wesley's death in 1791 that the Eucharist was administered in some Methodist meetings on Sundays on a regular basis. The soteriological dimension was winning out in its relationship of tension with the ecclesiological dimension. In fact, by 1797 the soteriological dimension would win out almost completely (which will be discussed below). However, the same tension between the necessity to receive the Eucharist and the necessity to receive it in an Established Church would be resolved in a completely different manner in America. And it is to that continent that we now turn.

---

41. Ibid., 1.381–2, emphasis included.
42. Ibid., 1.545.

Section III

# American Methodism: Immigrant Society

Chapter 6

# Eucharistic Tensions Prior to 1784

## UNOFFICIAL BEGINNINGS

It is almost impossible to give a definitive date for the beginnings of Methodism in America. This is because the Methodist movement in the New World, much like its parent-movement in the Old World, was not one that was definitively planned and implemented. In a completely organic way, it simply grew. Nathan Bangs, an early American Methodist and author of one of the earliest histories, recorded that "The introduction of Methodism into these United States was attended with those circumstances which show how great events often result from comparatively insignificant causes. Like the entire structure of Methodism, it originated without any foresight of man, without any previous design in the instruments to bring about such an event, and without any of those previously devised plans which generally mark all human enterprises."[1] What is known by historical record is that by 1766 there were two societies in what would become the United States: one in New York and one in Maryland. Differing generations of scholarship have placed primacy of foundation back and forth between New York and Maryland. William Warren Sweet noted, "As a matter of plain fact, it is a type of controversy that can never be definitely settled, since the necessary documents on both sides are lacking, and for that reason there can be no historical proof for either contention."[2] But one thing is certain: the society

---

1. Bangs, *History*, 46.
2. Sweet, *Methodism*, 50.

founded in New York was the first properly constituted Methodist Society in North America.

Philip Embury, the man most responsible for founding the New York society, was an Irish immigrant. He was one of the Irish Palatines. These were a group of some 13,000 refugees and their descendants who fled the Lower Palatine region of the Rhine in 1709 due to persecution by the Roman Catholic King Louis XIV of France.[3] They were Protestants and, once settled in Ireland, made a fertile ground for Methodist preachers when, following the example of John Wesley himself, those relentless and industrious preachers began their work in Ireland. Embury, along with many other Irish Palatines, became Methodist. He became a local preacher and was even set aside to be a reserve itinerant preacher in 1758. It is believed that Embury helped on the construction of the Methodist chapel in Courtmatrix in Ireland, being a young carpenter at the time.[4] By 1760, with the intention "to better themselves,"[5] Embury and several others decided to emigrate to New York. "Sometime in the middle of June they sailed from Limerick on the schooner *Pery*, and nine weeks later landed in New York."[6] According to Bangs, when these Irish Methodists arrived in New York, "They were strangers in a strange land; and not finding any pious acquaintances with whom they could associate, they gradually lost their relish for divine things, and sunk away into the spirit of the world."[7] Cooney described the situation succinctly by stating, "These were the first Methodists to arrive in America, and finding no Methodist society there, they did nothing about it for several years."[8]

Among those immigrants was the woman most responsible for founding the New York society, Barbara Heck. Heck was also an Irish Palatine and a Methodist. There is anecdotal evidence found in almost all accounts of the foundation of this Methodist society that it was at the instigation of Heck that Embury started the society in New York. Several years after their arrival in New York, so the story goes, Heck came home one evening to find a card game in her house. In some tellings of the story Embury is one of the participants in the game, in some he is not present. She threw the cards into the fire, and then either turned to Embry (if he was there) or went to his house (if he was not there) and told him "that if he did not preach to the

---

3. Daniels, *History*, 380.
4. Cooney, *Methodists in Ireland*, 231.
5. Ibid., 231.
6. Ibid., 232.
7. Bangs, *History*, 47.
8. Cooney, *Methodists*, 232.

little group they would all go to hell, and God would require their blood at his hands."[9] In the face of such persuasive encouragement, shortly thereafter Embury began to preach and the society began to grow.

At first, Embury's preaching was limited to his own family, the Heck family and their servant, and a few other (up until that point non-practicing) Irish Methodists. These meetings were in Embury's or Heck's home and very quickly outgrew the space available. Sweet related the steady growth thus, "Conversions became of frequent occurrence. Three musicians from the British regimental band, located at the neighboring barracks, joined the group, and soon became active helpers. The superintendent of the almshouse invited Embury to preach there, and several of the inmates were enrolled as members of the society."[10] At this point, around 1766, this newly reconstituted and reinvigorated group of Methodists rented a room near their homes in which to preach and pray for the salvation of, not only their own souls, but the souls of all those around them. Embury continued to preach and exhort his hearers, and their numbers continued to grow. The growth was not exponential, but it was steady. And then a new person joined the society for worship, and this person was wearing a British military uniform.

The British military, which less than ten years later would be the embodiment of an oppressive regime for most Americans, contributed to the establishment of American Methodism in the personage of Captain Thomas Webb. Webb had been converted through hearing one of John Wesley's sermons in Bristol in 1765 and it was quickly noted that he had the gifts of a preacher. Wesley very readily convinced Webb to accept a license to preach.[11] Captain Webb ended up in America as the Barrack-master in Albany, New York and while there, "opened his house for religious services, conducted by himself."[12] He had heard about the fledgling society in New York and, in February of 1767, he arrived at the society meeting in New York and offered his help and leadership to this growing group of Methodists.[13] Because of the novelty of a preacher in uniform, crowds grew rapidly, so rapidly in fact that the society needed to find yet another, larger room to contain all those who wished to attend. It is at this point that the society began renting a rigging loft on Williams Street.[14] Thomas Taylor, a Methodist layman in New York, in a letter he wrote to John Wesley on April 11,

9. Ibid., 233.
10. Sweet, *Methodism*, 54–55.
11. Daniels, *History*, 387.
12. Stevens, *History of the Methodist Episcopal Church*, 1.62.
13. Sweet, *Methodism*, 55.
14. Bangs, *History*, 50.

1768 asking for more help in planting and growing Methodism, recounted Webb's joining the group in New York by writing, "[Webb] found them out and preached in his regimentals. The novelty of a man preaching in a scarlet coat soon brought greater numbers to hear than the room could contain."[15]

As the crowds continued to grow, and as Embury and Webb preached regularly on Thursdays and Sundays, the society decided it was time to build a preaching house. After a fortunate turn of events, they ended up purchasing property on Johns Street rather than leasing land elsewhere, and the Wesley Chapel was built in 1768, just two years after Embury's first sermon in New York. Taylor, in his letter to Wesley, described the turn of events thus

> Great numbers of serious people came to hear God's word as for their lives. And their numbers increased so fast that our house for this six weeks past would not contain the half of the people. We had some consultations how to remedy this inconvenience, and Embury proposed renting a lot of ground for twenty-one years . . . A young man, a sincere Christian and constant hearer . . . offered ten pounds to buy a lot of ground . . . There are eight of us, who are joint purchasers.[16]

Due to religious and zoning regulations, Wesley Chapel was not allowed to be officially consecrated as a preaching house, but nevertheless, the New York Society had their own worship space, and all of this was accomplished by the drive and determination of lay preachers and local Methodists. Not one official representative of Wesley's connection or of a Methodist conference had yet reached the shores of America.

This society in New York was the first proper Methodist society in that it held to John Wesley's principle of union with established churches, most visibly demonstrated in not having the sacraments within its worship or at its meetings.[17] The Methodists of New York had to attend an established Church to receive the sacraments. For most of the Methodists of this early period either in America or the United Kingdom, that would mean they would have to attend the Church of England to be baptized or receive the Lord's Supper. In the case of Embury and his group, they were affiliated with Trinity Lutheran Church in New York, most likely because of the German cultural connection between the Lutherans and the Irish Palatines.[18]

At the same time Embury, the other Irish Palatines, and Webb were organizing themselves into a Methodist society in New York, another Irishman

15. Richey, Rowe, and Schmidt, *Methodist Experience in America*, 49.
16. Ibid., 50.
17. Wesley, *Works* (Jackson), 8.280.
18. Sweet, *Methodism*, 53–54.

named Robert Strawbridge was busy about his work of creating a Methodist society in Maryland, around Sam's Creek in Frederick County. Like Embury, Strawbridge was a local preacher in Ireland. Unlike Embury and Heck, however, Strawbridge was not an Irish Palatine; he was not even Protestant prior to becoming a Methodist. Strawbridge converted to Methodism from the Roman Catholic Church, and it appears that he was disowned by his family for the conversion. William Crook, an Irish Methodist presbyter, made several historical enquiries in preparation for a work entitled *Ireland and the Centenary of American Methodism* in 1866, and when he "visited the area [of Strawbridge's origin] in the hope of finding something about his childhood, he found some people who remembered his family, but of Robert himself they had never heard. It would seem as though after his desertion of their faith, his family never mentioned him again."[19] When Strawbridge moved to Terryhoogan, he had an extra room built at the end of his house for the visiting Methodist preachers to use. John Wesley, himself, made use of this room for the first time in 1758.[20] On May 9, 1758 Wesley recorded his use of it by writing, "The room built on purpose for us here, is three yards long, two and a quarter broad, and six foot high. The walls, floor, and ceiling are mud; and we had a clean chaff bed."[21]

No one quite knows when Strawbridge emigrated from Ireland to Maryland (with dates ranging from 1760 to 1765), but it is known that by 1766 he had set up the beginnings of his Methodist society in the region. He built a meetinghouse, dubbed the "Log-Meeting House," near Pipe Creek,[22] and Strawbridge took it upon himself not only to begin a Methodist society, but also to supply that society with the sacraments of baptism and the Lord's Supper. It is difficult to discern the logic or reasoning behind such a decision on the part of Robert Strawbridge. It may be that he simply was a maverick and felt he should and could do as he wished, whatever the rules may say to the contrary. It may be that, coming from an Irish Catholic background, Strawbridge had no love for the Church of England and could not see fit to submit himself or his converts to its care, even though around America where he settled, the Church of England was almost the only Church available for people to attend. Or it may simply have been a matter of pride. Francis Asbury said at the Quarterly Meeting in Mills Creek in 1775, "Mr. Strawbridge discovered his independent principles, in objecting to our discipline. He appears to want no preachers: he can do as well or better than

19. Cooney, *Methodists*, 232.
20. Ibid.
21. Wesley, *Works*, 21.146.
22. Bangs, *History*, 60.

they. But it is likely self-sufficiency is the spring of all this."[23] Whatever the reason for Strawbridge's administering the sacraments contrary to Methodist rules and discipline, he would prove to be a thorn in the side of John Wesley's official representatives and missionaries for years to come.

It should also be noted that there were two more unofficial Methodist ambassadors to America before and during the time Wesley's official representatives ministered on the North American continent, namely Robert Williams and John King. Williams did have permission by John Wesley to come and minister in America, but he was neither officially sent by a conference nor was he supplied with any remuneration for his travel expenses by the Methodist connection; in fact he had to sell his horse to discharge his debts prior to his travels.[24] Williams arrived and began his ministry in 1769 by assisting Embury in New York and, once Richard Boardman arrived, he "made his way southward."[25] Williams also assisted Strawbridge and became the first person to bring Methodism to Virginia and North Carolina.[26] John King, like Embury and Strawbridge, came of his own accord and also arrived in 1769. King also assisted Strawbridge and then became the first Methodist preacher in Baltimore, the city that was to become the bastion of Methodism in the early period of American independence.[27] By the time Wesley's official missionaries arrived, "Methodism had been planted in Maryland, Delaware, New Jersey, Pennsylvania, and New York" by these unofficial ambassadors of Methodism.[28]

## OFFICIAL BEGINNINGS

As noted above, on April 11, 1768 a member of the New York society, Thomas Taylor, wrote to John Wesley asking for help with the ever-expanding ministry among Methodists in America. He apparently was not the only one who made the same request. Wesley received numerous letters from different locations throughout America. They came in from New York, Maryland, and Charlestown and were from Taylor, Captain Webb, and a layman named Thomas Bell.[29] They all had the same concerns. Through the work of Embury and Webb, there were now Methodists in New York,

23. *JLFA*, 1.163.
24. Sweet, *Methodism*, 58.
25. Ibid.
26. Ibid.
27. Ibid., 59.
28. Ibid.
29. Kinghorn, *Heritage*, 30.

New Jersey, Pennsylvania and Delaware, and the societies kept growing.[30] Through the work of Strawbridge and Williams, there were Methodists in eastern Maryland, Delaware, Pennsylvania and Virginia.[31] While admiring the work of God in this growth, and giving ample credit to Embury and Webb, Taylor gives a good summation of the situation and their need.

> I must importune your assistance, not only in my own name, but also in the name of the whole society. We want an able and experienced preacher; one who has both gifts and grace necessary for the work. God has not, indeed, despised the day of small things. There is a real work of grace begun in many hearts by the preaching of Mr. Webb and Mr. Embury; but although they are both useful, and their hearts are in the work, they want many qualifications for such an undertaking; and the progress of the gospel here depends much upon the qualifications of preachers.[32]

John Wesley and the Methodist Conference at Leeds responded to this request from the Methodists in America for help by sending two missionaries, Richard Boardman and Joseph Pilmore. Both of these men were itinerant ministers in full connection with the Conference, Boardman having been an itinerant for six years prior to his being sent to America and Pilmore itinerating for four years;[33] and because of Boardman's seniority, it was to him that the leadership of the two, and the whole of the Methodist societies in American was given.[34] Joseph Pilmore recorded in his journal that the call for missionaries to America was first read to the Methodist conference in 1768 in Bristol, and that the preachers were encouraged to consider the call for one year. By the 1769 Conference at Leeds, Pilmore had decided that "I could not be satisfied to continue in Europe. A sense of duty so affected my mind, and my heart was drawn out with such longing desires for the advancement of the Redeemer's kingdom that I was made perfectly willing to forsake my kindred and native land, with all that was the most near and dear to me on earth, that I might spread abrode [sic] the honours of his glorious Name."[35]

Under the leadership and guidance of Boardman and Pilmore, the existing societies grew and new ones were formed. The society in Philadelphia,

---

30. Stevens, *History of the Methodist Episcopal Church*, 1.66.
31. Ibid., 1.73.
32. Bangs, *History*, 57.
33. Daniels, *History*, 406.
34. Stevens, *History of the Methodist Episcopal Church*, 1.100.
35. Pilmore, *Journal*, 15.

begun under Captain Webb as he itinerated, outgrew the building they used and bought a shell of what would have been a German Reformed church building, but had been left incomplete due to their lack of money. It was auctioned and sold to "a Gentleman's son" who, according to Pilmore, was "*non compos* [sic] *mentis*" and then sold to the Methodists by said Gentleman, and all at a price much less than the value of the building.[36] This church building, St. George's Church, is today the oldest Methodist facility in continual use in America.[37] These missionaries continued to spread Methodism to more and more areas of the American colonies, going as far as South Carolina.[38]

Despite being itinerants, and spreading Methodism further than before, both essentially settled within either New York or Philadelphia and the scope of itinerating for them was to switch locations frequently, usually three times a year. This presented the Methodist movement on the North American continent with both fortune and misfortune. On the one hand, the Methodist societies in larger areas such as New York and Philadelphia had easy access to Established churches in which the Methodists could receive the sacraments. Pilmore records in his *Journal* that the Philadelphia Methodists were welcomed to receive the Lord's Supper frequently at St. Paul's Church.[39] Pilmore described one such occasion on November 5, 1769 in which he recorded, "We had a blessed time at St. Paul's at the Sacrament—my soul did truely [sic] eat Christ's flesh and drink his blood, and found it *meat indeed*."[40] On the other hand, this sacramental access came at the price of not spreading "scriptural holiness across the land," by not founding new societies in new areas outside of these cities. This was a topic with which one of the next official missionaries, Francis Asbury, would take issue.[41]

As even more requests were made by Boardman, Pilmore and Webb for extra missionary help for the growing Methodist presence in the Colonies,

---

36. Ibid., 27–28. According to Pilmore, the building cost more than £2000 to construct, was sold to the insane son at auction for £700, and was bought by the society from his father for £650.

37. Kinghorn, *Heritage*, 32.

38. Ibid., 33.

39. Pilmore, *Journal*, 28.

40. Ibid., 25.

41. This is not to say that Pilmore and Boardman never moved beyond the confines of New York or Philadelphia. In fact, Stevens recorded that, because of Asbury's instigation, Pilmore actually traveled as far south as Savannah, Georgia to expand Methodism's reach. See Stevens, *History of the Methodist Episcopal Church*, 1.131 and Pilmore, *Journal*, 134–82 for his "Southern Journey."

the Methodist Conference in Bristol sent Francis Asbury, along with Richard Wright, to America as official missionaries in 1771.[42] Asbury was an itinerant for five years prior to being sent to America, where he would spend the rest of his life in the Methodist ministry. Wright itinerated for one year prior to setting sail for the New World and his ministry in America lasted only three years before he returned to England.[43] Able Stevens recorded of Wright, "We know but little of his history, scarcely more indeed than that he accompanied Asbury . . . and that in 1774 he returned to England, where, after three years spent in the itinerancy, he ceased to travel, and totally disappeared from the published records of the denomination."[44] Due to Francis Asbury's importance for American Methodism, a more in-depth look at him will be found below.

After Asbury and Wright, Webb petitioned the 1772 Methodist Conference in Leeds in person (being back in the Old World) for even more missionaries. Accordingly, Wesley asked for volunteers, and sent Thomas Rankin and George Shadford in 1773. Rankin was sent with the authority to become "General Assistant or Superintendent of the American Societies, for he was not only Asbury's senior in the itinerancy, but was an experienced disciplinarian."[45] Finally, the last official missionaries Wesley sent to America were Martin Rodda and James Dempster in 1774.[46] Dempster itinerated for ten years prior to coming to America and Rodda itinerated for twelve years. Each of Wesley's missionaries brought something different to the emerging American Methodist movement. Rankin was a strict disciplinarian and one who thoroughly enforced Wesley's leadership over Methodism as a whole, something that was sorely needed as Asbury encountered difficulty implementing the many aspects of Wesleyan polity.[47] Shadford was eloquent and passionate and had a "readiness for any opportunity of usefulness."[48] Rodda brought persecution, as he was a staunch royalist and decried against the revolutionaries as much as he preached for God, being "accused of having circulated over his circuit, in Delaware, the royal proclamation against the American patriots."[49] And Dempster brought a reminder to the itinerants to be ever committed to the itinerant ministry,

---

42. Stevens, *History of the Methodist Episcopal Church*, 1.110.
43. Sweet, *Methodism*, 64.
44. Stevens, *History of the Methodist Episcopal Church*, 1.119.
45. Ibid., 1.142.
46. Kinghorn, *Heritage*, 33.
47. Stevens, *History of the Methodist Episcopal Church*, 1.142.
48. Ibid., 1.242.
49. Ibid., 1.265.

as he settled and married and became Presbyterian within one year of arriving in America, becoming a minister within that denomination in New York.[50] Indeed, most of Wesley's missionaries left Methodism or America—or both—during the Revolutionary War. Boardman and Pilmore left for England in 1774, although Pilmore returned as a Protestant Episcopal Church clergyman in Philadelphia and New York after the Revolution was over. Wright left America in 1774, Webb in 1775, Rankin in 1777, Rodda in 1777 (having to be smuggled out to the British Fleet by slaves for fear of his life),[51] and Shadford in 1778.

## OUTSIDE HELP

During the Colonial Period, the American Methodists did receive help from those who were not Methodists, most notably Anglican clergy in America. It is a misnomer to state that all Anglican clergy were antipathetic to the idea of Methodism, especially in its early days on the North American continent. After all, just as Methodists saw themselves as primarily members of the Church of England, so did some of its priests see the Methodists as their members.

One prime example of the help Anglicans offered the Methodists was in the building of the first meetinghouse in New York on John's Street. First, the land that was purchased was initially leased by the Methodists for two years on the understanding that, after the two-year period was concluded, they could purchase the land outright.[52] The person from whom they leased/purchased the land was Mrs. Mary Barclay, the widow of the rector of Trinity Anglican Church, Rev. Henry Barclay.[53] In addition, three of the persons named on the subscription paper to raise funds for the purchase and building of the preaching house were Rev. Dr. Samuel Auchmuty, Rev. John Ogilvie, and Rev. Charles Inglis, all of whom were priests at Trinity Church.[54]

In addition to this help early in the life of American Methodism, there were also some Anglican clergymen who proved extremely helpful further south in the Virginia area in later years. Among these Anglicans were Devereux Jarratt and Archibald McRoberts. These two rectors of neighboring

50. Ibid., 1.264.
51. Ibid., 1.265.
52. Wakely, *Lost Chapters*, 55–56.
53. Ibid., 54.
54. Ibid., 69. It is also worth noting that Mrs. Barclay was also a contributor to the fund.

parishes in Virginia helped lead a revival that spanned the years of 1770 through 1776. During this time, Methodists and Anglicans helped one another, and the number of Christians grew. Jarratt had begun to organize his parishioners who were spiritually awakened into societies, not unlike Wesley's work, in 1774. As these continued to grow, being attended upon by the likes of Thomas Rankin and George Shadford, the revival was officially brought under the auspices of the Methodists in 1775 when,

> After Mr. Shadford had been about eight months in the circuit, Mr. Jarratt desired his parish might be included in it; that all who chose it might have the privilege of meeting in class, and being members of the society. He soon saw the salutary effects. Many that had but small desires before, began to be much alarmed, and laboured earnestly after eternal life. In a little time numbers were deeply awakened, and many tasted of the pardoning love of God. In a few months Mr. Jarratt saw more fruit of his labours than he had done for many years. And he went on with the preachers hand in hand, both in doctrine and discipline.[55]

So, Methodists helped the Established Church, and the Established clergy worked with the Methodists to continue the good work.

It is also important to note that this attitude was also found after the American Revolutionary War had concluded. In *The Methodist Magazine* in 1823 several letters from Uzal Ogden to Francis Asbury were printed. Ogden was a priest with the Church of England, sent to New Jersey as a missionary with the Society for the Propagation of the Gospel in Foreign Parts. On July 10, 1783 Ogden wrote, "I am happy to mention, that the clergy of our church, in this state, are disposed to be friendly to the Methodists, and, with cheerfulness, if called on, will administer to them the divine ordinances."[56] If it was just Ogden, this would be one more priest who was willing to help the Methodists; if, as the letter implies, it was most of the priests in New Jersey, then it was several more that were willing to be of service to the American Methodists. Either way, it is important to note that American Methodists did have access to the sacraments to a certain degree, and therefore were not in a complete vacuum with respect to them.

---

55. *JLFA*, 1.220.
56. In *Methodist Magazine*, 29.

Chapter 7

# American Methodist Leadership

## FRANCIS ASBURY

FRANCIS ASBURY IS UNIQUE among the missionaries Wesley sent to America. He was the only one that stayed. Asbury alone continued in America and provided leadership and direction to the American Methodist societies. Robert Tuttle, writing of Asbury, said, "Few others could be compared so favorably with Wesley in the advancement of Methodism."[1] He was born on August 20 or 21, 1745, which put him at twenty-six years of age when he first set foot on American soil. He was "awakened before [he] was fourteen years of age"[2] and soon afterwards met the Methodists. When Asbury first encountered Methodist worship, he "soon found this was not the Church—but it was better. The people were so devout—men and women kneeling down—saying *Amen*. Now, behold! they were singing hymns—sweet sound! Why, strange to tell! the preacher had no prayer-book, and yet he prayed wonderfully! What was yet more extraordinary, the man took his text, and had no sermon-book: thought I, this is wonderful indeed! It is certainly a strange way, but the best way."[3] This self-reflection on his Methodist conversion may be considered one among many pieces of evidence from Asbury's writings that show a bias against formalism and ritual. How this will impact the sacramental tensions to come will be seen below.

1. Tuttle, *Giant Shoulders*, 31.
2. *JLFA*, 1.721
3. Ibid.

From this experience onward, Asbury became more closely associated with Methodism. He became a local preacher and then an itinerant, serving the circuits containing "Derbyshire, Staffordshire, Warwickshire, Worcestershire, and indeed almost every place within my reach, for the sake of precious souls."[4] Through this experience, specifically at the Colchester Circuit,[5] Asbury was no stranger to internecine fighting within a society. The society members at Colchester turned on themselves in a major disagreement in 1763. By the time Asbury was appointed to this circuit, there was peace in the society, but, as Wesley recorded, "yet they had not the life which they had once: a loss of this kind is not easily recovered."[6] Asbury was on this circuit during the 1767–8 period and would have seen what damage can occur to a society that fights among itself, and as will be seen below, this kind of problem was something he would have to manage first-hand in the coming years in America. Nor was Asbury a stranger to frequent reception of the Lord's Supper, as John and Charles Wesley's compromise of administering the Lord's Supper every other week in Bristol occurred in October of 1770 (one year prior to Asbury's departure for America), when Asbury was on the Wiltshire circuit, near Bristol.[7] These specific instances, along with Asbury's five years' experience in itinerant ministry, would shape his understanding of what it means to be a Methodist as he embarked for the New World.

It did not take long for Asbury to begin to sense a difference in priorities for the ministry between Pilmore, Boardman and himself once he arrived in the New World. Asbury arrived in America on October 27, 1771 and on November 21 wrote in his Journal, "At present I am dissatisfied. I judge we are to be shut up in the cities this winter. My brethren seem unwilling to leave the cities, but I think I shall show them the way."[8] This was not to be the last instance of differing opinions between the men on the direction and scope of Methodism in America. At the Quarterly Meeting held at Joseph Presbury's home near Aberdeen, Maryland on December 22, 1772 Asbury recorded this exchange:

> 5. Will the people be contented without our administering the sacrament? John King was neuter [sic]; brother Strawbridge pleaded much for the ordinances; and so did the people, who appeared to be much biased by him. I told them I would not

4. Ibid., 1.722
5. Ibid., 3.3 compare with Wesley, *Works*, 21.435, 22.29, 22.70, 22.107.
6. Wesley, *Works*, 22.107.
7. *JLFA*, 3.8n.
8. Ibid., 1.10.

agree to it at that time, and insisted on our abiding by our rules. But Mr. Boardman had given them their way at the quarterly meeting held here before, and I was obliged to connive at some things for the sake of peace.[9]

This shows a friction already present between Asbury and Strawbridge as well as those who would side with Strawbridge, which in this case included Boardman, over the issue of the sacraments. It is also interesting to note that, while the debate may not have gone Asbury's way, three days later he attended the Established Church and received the sacrament as per "our rules,"[10] demonstrating how a good Methodist ought to approach the issue of the sacraments. This most likely was Asbury's last salvo in this round of the sacramental debate. Thus, the main sacramental issue at the Quarterly Conference of 1772 for Asbury was whether Strawbridge was following the rules of the societies, not whether people were experiencing God's grace in the Eucharist.

Yet for all of Asbury's arguing against the administration of the sacraments by the Methodist preachers, an argument which he would make even more forcefully over the next eight years, this must not be construed as Asbury being in any sense anti-sacramental. William Wade has argued that,

> We maintain that the limitation and restrictions placed upon native American Methodist preachers in regard to the sacraments were primarily the result of Asbury's personal attitudes upon the necessity and the desirability of the sacraments and the question of polity. Asbury was to thwart this native grass-roots American desire for a sacramental life in the 1779–80 controversy by his calling of the Delaware Conference and subsequent ultimatum to the southern brethren of the Virginia circuits who comprised the vast majority of the American Methodists of this time. The action of the 1792 *Discipline* which was again to restrict the administration of the sacraments to ordained clergy while at the same time authorizing a new order designated as "Preachers," favored a non-sacramental worship life among American Methodists in which preaching, not the Lord's Supper, was to predominate. We would suppose that Asbury is the man most responsible for this turn of events in the Methodism of America.[11]

---

9. Ibid., 1.60.
10. Ibid.
11. Wade, "History of Public Worship," 171.

Wade's analysis of the situation extrapolates from instances such as the one above between Asbury and Strawbridge, and places culpability for what he perceives to be an anti-sacramental nature of the Methodist Episcopal Church squarely on Asbury's shoulders. His analysis contrasted selected passages from Asbury's *Journal* with that of Joseph Pilmore's *Journal* and arrived at the conclusion that Asbury swayed the American Methodists in "his own unconcern for the importance of the sacrament."[12] Wade also made the statement that, "Finally we must note that Asbury's attitude was *not* that of many early American Methodists who had a great desire for the sacraments."[13]

While Asbury is on record as endeavoring to stop the American Methodists from administering the sacraments (which will be discussed in Chapter 8), the only way the conclusion Wade has made can be reached, that Asbury influenced the American Methodists to turn their backs on Wesley's admonition for a sacramental new Church and create one devoid of significant appreciation for the sacraments, is to see Asbury and his actions through a limited reading not of Francis Asbury, but of John Wesley. As stated before, John Wesley had two fundamental dimensions to his theology of the Eucharist, one being soteriological and functioning as a means of grace, and the other being ecclesiological and functioning as a marker of a true Church. For Wade to understand Asbury as being anti-sacramental, one would have to see Asbury in light of Wesley's soteriological dimension of Eucharist only, and that is precisely what Wade has done. Wade wrote a section in his research entitled *John Wesley's Eucharistic Thought*, which covered such topics as Wesley's understanding of the nature of the Eucharist, his injunction for "constant communion," his understanding that the Eucharist could be a converting ordinance, and finally Wesley's *Sunday Service* with respect to the Eucharist. The research covers ten pages in his dissertation and dealt exclusively with what this study has called Wesley's soteriological dimension to his Eucharistic theology. There is no mention of his ecclesiological dimension of Eucharistic theology at all.[14] Wade then took this uni-dimensional approach to Wesley and used it as the canon by which Asbury's Eucharistic understanding was to be judged. By this canon, then, Wade found Asbury wanting in what he framed as an appropriately Wesleyan understanding and appreciation of the Eucharist.

This does not reflect the reality of the situation, though. Francis Asbury, while not as explicit as Wesley in theological discourse and understanding,

12. Ibid., 159.
13. Ibid., emphasis included.
14. Ibid., 77–86.

was not uni-dimensional in his Eucharistic approach, just as Wesley was not uni-dimensional. Rather, Asbury had an opposite ordering of these dimensions of the Eucharist in his thought as Wesley did. For Asbury, the Eucharist primarily had an ecclesiological function, and secondarily a soteriological function. As this study progresses, Asbury's ecclesiological dimension of the Eucharist (as well most of American Methodism's ecclesiological understanding of the sacrament) will be detailed; therefore, it is important to illuminate his soteriological understanding here, thereby showing that he did, indeed, have such an understanding of the Sacrament. First, there is the possibility presented to Asbury to leave America and go to Antigua as a Methodist missionary on that island in 1775. Asbury recorded his thoughts on the matter:

> I received a letter from Miss Gilbert at Antigua; in which she informed me, that Mr. Nathaniel Gilbert was going away; and as there are about three hundred members in society, she entreats me to go and labour amongst them. And as Mr. Wesley has given his consent, I feel inclined to go, and take one of the young men with me. But there is one obstacle in my way—the administration of the ordinances. It is possible to get the ordination of a presbytery; but this would be incompatible with Methodism: which would be an effectual bar in my way.[15]

If the ordinances (sacraments) were not of value to Asbury, so much so that he would try to undermine Wesley's injunction to receive them constantly (as Wade's reasoning delineated), there is no reason why Asbury's inability to administer them should have prevented him from going to Antigua. Rather, the more logical conclusion is that Asbury did place value on the sacraments, thus the "bar in my way" of not being able to administer them in that setting. Next, there is a discussion Asbury recorded with a Baptist in 1776 specifically concerning baptism, but the sacramental implication can be drawn for the Eucharist as well. Asbury wrote, "O, the policy of Satan! Some he urges to neglect the ordinances altogether; others he urges to misunderstand them, or make additions to them."[16] Baptist misunderstandings of the sacraments and total neglect of the sacraments are both seen as equally evil in Asbury's sight. In the same frame of reference, Asbury recorded an instance in 1779 in which Methodists were accused of neglecting the ordinances. Asbury wrote, "I met with an old man who had strange notions about the Methodists' rejecting the ordinances, and pulling

---

15. *JLFA*, 1.149.
16. Ibid., 1.176.

down the Church; whom I endeavoured to set right."[17] This old man's "notions" were almost exactly what Wade accused Asbury of perpetrating in his thesis. If Wade was correct, it would not be likely that Asbury would have "endeavoured to set right" this man, for the old man would have been correct and Asbury would have been obliged to agree with him.

Not one month after the exchange with the "old man," on October 30, 1779, Asbury "preached a sacramental sermon from 1 Cor. xi, 28–30; was directed to the awful consequence of an unworthy, and the blessings of a proper, receiving it."[18] Again, if Asbury did not value the Lord's Supper as a means of grace, it would not be logical for him to have preached a sermon concerning it on a Saturday, and then go on a Sunday with his Methodists to the Established Church to receive it. In March of the following year, Asbury recorded a situation that may have just as easily come from the hand of John Wesley concerning the Methodists in England. Asbury wrote on March 26, 1780, "Rode to church [Christ Protestant Episcopal Church, Dover, Delaware], where we had a smooth, sensible discourse on 1 Peter i, 3. I attended the communion—communicants increase daily, for people get awakened by us; when this is the case, they go to the Lord's Supper."[19] Here is the same phenomenon in America as in England, namely that the Methodists understand the soteriological dimension of the Eucharist and flock to the Established Church to receive it accordingly. If Asbury did not agree with this understanding, it is not likely he would have recorded this event as something of which to be proud. In addition to being proud of this example of Methodist Eucharistic piety, Asbury preached on it. On February 7, 1782 Asbury wrote, "I find no preaching does good, but that which *properly presses the use of the means*, and urges holiness of heart; *these points I am determined to keep close to all in my sermons*."[20] Asbury was not the anti-sacramentalist Wade portrayed him as being. Finally, Asbury recorded an incident later in the same year that is extremely illuminating concerning the American Methodist understanding of the Eucharist and its piety. On August 22, 1782 Asbury recorded

> I went to St. Paul's; and to my great surprise, in comes my old friend Barton. He was brought up a Churchman, and was awakened without human means: observing that ministers and members in that Church were dead and careless, and finding some living testimonies among Friends, he was induced to join

17. Ibid., 1.316.
18. Ibid., 1.319.
19. Ibid., 1.342.
20. Ibid., 1.420, emphasis added.

them, and thus adhered, for twenty years, becoming a public speaker among them. He is now jealous for the Lord's ordinances; he says he could never fully give them up, and must now come to the Methodists.[21]

Here is a man who was raised in the Church of England, became a Quaker, and became convinced that he must join the Methodists so that he could have his piety *and* receive the sacraments. Again, if Asbury were anti-sacramental, this account would contradict his own understanding of the importance of the sacraments. If one's goal were to reduce the frequency of the sacraments in the life of the Church, it would not be logical to include an instance when someone joined the movement precisely because of the ability to receive the sacraments while in its fellowship. And while these instances show that Asbury did, indeed, have a soteriological dimension to his Eucharistic understanding and piety, it will be the ecclesiological dimension that will inform and direct most of his decisions regarding the sacraments and the American Methodists. Those instances, and that dimension to Asbury's Eucharistic piety, will be explored fully below, but before that analysis is done, it is necessary to delineate what options existed for Methodists to have access to the sacraments prior to forming their own Church.

## THE COLONIAL GENERAL CONFERENCES

On July 13, 1773, the first General Conference was held for the Methodist societies in America, and was convened in Philadelphia. Those present were Thomas Rankin, George Shadford, Joseph Pilmore, Thomas Webb, Richard Boardman, Richard Wright, John King, Abraham Withworth, Joseph Yearby, and Francis Asbury.[22] It is most likely the reason this was the first General Conference was due Asbury's opinions of Boardman and Pilmore and their prior action (or lack thereof) as missionaries on the continent, which led to hurt feelings and a defensive posture on the part of Boardman and Pilmore. Asbury recorded, "There were some debates amongst the preachers in this conference, relative to the conduct of some who had manifested a desire to abide in the cities, and live like gentlemen. Three years out of four have been already spent in the cities. It was also found that money had been wasted, improper leaders appointed, and many of our rules broken."[23]

---

21. Ibid., 1.433.

22. Ibid., 1.85, although Asbury arrived one day late and so the proceedings were postponed until the following day.

23. Ibid.

Pilmore, concerning the same conference, recorded, "As Mr. Boardman and I had been shamefully misrepresented to Mr. Wesley, and Mr. Rankin sent over to take the whole management upon himself, it was expected we should have pretty close work."[24] Since it was evidently Asbury's criticisms of his predecessors to America and their rebuttal to those criticisms that instigated this conference, it makes perfect sense that the business of the conference was postponed until the following day when Asbury arrived.[25] Both the issues of not circulating outside of the cities and the allowance by Boardman for Strawbridge to administer the Lord's Supper have already been mentioned above. Rankin evidently thought a General Conference would lay these issues to rest, as he was a strict disciplinarian and one thoroughly committed to John Wesley's scheme of doctrines and disciplines. Therefore, since Wesley held conferences for the Methodists in England to solve disputes and set doctrine and practice, Rankin would hold conferences for the Methodists in America for the same purposes.

At this conference, not surprisingly given Asbury's displeasure concerning the outcome of the 1772 Quarterly Conference referenced above, the issue of the sacraments was presented. According to the minutes

> The following rules were agreed to by all the preachers present: 1. Every preacher who acts in connexion with Mr. Wesley and the brethren who labour in America, is strictly to avoid administering the ordinances of baptism and the Lord's Supper. 2. All the people among whom we labour to be earnestly exhorted to attend the church, and to receive the ordinances there; but in a particular manner, to press the people in Maryland and Virginia, to the observance of this minute.[26]

This seems to lay the issue to rest as far as administering the sacraments, but Asbury recorded a different decision made by the conference. Asbury wrote, "No preacher in our connexion shall be permitted to administer the ordinances at this time; except Mr. Strawbridge, and he under the particular direction of the assistant."[27] The Assistant was Rankin, who was himself a layman, but he was closest to Wesley in matters of authority in America. The differences between these two accounts are striking, and lead to the general atmosphere of confusion concerning the sacraments in these early years of the Methodists in America. Also striking is the fact that this

---

24. Pilmore, *Journal*, 210.
25. Ibid.
26. Hitt and Ware, *Minutes*, 5.
27. *JLFA*, 1.85.

allowance was made for Strawbridge, since he was not even present at the meeting!

While this Philadelphia conference does shed light on the concern among Methodists around the sacraments, what it does not do is give any explicit theological reasoning as to the decision reached concerning the sacraments. There is no indication as to why Strawbridge saw it as necessary to administer the sacraments. There is, however, the implied ecclesiological dimension of the Eucharist present in the decision that Methodists ought to "attend the church" to receive the Lord's Supper. This implication is especially clear with the injunction that "the observance of this minute" was to have special authority in Maryland and Virginia where the Church of England was the Established Church. However, this ecclesiological piety is only implied, and there is no explicit theological reason given for the decision, only the decision about the administration of the sacraments.

This was the last time Robert Strawbridge would appear in the minutes of a Methodist conference. Asbury received several letters on June 24, 1774, "But one of these letters informed me that Mr. Strawbridge was very officious in administering the ordinances. What strange infatuation attends that man! Why will he run before Providence?"[28] Because of this breach of discipline, Strawbridge was subsequently dropped from the list of preachers precisely because he would not abide by the decisions of the conference and the discipline of the Methodists and refrain from administering the sacraments. Even so, it seems that Strawbridge had one last opportunity to re-enter the Methodist fold in 1775, but again he chose not to submit to the Methodist discipline. As noted above, Asbury's opinion was that Strawbridge's reason was simply pride. Asbury recorded of him, "He appears to want no preachers: he can do as well or better than they. But it is likely self-sufficiency is the spring of all this."[29] With this rejection by Strawbridge, his connection with the Methodists was effectively over, although some of his followers rejoined the Methodists after his death. Asbury recorded one such instance in September 1781, while also including that his personal opinion of the reason the man died was because he was prideful. Asbury wrote, "I visited the Bush chapel. The people here once left us to follow another [Robert Strawbridge]: time was when the labours of their leader were made a blessing to them; but pride is a *busy* sin. He is now no more: upon the whole, I am inclined to think the Lord took him away in judgment, because he was in a away [sic] to do hurt to his cause; and that he saved him in mercy,

---

28. Ibid., 1.120.
29. Ibid., 1.163.

because from his death-bed conversation he appears to have had hope in his end."[30]

While Strawbridge may have been excluded from the Methodist connection for failing to abide by its rules, nevertheless, the issue of the sacraments was not over with the decision in 1773. While the record is calm concerning the sacraments for the following three years (1774–1776), in 1777 at the General Conference in Deer Creek, Maryland, or more precisely at a preparatory meeting, just before the conference, the issue of the sacraments was raised once again. By this point, the American Revolution was being fought throughout the colonies and many loyal English, the Anglican clergy among them, had fled to England or other British holdings in the New World. As such, while there was an inconvenience to receiving the sacraments from an Anglican Church before 1777, now there was an almost absolute dearth of possibilities for most Methodists to receive them.

It was at this time Asbury recorded that "it was asked whether we could give our consent that Mr. Rankin should baptize, as there appeared to be a present necessity."[31] While Asbury's record showed that this was concerning Baptism and not the Eucharist, other reports by William Watters, the first native-born itinerant, and Freeborn Garrettson, one of the most prominent of the early American Methodists, included the Lord's Supper with the proposal. Watters recorded thus

> It was also submitted to the consideration of this conference, whether in our present situation, of having but, few ministers left in many of our Parishes, to administer the ordinances of Baptism, and the Lord's supper, we should not administer them ourselves, for as yet we had not the ordinances among us, but were dependent on other denominations for them. Some received them from and communed with the Presbyterians, but the greater part with the Church of England. In fact we considered ourselves at this time as belonging to the Church of England, it being before our separation, and our becoming a regularly formed Church. After much conversation on the subject, it was unanimously agreed to lay it over for the determination of the next conference, to be held in Leesburg, the 19th day of May.[32]

Even if it was solely concerning the issue of Baptism, and not the Lord's Supper, for a group of preachers who had denied the administration of the sacraments by themselves for at least five years prior to this, it is

30. Ibid., 1.410–11.
31. Ibid., 1.239.
32. Watters, *Short Account*, 30.

an important step towards questioning their ability for administering any sacraments, including the Lord's Supper. What is particularly interesting in this instance, however, is who made the original proposal for Rankin to baptize. Freeborn Garrettson, in his Semi-Centennial sermon of 1826, stated, "In conference the question was asked, I think by Mr. Rankin, Shall we administer the ordinances?"[33] Thomas Rankin, himself, proposed that the sacraments (apparently not just baptism) be administered by Methodist itinerants. For the strict Rankin, who always endeavored to follow the Methodist discipline as set out by Wesley, this is a remarkable step in the sacramental issue. The official minutes of the Deer Creek Conference record the decision as thus

> Q. 7. As the present distress is such, are the Preachers resolved to take no step to detach themselves from the work of God for the ensuing year?
>
> A. We purpose, by the grace of God, not to take any step that may separate us from the brethren, or from the blessed work in which we are engaged.[34]

In the official minutes we have the first glimpse of a theology for the sacraments. Up until this point, the Eucharistic piety of the American Methodists was not to administer the sacraments themselves. This question and answer in the Deer Creek minutes of 1777 had the beginnings of a theological explication of why that piety was practiced. The primary issue here is ecclesial. If the Methodists began administering the sacraments, they would effect a break and a separation between them and "the brethren" of the Established Church and the Methodists in the Old World still abiding by the discipline laid out by John Wesley and agreed upon at each conference in England. This is the ecclesiological dimension of Wesley's Eucharistic theology coming to the fore in American Methodist Eucharistic piety. And while the minutes from the conference seem to have a definitive answer to the question of sacramental administration, Watters showed that the conference did not see this as conclusive. The Methodists in conference knew that the issue would need to be debated further at the following conference in 1778.

The Methodists in conference the next year continued the debate as if they had never stopped for an intervening year of ministry. The 1778 conference was unique in that this was the first American Methodist conference presided over and attended by exclusively native-born itinerants. Watters

---

33. Garrettson, *American Methodist Pioneer*, 390.
34. Hitt and Ware, *Minutes*, 14.

presided over this conference while he was twenty-six years old, being the one itinerant with the most experience at the present time.[35] All of Wesley's official (and most unofficial) missionaries, except Asbury, were now either gone from the Methodist connection in America, or gone from America. Asbury was, in essence, confined to Delaware as of March 10, 1778. He would not take an oath of allegiance to the State of Maryland, and Delaware had no such oath requirement.[36] Thus, Asbury was not able to attend the conference, which met on May 19, 1778 in Leesburg, Virginia for fear of being arrested if he left Delaware.

Just as Watters recorded from the previous year, this conference took up the debate concerning the sacraments and was just as contentious over the issue as the Deer Creek Conference had been. In fact, as Abel Stevens had noted, "Besides this controversy [over the sacraments] we have intimations of no other business, done at the session, except the appointment of two 'general stewards' to receive and distribute its collections"[37] and raising the itinerants' salary due to depreciation of the currency during the war. As for the issue of the sacraments, Watters explained, "As the consideration of our administering the ordinances were at the last conference laid over till this, it of course came on and found many advocates. It was with considerable difficulty that a large majority was prevailed on to lay it over again, till the next conference, hoping that we should by then be able to see our way more clear in so important a change."[38]

Again, there is no discussion about the sacraments as being a means of grace. The debate was centered on the subject of the American Methodists relationship to the English Methodists and John Wesley. Just as with the prior year, the debate over the Eucharistic piety of these Methodists revolved around the ecclesiological dimension of Eucharistic theology. The key issue for these Methodists was whether they had the ecclesial authority to take administration of the sacraments into their own hands. Even though this issue was "laid over" (or tabled) once again, it would finally come to a head the following year at the conference in Flauvanna, Virginia. It is to this conference that we now turn.

35. Ibid., 1.
36. *JLFA*, 1.267.
37. Stevens, *History of the Methodist Episcopal Church*, 2.46.
38. Watters, *Short Account*, 36.

Chapter 8

# Sacramental Schism: Flauvanna 1779

## THE BACKGROUND

AMERICAN METHODISTS, FROM ROBERT Strawbridge to the General Conferences, debated the subject of the proper place and administration of the sacraments almost from the time they landed in the New World. As Lester Ruth has commented, "Early American Methodism was a movement which clamored for the sacraments."[1] William Wade stated, "the American Methodists had a burning desire for the administration of the sacraments among their number."[2] Indeed, first Quarterly Meetings' minutes then General Conference meetings' minutes show this clamoring and desire to be true. The question that one must ask, though, is *why* the Methodists "clamored for the sacraments" year after year. How one answers that question will greatly impact one's interpretation of the events of the Flauvanna Conference of 1779, the fallout from that conference, and the general rationale for American Methodist Eucharistic piety, practice, and understanding for the rest of the period under discussion in this study (and perhaps even beyond the bounds of it).

The decision of the Flauvanna Conference is well known: the Methodist preachers in attendance voted to form a presbytery, ordain themselves, and administer the sacraments to the Methodists under their care. Jesse Lee succinctly stated that the southern itinerants "concluded that, if God had called them to preach the Gospel, he had called them also to administer the

---

1 Ruth, "Reconsideration of the Frequency," 58.
2. Wade, "History of Public Worship," 160.

ordinances of baptism and the Lord's supper."[3] What is lacking in scholarly consensus is the rationale for these decisions. There are scholars who understand the Flauvanna Conference in the context of the continuing struggle for the sacraments that began with Robert Strawbridge. Daniels writes on the subject, "Five years before this [the Christmas Conference of 1784], in 1779, the preachers in the South proceeded to ordain themselves by the hands of three of their senior members, unwilling that their people should longer be denied the Lord's Supper, and their children and probationary members the rite of Baptism . . . Thousands of their children were unbaptized, and the members of the Societies in general had not partaken of the Lord's Supper for many years; some of them never."[4] Holland McTyeire said, "The people more and more clamored for the sacraments at the hands of their pastors . . . American Methodists could not see why they should be deprived of a whole gospel . . . why must they wait on the pleasure of men who could not understand their distant situation, or sympathize with their wants, for the sacraments?"[5] A.B. Hyde stated, "Our people had no doubt of their right to have these [sacraments] administered by the preachers; the only doubt was of its expediency. After several postponements, it had a hearing at Flauvanna."[6] These historians' themes have been recently picked up by Karen Westerfield Tucker in her assessment of Flauvanna. Tucker writes, "The Eucharist was thus an intrinsic part of the evangelical Wesleyan revival. Wesley recognized that in America 'for some hundred miles together there is none either to baptize or to administer the Lord's supper' (cf. Wesley's letter to *Our Brethren in America*), and that the Methodists longed for the sacraments from their own preachers—a privilege debated from 1772 and a matter that came to a head with the southern preachers' decisions at the Flauvanna Conference in 1779."[7]

These scholars' interpretations of the circumstances that led to the action taken at the Flauvanna Conference in 1779 illustrate two distinct points. First, in this line of reasoning that the American Methodists held a deep desire to receive the sacraments, it is only logical to assume the preachers would embark upon the plan which they agreed at this conference, and the disruption of that plan by Asbury and the northern preachers ought to be questioned for its motives. Second, and much more importantly, however, is that this position has as its main antecedent, a limited reading of Wesley

3. Lee, *A Short History*, 69.
4. Daniels, *History*, 468.
5. McTyeire, *Methodism*, 315.
6. Hyde, *Methodism*, 404.
7. Tucker, *Worship*, 119.

and not the American Methodists themselves, as evidenced by Tucker's quotation of Wesley above.[8] This is the same limited reading of Wesley that William Wade made when he conducted his research, and which has been described above. It is a limited reading that allows only for the soteriological dimension of the Eucharist to inform why those American Methodists desired the sacraments.

There are other scholars who see the rationale for the decisions at Flauvanna with not quite so singular motives. Dee Andrews sees this as more of an issue of culture than ministry. She wrote, "The sacramental controversy—ostensibly a struggle over the powers of Methodist ministry but also a cultural contest between Strawbridge's democratic Irish Methodism and Asbury's loyalty to Wesley's authoritarian 'old plan'—continued unsatisfactorily resolved . . . "[9] Frederick Norwood sees political dimensions within the decision. He stated, "As it turned out the crisis involved not only the sacraments, but also the relation of Methodists to the Church of England and the authority of Asbury as general assistant—to say nothing of the authority of Wesley in England, at this time almost totally out of touch with his American followers."[10] As well, John Wigger has stated

> The sacramental crisis [presented by the Flauvanna Conference] had much to do with the separation of English and American society reflected in the Revolution. When the southern preachers, mostly Virginians, met for the 1779 annual conference in Fluvanna County, Virginia, neither Asbury nor any other northern preacher except for William Watters attended because of the war. At the Fluvanna conference the southern preachers voted to ordain one another to administer the sacraments of baptism and the Lord's supper. This represented a clear break from Wesleyan practice, indicating among other things how little authority Asbury actually commanded in the South at the time.[11]

While it is important to keep these two differing views of Flauvanna in mind, that the motives were sacramentally driven or that the motives were somehow culturally or politically driven, it is equally important, as stated before, to allow the American Methodists to speak for themselves. And when that allowance is made, it will be seen that seeing this in a sacramental/

---

8. It should be noted as well that this quotation from Wesley was written in 1784, not 1779. Tucker is using a later statement of Wesley to justify a decision made by American Methodists (who had never met Wesley!) five years prior.

9. Andrews, *Methodists*, 64.

10. Norwood, *American Methodism*, 91.

11. Wigger, *Heaven*, 23.

cultural dichotomy is too simplistic for an actual understanding of what transpired. The stage had been set for at least the prior two years concerning the steps that were about to be taken in 1779. Each Annual Conference prior to this one took up the issue of the sacraments, and each one decided to wait another year before making a decision. By 1779 the wait was over. There were two conferences that year, one in the north and one in the south, both arriving at opposite conclusions on the issue, and both declaring the other conference's conclusions invalid.

## THE CONFERENCES OF 1779

The year 1779 is distinct in the history of the Methodist movement in America for several reasons, among the first being there were two conferences that year, and secondly, those conferences produced the first schism (albeit short-lived) in American Methodism. The regularly scheduled conference for 1779 was the one that took place in Flauvanna on May 18, 1779. This is the only conference that was authorized to meet to discuss issues of Methodist discipline and polity by the previous conference. However, there was another conference that met one month prior to this, on April 28, 1779 at Judge Thomas White's residence in Delaware under the leadership of Francis Asbury.

Since the departure of Thomas Rankin for England in 1777, Asbury had been acting as *de facto* Assistant for the societies in America. This was expected by most Methodists since it was a position he had held prior to the arrival of Rankin, and now it was only fitting he exercise it once again with Rankin's absence. The problem, however, was that Asbury was English, which made him suspect of supporting the English during the Revolution. Asbury also "could not persuade himself to take the required oath of allegiance to the state of Maryland,"[12] and thus because of suspicion and an unwillingness to appease that suspicion by the oath, Asbury put himself in voluntary seclusion at Judge White's home. Because of this seclusion, Asbury was not able to attend the Leesburg Conference of 1778, nor would he be able to attend the officially called Flauvanna Conference in Virginia for 1779, and knowing that the issue of the sacraments was going to be raised once again (with a decision most likely to be made), he decided the best course of action would be to try and obstruct any decision concerning the sacraments taken at that conference by holding a "preparatory conference" in Kent County, Delaware under his leadership and for the northern

---

12. Bangs, *History*, 124.

preachers who may or may not have been able to attend the Virginia conference because of the war situation.

Asbury recorded the proceedings of his conference with one entry, dated Wednesday, April 28, 1779, "Our conference for the northern stations began at Thomas White's. All our preachers on these stations were present, and united. We had much prayer, love, and harmony; and we all agreed to walk by the same rule, and to mind the same thing. As we had great reason to fear that our brethren to the southward were in danger of separating from us, we wrote them a soft, healing epistle."[13] The official minutes of this conference do not give much more information than what Asbury reported.

> Question 8. *Why was the Delaware conference held?*
>
> Ans. For the convenience of the preachers in the northern stations, that we all might have an opportunity of meeting in conference; it being unadvisable for brother Asbury and brother Ruff, with some others, to attend in Virginia; it is considered also as preparatory to the conference in Virginia. Our sentiments to be given in by brother Watters.
>
> Question 10. *Shall we guard against a separation from the church, directly or indirectly?*
>
> Ans. By all means.[14]

Shortly after this conference, Asbury tried a direct approach in appealing to the southern preachers. On May 3, 1779, he wrote a personal letter, apart from the "healing epistle" of the conference, trying to stave off a schism. Asbury recorded, "Yesterday we had some melting under the word, at the house of Edward White, and today I wrote John Dickins, to Philip Gatch, Edward Dromgoole, and William Glendenning, urging them, if possible, to prevent a separation among the preachers in the south—that is, Virginia and North Carolina. And I entertain great hopes that the breach will be healed; if not, the consequences may be bad."[15]

William Watters, the "brother Watters" of the official minutes, holds a singular place in these deliberations, as he was the only travelling preacher to attend both the Kent Conference and the Flauvanna Conference. He is the same young preacher, the first native Methodist preacher in full connection in North America, who presided over the Leesburg Conference in the prior year and convinced the preachers to defer the decision concerning the sacraments to this year. And he very nearly did not attend the conference

---

13. *JLFA*, 1.300.
14. Hitt and Ware, *Minutes*, 19.
15. *JLFA*, 1.300.

in the north. Watters recorded, "A few weeks before the annual conference came on, Mr. Asbury and the preachers east of the Potomac assembled in conference at Thomas White's in Delaware, the 28th April 1779. I had no notice sent me, and was in a very weak state of health from a bowel complaint, with which I had, for two months been afflicted. Yet I determined if possible to get there."[16]

The reason Watters gave for endeavoring so purposely to attend the conference was that "One of my objects in attending this meeting was to get Mr. Asbury to attend the regularly appointed conference" at Flauvanna.[17] Unfortunately, it was not the case that Asbury could attend the conference in Virginia. Watters desired Asbury's leadership and voice at Flauvanna on account of what he knew would happen in Asbury's absence. Watters stated

> From my particular knowledge of all the preachers, I foresaw what would be the consequences of the subject of the ordinances which had been so warmly debated the two preceding conferences, and which I was fully satisfied a number of them were determined to adopt at the ensuing conference, though it were at the expense of an entire division. My great concern was not whether we should or should not adopt them; but on account of the division that I was satisfied would take place at their being adopted. I could freely and without hesitation have agreed either way to have prevented what I considered one of the greatest evils that could befall us. This important matter lay with solemn weight day and night on my mind and caused me many sleepless hours. Nothing to me, appeared more formidable, and leading to more terrible consequences than introducing unscriptural doctrines into, or dividing, the Church of Christ. I finally came to a determination to endeavor by every means in my power to prevent a division: or if that could not be done, to stand in the gap as long as possible. I had no sooner come to this determination than the peace and witness I felt within fully satisfied me that I was on the ground on which the Lord set me, and that through his grace neither friends nor foes, rough nor smooth usage, should prevent me from endeavoring to hold those together, whom God had joined.[18]

This statement by Watters is extremely illuminating given the differences of scholarly opinion surrounding the circumstances leading up to the Flauvanna Conference. If, as some suggest, the American Methodists were

16. Watters, *Short Account*, 37–38.
17. Ibid.
18. Ibid.

endeavoring to fulfill their decade-long dream of receiving the sacraments because they had such a high sacramental piety that called for reception of them, it would be reasonable to see that in the thoughts of Watters. Yet that sentiment is not there. The overriding concern Watters had for what was about to transpire in Virginia was "introducing unscriptural doctrines into, or dividing, the Church of Christ." To use the language of this study, the soteriological dimension of Eucharistic piety and theology for the American Methodists was simply not a factor in Watters' assessment of the situation. The actual administration of the sacraments was an issue with which Watters had no stated opinion, and with which he could agree to administer them or not to administer them. The main concern was the ecclesiological dimension of Eucharistic piety. As the soteriological dimension gained ascendancy in England, the ecclesiological dimension was gaining ascendancy in America. As will be seen further, Watters was far from being the only American Methodist to see the situation from this perspective. There was much more going on in Flauvanna than a "clamor" for the sacraments.

## THE DEBATE

The American Methodists of the period debated the Flauvanna decision both prior to the conference and subsequent to it. There are numerous instances in their autobiographies and letters that demonstrate the issue at stake was not one of soteriology or grace, but rather ecclesiology and independence. Flauvanna in 1779 was, in essence, the Methodist preachers' own version of the American patriots' Philadelphia in 1776 in being a declaration of independence from the Church of England, although none would use that language. Those southern preachers that made up the membership of this conference used the issue of the sacraments to create their own Church. Especially illuminating on this point is a reflection Francis Asbury made in his *Valedictory Address to William McKendree* in 1813 on this period in the history of the Methodist movement in North America. Asbury wrote that "At this time the Methodists were, among others, not organized and had not the ordinances among us. As some in pleasantry said: 'We are a Church, and no Church.'"[19] This is especially enlightening concerning another statement that Asbury added as a note in his Journal when writing about the events of Flauvanna. He wrote that "American Methodists, both ministers and people, wished to have such [ordained] ministers among them, that they might partake, *like other Christian societies*, of the ordinances of the Church

19. JLFA, 3.476–77.

of God."[20] For Asbury, the issue was being fully a Church, like other Christian groups. The issue had very little, if anything, to do with the Eucharist as a means of grace.

Equally poignant are several letters to Stith Parham concerning the decision made at Flauvanna. Parham was an itinerant in full connection with the Methodists, and was not in attendance at the Flauvanna Conference. Immediately following the conference, Philip Gatch sent a letter to Parham inquiring as to his opinion on the decision made. Gatch wrote, "I expect you are acquainted with what was done at Conf. I should be glad to know your opinion concerning it by letter when you are at Petersburg."[21] While that inquiry in and of itself does not allow for any interpretation beyond simple curiosity, taken with another letter Parham received, it would seem that Gatch was quickly trying to solidify support for the separation that was effected at Flauvanna. Parham evidently agreed with the step taken at that conference and, following Gatch's example with himself, wrote to another prominent preacher who was not in attendance, Edward Dromgoole, and inquired of him as to whether or not he was in agreement as well. Parham sent him a letter, the substance of which can be discerned from Dromgoole's response, seeking support for the decision that was made. Dromgoole responded on February 21, 1780 to Parham thus

> I am at times distressed, under an apprehension of real religion degenerating into a party spirit. I am sorry to find that the sweet union which has so long subsisted among us is likely to be broken. I hope I never shall be of a contentious spirit, because I know it is an enemy to divine and brotherly love.
>
> You advance one argument to countenance or support a dissention: "It seems strange that we should contend for a union with a church that apparently has none of the power, and to [sic] little of the form of godliness."
>
> My dear brother, you are to look at the truth, and maintain it, without considering who does, or does not hold it. If we are to separate from every form or plan which is held by the wicked, then we must part with our reason, and give up the Bible: for wicked men hold with both. Now if you verily believed that the Church of England was more apostolic in her form than any other would you secede from that form, because maintained by many ungodly persons?[22]

20. Ibid., 1.378, emphasis added.
21. Parham, Papers.
22. Ibid.

This letter shows that the reason for the steps taken at Flauvanna was to separate from the Church of England. The issue of the sacraments was the catalyst for the decision, as shown in the official reason given for the decision: "Because the Episcopal Establishment is now dissolved and therefore in almost all our circuits the members are without the ordinances, we believe it to be our duty"[23] to ordain ourselves. But it is most closely John Wesley's ecclesiological understanding of the Eucharist that was used by the American Methodists in making their decision to conduct their own ordinations, not a soteriological understanding.

William Watters confirms this understanding when he wrote

> I was the only preacher in connection who attended both conferences. I felt a heavy heart at both, and could not but wonder at seeing some of the best men that I ever knew so little concerned, to appearance, at what to me was *one of the greatest matters in the world*. Several of the southern preachers complained that there had been an illegal conference held to keep as many of the northern preachers from conference as possible, lest they should join with them in adopting the ordinances. After much loving talk on the subject all but a few determined on appointing a committee to ordain each other and then all the rest. The few who did not agree to what was done, who were not confined by families, came in company with me, and took their stations more to the north.[24]

For Watters, "one of the greatest matters in the world" was the division of the Methodist societies in North America. Nowhere in the discussion of this conference did anyone speak of the Eucharist in any way remotely similar to Wesley's soteriological understanding. Ironically, this was a perfect use of Wesley's ecclesiological understanding of the Eucharist, as by giving themselves the authority to administer the sacraments, they knew they would be proclaiming their independence from the Church of England. At stake in the decision for ordinations and administration of the sacraments is the relation of American Methodists to the Church Universal. Was it to continue to be subordinated to the Church of England, or was it to be a Church in its own right?

The key to understanding this reading of what happened in Virginia in 1779 comes from one of the central players in the entire controversy, Philip Gatch.[25] Gatch became an itinerant in 1772, the same year as William

---

23. Gatch, Papers.

24. Watters, *Short Account*, 38, emphasis added.

25. Jesse Lee stated, "the most influential preachers in that separation in favour of the ordinances were Philip Gatch, John Dickins, and James O'Kelly" (*History*, 73).

Watters, and like Watters, was a native born American preacher.[26] Gatch was the leader of the conference itself[27] and it is through his own notes that we have an accurate account of the minutes for the conference. Gatch was elected to be one of the four preachers who made up the oversight Committee. This committee would have the authority to lead the new Church they were creating. He was also selected to be one of the three preachers who were a part of the initial presbytery, which ordained themselves and then proceeded to ordain all others at the conference who agreed to be ordained. It is in Gatch's recorded minutes of the conference that has a telling passage.

> Q 16. Is it proper to have a Committee?
>
> A. Yes, and by the vote of the preachers.
>
> Q. 17. Who are the Committee?
>
> A. P. Gatch, Jas. Foster, Leroy Cole and Reuben Ellis.
>
> Q. 18. What power do the preachers rest in the Committee?
>
> A. They do all agree to observe all the resolutions of the said Committee so far as the said Committee shall adhere to the Scriptures.[28]

This does not seem to reveal much of anything except for the fact that the oversight Committee was to be followed insofar as they followed the teachings of Scripture. Many of the most widely read and used history books of early Methodism in America, in fact, leave the issue at this point. One of the main reasons for this is that one of the major resources for these minutes comes from John Tigert's *A Constitutional History of American Episcopal Methodism*, in which he has these minutes printed as quoted above.[29] However, that is not the way in which the answer to Question 18 above was originally worded. Philip Gatch recorded the original in his journal, as he took the minutes of the conference. According to the original, the oversight Committee was to be followed insofar as they followed "the Methodist Discipline."[30] Those words were crossed out and replaced by the single word "Scriptures." Considering this fact, Flauvanna was not only a declaration of independence from the Church of England; it was also a declaration of independence from John Wesley, Francis Asbury, and Methodism itself.

26. Daniels, *History*, 440.
27. Stevens, *Compendious History*, 160.
28. Gatch, Papers.
29. Tigert, *Constitutional History*, 106.
30. Gatch, Papers. There is another sentence crossed out beneath "Methodist Discipline" which is not legible.

These preachers were going to form a separate Church, free from all previous entanglements. And this had nothing to do with a high sacramental piety. It had everything to do with an understanding of the sacraments in which the due administration of them demarcated an official Church, not just a renewal society within a Church. It was a cultural and political decision that was informed and supported by a specific sacramental piety, an ecclesiological one.

## THE FALLOUT

The decision at Flauvanna to form a separate Church, one of the benefits of which was the ability to provide American Methodists with access to the sacraments, was both applauded and derided. There were many in the southern colonies that vigorously applauded the decision, most in Virginia Colony where the Church of England was the official "state" Church, and, ironically, where the Methodists received the most help and encouragement from Anglican priests such as Jarrett and McRoberts. The preachers went about enthusiastically baptizing their members and administering the Lord's Supper as often as they could so do. The fact that this step was most welcome precisely where the Methodists received the most help from the Established Church ought to point to the fact that there was more than access to the sacraments that was at stake in this decision. It should also be noted that not every southern Methodist agreed with the decision. Stith Parham received a letter from Richard Ivey, who was appointed to the Brunswick Circuit in Virginia for the 1779–80 year on August 13, 1779, three months after the Flauvanna Conference, in which he wrote (with very poor grammar), "It is a great thing to be a saint but it is greater to know properly how to instruct saints. The People in my Circuit some is happy[,] others formal. I fear we have many things to struggle with. May God bring order out of confusion."[31] The confusion had arisen due to the introduction of the sacraments on this circuit.

Nevertheless, the response in the south was generally most favorable. Jesse Lee wrote

> The preachers thus ordained, went forth preaching the gospel in their circuits as formerly, and administered the sacraments wherever they went, provided the people were willing to partake with them. Most part of our preachers in the south, fell in with this new plan; and as the leaders of the party were very zealous, and the greater part of them very pious men, the private

31. Parham, papers.

members were influenced by them, and pretty generally fell in with their measures. However, some of the old Methodists would not commune with them; but steadily adhered to their former customs.[32]

This passage shows the "confusion" that Ivey encountered on his circuit.

Lee also wrote that "the preachers in the south were very successful in their ministerial labours, and many souls were brought to God in the latter part of that year . . . These things all united to confirm the preachers in the belief, that the step they had taken was owned and honoured of God."[33] Philip Gatch, in commenting upon the action taken at Flauvanna, wrote of the results on the circuits, "I believe it was of the Lord for he greatly blessed us."[34] This was the common opinion in the southern societies. This opinion was so great among those who made the decision to administer the sacraments that the idea of an increase in membership of the societies became fact to many people. Yet the facts say contrary, there being a net decrease of members in all the circuits for this year.[35] This opinion has carried over to somewhat more recent times as well, with Herbert Asbury writing about this action

> The news of the establishment of the presbytery [of Philip Gatch, Rueben Ellis, James Foster and LeRoy Cole at Flauvanna] was received gladly; throughout Virginia, Maryland, and North Carolina there was great rejoicing when the word spread that the faithful could now be baptized and enjoy the emotional and spiritual cannibalism of the Lord's Supper. The preachers, invested with all the authority possessed by ministers of regular churches, hasten into their circuits, and for almost a year Virginia and Maryland were aflame with revivals, the societies in these sections showing phenomenal increases in membership.[36]

Even John Wigger says of the south in this period that it was "the movement's fastest growing region,"[37] and yet the statistics prove otherwise. Such was the enthusiasm for this course of action that the facts do not speak for themselves in the matter.

In the north, the response to the Flauvanna Conference was decidedly less enthusiastic. While it has been shown above that the southern societies

32. Lee, *A Short History*, 69–70.
33. Ibid.
34. Gatch, Papers.
35. See Appendix B.
36. Asbury, *Methodist Saint*, 126.
37. Wigger, *Heaven*, 24.

viewed the issue of the sacraments in light of Wesley's ecclesiological understanding of the Eucharist, it can be seen by the response of Francis Asbury and the northern societies that they were operating under the same assumptions. The decision at Flauvanna was seen as a schism within Methodism, and one that had to be repaired, if possible, not celebrated as the southern preachers were doing. Francis Asbury's immediate response upon hearing of the Flauvanna Conference's decision was recorded on June 30, 1779. He wrote, "I received the minutes of the Virginia Conference [at Flauvanna], by which I learn the preachers there have been effecting a lame separation of the Episcopal Church, that will last about one year. I pity them: Satan has a desire to have us, that he may sift us like wheat."[38] It was at this time that Asbury wrote the only book (besides his journals) that he did. It was an abridgement of two different books, *Heart Divisions: the Evil of our Times* by Jeremiah Burroughs and *The Cure of Church Divisions* by Richard Baxter, the majority of Asbury's work coming from the former.[39] This abridgment was put forward by Asbury to remind the southern societies that they had, in fact, separated from Methodism in general, and from the northern societies and himself in particular. One passage that Asbury left intact from Burroughs' work dealt with the sin of *rashness* and how it can cause divisions among Christians:

> Rashness causes men suddenly to provoke others; whereas, did they consider what ill consequences might come of it, they would forbear. Rash men quickly take hold of the sword of justice to hack and hew; they think that what they do is according to reason; but they do not wisely weigh things in the balance of justice. Remember, justice hath a balance, as well as a sword . . . Rash men presently think they understand all that can be known in such a business, and thence presume to make sudden determinations; but, as over-hearty digestion causes wind, and brings much trouble to the body; so do over-hasty resolutions to men's spirits, and societies.[40]

Yet another passage Asbury retained concerned, not an attitude within the heart that he thought shed light on the reason for the southern preachers' schism, but a practice that led to the same; namely *needless disputes*.

---

38. *JLFA*, 1.304. It may be that Asbury had some commentary inserted in this entry for publication, trying to smooth over the effect of the separation by "predicting" it would only last one year.

39. Which was published under the title *The Causes, Evils and Cures of Heart and Church Divisions*.

40. Asbury, *Divisions*, 44–45 and Burroughs, *Heart-Divisions*, 136.

"When men have got a little knowledge, they think it is a fine thing to be arguing and disputing in matters of religion: unnecessary disputes are their necessary practice, for they shall be accounted as nobody, if they have not something to object against almost every thing; but in this way of theirs they shall be accounted knowing men, men who have an insight into things, who understand more than ordinary men do: hence they turn all their religion into *disputes*, and by them they grow giddy."[41]

Extremely interesting for this study, however, is one passage that Asbury conspicuously deleted from his abridgement. In the section entitled "To the Reader," Burroughs wrote, "Those things which God himself ordains for union (the Sacraments) are by man's corruption made the occasion of great contention in the Christian world. No marvell [sic] then that what comes from man's sincerest intentions and best endeavours be turned quite crosse [sic]."[42] In fact, all uses of the Lord's Supper have been omitted in Asbury's edition.[43] For Asbury, the sacraments themselves were not the issue. The issue was seen as purely ecclesiological in nature. Nowhere in Asbury's treatment of the schism, even beyond this abridgement, are the sacraments seen as means of grace. Rather, the issue is consistently one of unity within the society and the unity of the society to the Church.

Asbury was not the only one to see the decision at Flauvanna in this manner. Devereux Jarratt wrote to Asbury complaining of the situation in Virginia. Asbury recorded

> I received a letter from Mr. Jarratt, who is greatly alarmed, but it is too late: he should have begun his opposition before. Our zealous dissenting brethren are for turning all out of the society who will not submit to their administration. I find the spirit of separation grows among them, and fear that it will generate malevolence, and evil speaking: after all my labour, to unite the Protestant Episcopal ministry to us, they say, "We don't want your unconverted ministers; the people will not receive them."

41. Ibid., 53 and ibid., 148, emphasis in Asbury alone.

42. Burroughs, *Heart-Divisions*, 3.

43. Also interestingly omitted is a passage that could have been used against Asbury and his objections to the southern preachers. Burroughs wrote, "A proud man opposes others, because they have begun such a work; and others, who are also proud, oppose him, because he hath begun it. The Senators of Rome could have been content to have admitted Christ to have been amongst the number of their gods, but only upon this, they refused because the motion began not with them; they are loth [sic] to break the yce [sic], to begin a good work, if they see any difficulty in it, and yet the cause of God must not goe [sic] on, Christ must not be admitted, if they have not been at the beginning" (114). One of the benefits of making the abridgement is being able to choose what is included and what is not included.

I expect to turn out shortly among them, and fear a separation will be unavoidable: I am determined, if we cannot save all, to save a part; but for the divisions of Reuben there will be great heart searchings![44]

Freeborn Garrettson wrote that

> The Methodists being only a society, who were mostly united (with respect to communion) to the church of England; and her ministers (especially in Virginia, and Carolina) in the time of the war were dispersed, so that a large body of people, under the name of Methodists, were in a great measure destitute of the ordinances of the Lord's house. In this case what was to be done? Our dear Virginia brethren thought it expedient to form themselves into a church, and have the ordinances among them; which they did in the year 1779. But it was contrary to the minds of the preachers to the North.[45]

What is extremely telling about this quotation is that Garrettson recognized the surface issue was one of the ordinances, and yet he also fully understood that the result was that the southern societies formed themselves into a separate Church. Again, this shows the prevailing understanding of the Eucharist in the American Methodist piety was one of ecclesiological function, not soteriology.

Finally, Jesse Lee recorded, "The preachers north of Virginia, were opposed to this step so hastily taken by their brethren in that south, and made a stand against it, believing that unless a stop could be put to this new mode of proceeding, a separation would take place among the preachers and the people. There was great cause to fear a division, and both parties trembled for the ark of God, and shuddered at the thought of dividing the church of Christ."[46]

This situation persisted until the Methodists once again met in separate northern and southern conferences in 1780. The minutes of the northern conference are direct and to the point. The first question set the tone for the conference when it asked, "What preachers do now agree to sit in conference *on the original plan, as Methodists*?"[47] From this point, the conference continued with several items of business that occurred every year, such as setting the appointments, condemning slavery and grain alcohol,

---

44. *JLFA*, 1.322.
45. Garrettson, *American Methodist Pioneer*, 104.
46. Lee, *A Short History*, 70.
47. Hitt and Ware, *Minutes*, 23, emphasis added.

and setting salaries for traveling preachers. Interspersed within this business, though, are several questions that pertain to the situation in the south.

> Quest. 12. Shall we continue in close connexion with the church, and press our people to a closer communion with her?
>
> Ans. Yes.
>
> Quest. 13. Will this conference grant the privilege to all the friendly clergy of the church of England, at the request or desire of the people, to preach or administer the ordinances in our preaching houses or chapels?
>
> Ans. Yes.
>
> Quest. 20. Does this whole conference disapprove the step our brethren have taken in Virginia?
>
> Ans. Yes.
>
> Quest. 21. Do we look upon them no longer as Methodists in connexion with Mr. Wesley and us till they come back?
>
> Ans. Agreed.
>
> Quest. 22. Shall brother Asbury, Garrettson and Watters attend the Virginia conference, and inform them of our proceedings in this, and receive their answer?
>
> Ans. Yes.
>
> Quest. 26. What must be the conditions of our union with our Virginia brethren?
>
> Ans. To suspend all their administrations for one year, and all meet together in Baltimore.[48]

The answer to Question 26 was actually a compromise. Philip Gatch and Reuben Ellis, both preachers who were a part of the oversight Committee and the original presbytery formed at Flauvanna, attended the northern conference in the hopes of convincing Asbury and those preachers in the north that the south's position was acceptable. Francis Asbury recorded the original answer to this question in his journal. He wrote

> Our conference met in peace and love. We settled all our northern stations; then we began in much debate about the letter sent from Virginia. We first concluded to renounce them; then I offered conditions of union. I. That they should ordain no more. II. That they should come no farther than Hanover circuit. III.

---

48. Ibid., 25–26.

> We would have our delegates in their conference. IV. That they should not presume to administer the ordinances where there is a decent Episcopal minister. V. To have a union conference. These would not do, as we found upon long debate, and we came back to our determinations; although it was like death to think of parting. At last a thought struck my mind; to propose a suspension of the ordinances for one year, and so cancel all our grievances, and be one. It was agreed on both sides, and Philip Gatch and Reuben Ellis, who had been very stiff came into it, and thought it would do.[49]

William Watters recorded the events and emotions at this conference in Baltimore. He wrote

> April twenty-fourth one thousand seven and eighty, our conference began in Baltimore for those preachers who rejected the administering the ordinances. Two of our brethren from below, Gatch and R. Ellis who had adopted the administering the ordinances, attended to see if anything could be done to prevent a total disunion, for they did not wish that to be the case. They both thought their brethren were hard with them and there was little appearance of anything but an entire separation. They complained that I was the only one who did not join them, that treated them with affection and tenderness. Before conference rose, it appointed Mr. Asbury, Garrettson and myself to attended their conference below, but as nothing less than their suspending the administering of the ordinances, could be the terms of our treaty with them, I awfully feared our visit would be of little consequence, yet I willingly went down in the name of God—hoping against hope.[50]

Here once again, the issue at hand for the Methodists intimately involved in the decisions of the Flauvanna Conference and an appropriate response to that conference revolved around the issue of ecclesial unity. The high sacramental piety that supposedly resulted in the "clamoring" for the Lord's Supper is absent.

There was much debate over this sacramental decision, and all the debate surrounded the unity and integrity of Methodism. What is extremely telling about the fallout from this decision is what is not said about it. Nowhere is there any mention of the Lord's Supper as being a means of grace that draws people closer to God, let alone the means of grace *par*

---

49. *JLFA*, 1.346–47.
50. Watters, *Short Account*, 40–41.

*excellence* as Wesley would describe it. The issue is solely ecclesial in nature. Even the idea of how Christ may or may not be present in the sacrament is not discussed; rather the issue is whether these Methodists have the right or authority to dissolve union with their northern brethren who disagree with them and form their own Church where the sacraments can be duly administered.

## Chapter 9

# Healing the Schism

### THE TEMPORARY SOLUTION

As agreed at the northern conference in Baltimore in 1780, the northern societies sent representatives to the southern conference, held in Manakintown, Virginia, and presented the north's ultimatum of suspending ordinations and administration of the sacraments for one year or no longer be considered Methodist. These men were Francis Asbury, Freeborn Garrettson, and William Watters. As they progressed south, Asbury noted, "We found the plague was begun; the good man Arnold was warm for the ordinances."[1] Three days later and closer to the southern conference, Asbury noted, "These people are full of the ordinances . . . I conducted myself with cheerful freedom, but found there was a separation in heart and practice. I spoke with my countryman, John Dickins, and found him opposed to our continuance in union with the Episcopal Church; Brother Watters and Garrettson tried their men, and found them inflexible."[2] Even here it can be seen that the real issue is not the ordinances in and of themselves, but the separation from the Methodist Societies, and thereby extension the Established Church, that the administration of the ordinances has caused. The soteriological dimension of Methodist Eucharistic piety from John Wesley's theology is completely absent in this dialogue between Dickins and Asbury, as well as in Asbury's assessment of the situation with respect to "the good man Arnold."

1. *JLFA*, 1.348.
2. Ibid., 1.349.

There are, unfortunately, no existent minutes from this meeting, but Asbury, Garrettson and Watters all recorded what happened at the meeting. The south initially rejected such a demand and resolved to be separated from the north. Watters recorded

> We found our brethren as loving and as full of zeal as ever, and as fully determined on all their former arguments, they now added (what with many was infinitely stronger than all the arguments in the world) that the Lord approbated, and greatly blessed his own ordinances, by them administered the past year. We had a great deal of loving conversation with many tears; but I saw no bitterness, no shyness, no judging each other. We wept, and prayed, and sobbed, but neither would agree to the other's terms.[3]

Freeborn Garrettson wrote that "we found the brethren in conference, fully persuaded in their minds that the Lord required us to be a separate church."[4] This is the most plain language definition of the reasoning behind the decision at Flauvanna in print. This issue was ecclesiological in nature.

Per Asbury's account, once the three of them arrived at the conference, an ally joined them in arguing for the southern societies to repair the breach in unity by abandoning the ordinances, Edward Dromgoole. Apparently, his response to Stith Parham was Dromgoole's final answer about the sacraments and he was not persuaded to join the southern preachers. Asbury thus wrote

> The conference was called: brother Watters, Garrettson, and myself stood back, and being afterward joined by brother Dromgoole, we were desired to come in, and I was permitted to speak; I read Mr. Wesley's thoughts against a separation: showed my private letters of instructions from Mr. Wesley; set before them the sentiments of the Delaware and Baltimore conferences; read our epistles, and read my letter to brother Gatch, and Dickins's letter in answer. After some time spent this way, it was proposed to me, if I would get the circuits supplied, they would desist; but that I could not do. We went to preaching; I spoke on Ruth ii, 4, and spoke as though nothing had been the matter among the preachers or people; and we were greatly pleased and comforted; there was some moving among the people. In the afternoon we met; the preachers appeared to me to be farther off; there had been, I thought, some talking out of doors. When we—Asbury,

---

3. Watters, *Short Account*, 40.
4. Garrettson, *American Methodist Pioneer*, 104.

> Garrettson, Watters, and Dromgoole—could not come to a conclusion with them, we withdrew, and left them to deliberate on the conditions I offered, which was, to suspend the measures they had taken for one year. After an hour's conference, we were called to receive their answer, which was, they could not submit to the terms of union. I then prepared to leave the house, to go to a near neighbour's to lodge, under the heaviest cloud I ever felt in America: O! what I felt!—nor I alone!—but the agents on both sides! they wept like children, but kept their opinions.[5]

Through all of this debate, tears, worship, and prayer, the issue at hand still was the union of the societies together and, secondarily, their union to the Established Church.

Miraculously, however, just before Asbury, Garrettson and Watters were about to leave and report the southern rejection to the northern societies, the southern conference changed its mind and accepted the terms of union, to give up the administration of the sacraments. This decision may owe much to the fact that Garrettson and Watters were praying upstairs from the conference and, doubtless, the preachers heard their petitions to God.[6] Asbury concluded his comments concerning this conference with the following

> We heard what they had to say; surely the hand of God has been greatly seen in all this: there might have been twenty promising preachers, and three thousand people, seriously affected by this separation; but the Lord would not suffer this; we then had preaching by brother Watters on, "Come thou with us, and we will do thee good;" afterward we had a love feast; preachers and people wept, prayed, and talked, so the spirit of dissension was powerfully weakened, and I hoped it would never take place again.[7]

Throughout all this debate, again, was the ecclesial concern of unity. There was no talk of the sacraments as a means of grace, no mention of their soteriological importance. For these preachers, the unity of the societies was more important than access to the means of grace *par excellence*. Rather than see the Eucharist as a means of grace, they saw it as the source of contention that drove a wedge between Methodist brothers. William Watters confirms this in his *Journal*, where he wrote,

---

5. *JLFA*, 1.349–50.
6. Ibid.
7. Ibid.

> I could not but say it is of the Lord's doing and it is marvelous in our eyes. I knew of nothing upon earth that could have given me more real consolation, and could not but be heartily thankful for the stand I had taken, and the part I had acted during the whole contest. I had by several leading characters, on both sides been suspected of leaning to the opposite. Could all have agreed to the administering the ordinances, I should have had no objection; but until that was the case, I could not view ourselves ripe for so great a change... We now had every reason to believe that every thing would end well: that the evils which had actually attended our partial division, would make us more cautious how we should entertain one thought of taking any step that should have the least tendency to so great an evil.[8]

Just as Watters stated one year earlier at the initial outbreak of the schism, the issue of the sacraments could have gone either way for Watters, and he would have been equally content. The great evil with which contention had to be made was the dissolution of unity amongst the Methodists themselves. The ecclesiological dimension of Eucharistic piety was the main, if not only, focus in this conflict and its resolution.

Not everyone acquiesced to the north's demands, however. There are recorded instances where both traveling preachers and local preachers would not give up administering the sacraments. Freeborn Garrettson recorded that

> I travelled (by the desire of the brethren) largely through the circuits, and my dear Lord was powerfully present in many places to heal. I met with much trouble from several who were not willing to give up the administration of the ordinances... Amelia, VA Quarterly Meeting began, here I had my hands full. Several of the local preachers had been breaking the rules—I mean administering the ordinances. I took them aside and told them plainly if they could not come under discipline they could not be of us. My greatest trial was from I. J. a travelling preacher who had gone out of the line of the gospel. His accuser was brought face to face; I did not know whether to send him to a circuit or not, he acknowledged his fault, we thought he might be dropped another quarter.[9]

Asbury recorded a similar instance when he wrote two months after the conference, "I find the *spirit of separation on account of the ordinances*, is

---

8. Watters, *Short Account*, 41.
9. Garrettson, *American Methodist Pioneer*, 118, 196.

very high among preachers and people; but I hope it will be checked."[10] It is important to point out that it was an attitude of separation that was brought about as a result of the sacraments that was the issue at hand, not the sacraments themselves. In this entire incident, from start to finish, ecclesial unity was the issue and the sacraments were symptomatic of a dissolution of that unity. Asbury also noted, "I met with five or six faithful souls on our fast day, and the Lord was present with us. There is considerable distress amongst our societies, caused by some of the local preachers, who are not satisfied unless they administer the ordinances without order or ordination, and the whole circuit appears to be more or less tinctured with their spirit."[11]

Probably the most interesting comment anyone made surrounding the entire situation came from Asbury. Eight days after the conference agreed to give up administering the ordinances, Asbury encountered many of the people in Virginia who were in favor of the Methodists administering the sacraments. Asbury reflected upon how to encourage the people to stop contesting for them and return to the "old plan" of Methodism, where the Methodists attend established churches for the sacraments. To do this, Asbury thought, "I see clearly that to press the people to holiness, is the proper method to take them from contending for ordinances, or any less consequential things."[12] If the soteriological understanding of the sacraments as means of grace were anywhere in the debate, it is most definitely absent in the above statement. Whereas John Wesley argued the Eucharist was one of the best ways to live the life of holiness, Asbury used the idea of seeking holiness to deflect people from want of the sacraments. This instance, along with the entire debate concerning the sacraments from the Flauvanna Conference through this following year, demonstrate that as of 1780, the early American Methodist understanding of the Eucharist was one of ecclesiology almost exclusively. The importance of this point cannot be ignored. This is the framework out of which the soon-to-be created Methodist Episcopal Church will work in relation to the sacraments.

It took the next two Annual Conferences, of 1781 and 1782, to finally put this schism completely behind them and continue forward in unity. At the 1781 Conference, April 24 of that year, William Watters recorded, "We rejoiced together that the Lord had broken the snare of the devil, and our disputes were all at an end . . . Mine eyes have seen thy salvation in healing the divisions that have been among us for these several years."[13] The reason

---

10. *JLFA*, 1.367, emphasis added.
11. Ibid., 1.417.
12. Ibid., 1.351.
13. Watters, *Short Account*, 46.

for his joy was that almost all of the southern preachers (Asbury recorded that it was all but one)[14] agreed together to continue the one-year moratorium on ordaining each other and administering the sacraments indefinitely. The schism had been healed. However, there were still instances of local preachers wanting to administer the sacraments, as referenced by Garrettson above. To finally put an end to this problem, when the 1782 Conference met on April 16 in Virginia and continued on May 20 in Baltimore, it was proposed in Virginia that the preachers sign a statement signifying their unity and allegiance to the "old plan" of Methodism. This was done and all preachers signed the document in Baltimore. In the words of Asbury, "the preachers all signed the agreement proposed at the Virginia Conference, and there was a unanimous resolve to adhere to the old Methodist plan."[15]

During the following two years, the topic of the sacraments was brought up infrequently. It would seem that the American Methodists were tired of fighting amongst themselves over this one issue. One letter of note stands out from this period, however. It is a letter from Francis Asbury to John Wesley concerning the sacraments written on September 20, 1783. In this letter Asbury commented that, since Methodists are made up of so many Christians of varying backgrounds, and since all of those backgrounds do not share the same opinion of the sacraments, until Methodists can adequately administer them to their own people, they could not emphasize the importance of sacraments for fear of losing members. Asbury wrote to Wesley

> I reverence the ordinances of God; and attend them when I have opportunity; but I clearly see they have been made the tools of division and separation for these three last centuries. We have joined with us at this time, those that have been Presbyterians, Dutch, and English, Lutherans, Mennonites, low Dutch, and Baptists. If we preach up ordinances to these people, we should add, "if they are to be had, and if not, there can be no guilt." If we do any other way, we shall drive them back to their old churches that have disowned them; and who will do all they can to separate them from us.[16]

With this letter, it is also necessary to consider a similar notion Asbury wrote to Wesley shortly after the temporary resolution of the entire affair on September 3, 1780:

---

14. *JLFA*, 1.402.
15. Ibid., 1.425
16. Ibid., 3.31.

> Since my last [letter] I have been travelling through the circuits in Virginia & North Carolina and according to my abilities have been confirming the souls of them which have believed, that they may walk by the same rule, and mind the same thing. That violence for assistants introducing the ordinances is much cooled, but yet I must say our people are under great disadvantages, tho [sic] not such as will vindicate an alteration of old Methodism and weak laymen acting as ministers. I think the want of opportunity suspends the force of duty to receive the Lord's supper.[17]

These two letters sum up the position the American Methodists took between 1780 and 1784 when John Wesley authorized the creation of the Methodist Episcopal Church: it is not a sin to neglect receiving the sacraments because they are not to be had among us, and even if they were to be had, they would cause more division than unity. Having had a taste of the sacraments, and the near schism because of it, the American Methodists let this issue drop until Wesley himself could cut through the Gordian knot of sacraments and unity and create a solution, the Methodist Episcopal Church.

## THE PERMANENT SOLUTION

The reconciliation that affected the end of the schism brought about by the Flauvanna Conference in 1779 was for the societies to desist administering the sacraments for one year while the American Methodists awaited direction from John Wesley. That direction finally came, not one year later in 1780, but five years later in 1784. That is not to say that Wesley did not try to resolve the situation prior to 1784. Quite the contrary, in August of 1780 Wesley wrote to the bishop of London, Robert Lowth asking for him to ordain a man for the Methodists specifically in America. The reason this request was made to the Bishop of London is because that bishop was the one that had ecclesial authority over the American Colonies.

    The Societies in America had requested of Asbury to seek an answer to the sacramental question from Wesley. Asbury wrote one letter shortly after the 1780 conferences, but it has been lost to history. He followed up that letter, assuming that it had been lost, with another on September 3, 1780. In this, Asbury laid out the desire of the American Methodists. "If we had an itinerant clergyman all our wants of ordinances would be supplied, but such a clergyman is a miracle; we have had but two in an age, yourself and Mr.

---

17. Ibid., 3.24–25.

Whitefield; the latter has left the world without successor so I fear will the former. I hope, dear sir, if ever there should be peace between Britain and America, if you should live to see that blessed period, nothing will prevent your coming and laying your bones in America as dear Mr. Whitefield has done."[18] One detail of this letter stands out in that Asbury requested, apparently at the desire of the American Methodists, that one single ordained itinerant minister would suffice for the desire of the sacraments among the American Methodists. Given the vastness of the American landscape and the geographic space between Methodist societies, the request of only one ordained minister shows that there was something besides a soteriologically motivated access to a means of grace as a main reason for the request.

Apparently, Wesley did receive Asbury's first letter, since he sent a follow-up letter to Bishop Lowth on August 10, 1780. In this letter, Wesley reminded the bishop that the American Methodists only requested the minister, not the salary to pay the minister. "They wanted no salary for their Minister; they were themselves able and willing to maintain him."[19] This is an important point since the ministers in the Church of England were supported by the cures to which they were sent. Since the Americans were requesting an itinerant minister, there would be no cure, and hence no salary. That the Methodists would supply the salary shows that, while they understood their dependence upon the Established Church for the ordinances, they did not wish to be entangled with it any more than was absolutely necessary.

The American Methodists were serious about wanting an ordained, itinerating minister. "They [the American Methodists] therefore applied, by me, to your Lordship, as members of the Church of England, and desirous so to continue, begging the favour of your Lordship, after your Lordship had examined him, to ordain a pious man who might officiate as their Minister."[20] The answer Wesley, and thus the American Methodists, received was overwhelmingly negative. Wesley recorded, "But your Lordship observes, 'There are three Ministers in that country already.'"[21] Apparently not being dissuaded by this rejection, Wesley reminded the bishop of a time in the past when he suggested to the bishop a specific man for ordination. Unfortunately, the bishop also rejected this man.

> Some time since, I recommended to your Lordship a plain man, whom I had known above twenty years, as a person of deep,

18. Ibid., 3.25–26.
19. Wesley, *Works* (Jackson), 13.142.
20. Ibid.
21. Ibid.

> genuine piety, and of unblamable conversation. But he neither understood Greek nor Latin; and he affirmed, in so many words, that he believed it was his duty to preach, whether he was ordained or no. I believe so too. What became of him since, I know not: I suppose he received Presbyterian ordination; and I cannot blame him, if he did. He might think any ordination better than none.[22]

Wesley ventured to remind the bishop of this by way of questioning the ministerial character of the "three Ministers in that country already." Wesley continued

> I do not know that Mr. Hoskins [the man mentioned above] had any favour to ask of the Society. He asked the favour of your Lordship to ordain him, that he might minister to a little flock in America. But your Lordship did not see good to ordain him: But your Lordship did see good to ordain, and send into America, other persons, who knew something of Greek and Latin; but who knew no more of saving souls, than of catching whales. In this respect also, I mourn for poor America; for the sheep scattered up and down therein. Part of them have no shepherds at all, particularly in the northern colonies; and the case of the rest is little better, for their own shepherds pity them not. They cannot; for they have no pity on themselves. They take no thought or care about their own souls.[23]

Despite this last salvo in the debate upon the presence and worthiness of the ministers in the American Colonies, Wesley was not able to convince Bishop Lowth to ordain anyone else for America.

Having failed to obtain results within the established channels of the Church, towards the end of 1784 John Wesley took matters into his own hands. In explaining the course of action he chose, he wrote, "for some hundred miles together, there is none, either to baptize, or to administer the Lord's supper. Here, therefore, my scruples are at an end."[24] For forty years Wesley asserted the Methodists would not separate from the Church of England. For forty years Wesley decried the idea of establishing Methodism as a Church of its own. And in 1784, due to the effects of the American Revolutionary War severing all governing ties between the American (now) States and England, Wesley himself was the one who facilitated the separation of the American Methodists from the Established Church. Such a

22. Ibid., 13.143.
23. Ibid.
24. Ibid., 13.252.

monumental decision as this, going against forty years of profession and belief, was neither made lightly, nor without significant cause. Wesley's "scruples were at an end" precisely because the Methodists ultimately under his care in America no longer had access to the sacraments. This was an intolerable situation for Wesley, as can be seen from a statement he wrote in his *Advice to the People Called Methodist*. Cautioning the Methodists not to look unfavorably on people who did not share the same opinion, Wesley nevertheless stated the position of the Methodists when he wrote, "You likewise lay so much stress on the use of those ordinances which you believe to be of God, as to confess there is no salvation for you if you willfully neglect them."[25] For Wesley, the issue concerning the absence of ordained ministers in America with the authority to administer the sacraments to his Methodists was about salvation itself.

William Warren Sweet, in his book *Methodism in American History*, relates the situation well. "Wesley had been kept informed as to conditions among American Methodists. He knew that many of them had not partaken of the sacrament for years, while the children of members were generally unbaptized. The possibility of the success and growth of American Methodism under such conditions would be slight, and this was doubtless the determining factor in the momentous step which John Wesley now took to provide the American Methodists with the sacraments."[26] Wesley's soteriological understanding of the sacraments (and the Eucharist in particular), led him to make a decision that brought him in tension with the Church of England because of his long standing explication of his ecclesiological understanding of the sacraments. If the American Methodists were going to have access to the means of grace, especially the Eucharist as the means of grace *par excellence*, then they would have to do so through their own separate Church order.[27]

On the surface, this appears to be the Flauvanna Conference *redividus*, only on the opposite side of the Atlantic, and originating with the founder

25. Wesley, *Works*, 9.126.

26. Sweet, *Methodism*, 102.

27. There is ample debate over Wesley's intensions surrounding the ordinations that followed this decision. There are scholars who argue successfully on both sides of the issue of whether or not he intended for the American Methodists to become an independent Church to the degree they did. For a well done treatment of the issue in the opinion that the Americans overstepped their mandate from Wesley in creating a Church, see Andrews, *Methodists*, specifically pages 66–72. In Andrews' estimation it was Thomas Coke who was the primary culprit for modifying Wesley's original intent, whatever that intent was. Nevertheless, for the purposes of this thesis, this study will assume that Wesley intended for the American Methodists to become an independent Church.

of Methodism himself, not merely some lay preachers whom he had never met. However, this is not the case for one main reason: the dominant and controlling view of the Eucharist. In Virginia in 1779, as has been shown above, the primary concern of the Methodists was that of separation from the Church of England. Those men wanted, for various reasons, to cut off ties with the Church of England. These reasons ranged from not wanting to be affiliated with the establishment of the (then) enemy to not wanting to receive the sacraments from the hands of (who they perceived to be) unconverted ministers. These Methodists already had the power of godliness among them, what they lacked was the form. It was in that vein that they chose the path of ordination to administer the sacraments. Ordination for the administration of the sacraments was the most expedient way to achieve their goal of independence from the Church of England.

Wesley, on the other hand, was primarily concerned that the American Methodists no longer had even a remote access to one of the greatest sources of the power of godliness in the Eucharist. His concern for the Americans led him to propose ordination for the administration of the sacraments because it was the most expedient way to achieve his goal of providing all the means necessary for the people under his care to press on towards holiness of heart and life. That the Flauvanna Methodists and John Wesley came to the same conclusion, but for radically different reasons, shows how intimately interconnected both the soteriological understanding and the ecclesiological understanding of the Eucharist can be. Yet despite the similar end, the distinction between the means of achieving that end must be understood. This will be the key to understanding the forthcoming new Church's Eucharistic piety and practice. Flauvanna saw the sacraments as the means of achieving a separate Church; Wesley saw a separate Church as the means of providing the sacraments. Therein lies the difference. For the former, the sacraments function primarily in an ecclesiological manner, helping demarcate what a true Church is. For the latter, a Church exists primarily to provide the sacraments precisely because of their soteriological importance in the life of a believer.

Wesley, confessing he had tried all other options, decided to take it upon himself to ordain ministers for the Methodists in America and endow them with the authority to perpetuate this new ordained ministry through subsequent ordinations. On September 1, 1784 John Wesley, Thomas Coke and James Creighton, all ordained presbyters in the Church of England, ordained Richard Whatcoat and Thomas Vasey (Methodist lay preachers) deacons. On the following day, they ordained the two elders and then ordained Coke as superintendent for the Methodists in America with the authority to ordain others there.[28] Even in the ordination certificate Wesley presented to Coke, the issue at stake for him was the absence of opportunity to receive the sacraments. Wesley wrote

> Whereas many of the people in the southern provinces of North America who desire to continue under my care, and still adhere to the doctrines and disciplines of the Church of England are greatly distrest [sic] for want of ministers to administer the sacraments of Baptism and the Lord's Supper, according to the usage of the said Church: and whereas there does not appear to be any other way of supplying them with ministers: Know all men, that I John Wesley think myself to be providentially called at this time to set apart some persons for the work of the ministry in America.[29]

Yet another reason Wesley decided upon this course of action can be inferred from the language in Coke's ordination certificate. Wesley, through these ordinations, created a new Church, separating the American Methodists from the Church of England, to prevent an even more portentous separation of the American Methodists from the English Methodists and Wesley himself. The American Methodists had already proven the fact that they would separate even from Wesley and the English Methodists if needs be by the way they constructed their separation at Flauvanna. As has been illustrated before, the only rule of guidance for the short-lived Virginia presbytery was Scripture. The connection to Methodism, and thus Wesley, having been crossed out in the minutes by the marking out of "Methodist Discipline" as the guiding principle for the authority of the oversight committee. So, in the interest of preserving cordial and filial unity among the Methodists, Wesley separated the American Methodists from the Church of England.

This is not to say that Wesley's ordinations were universally accepted. Wesley knew he had questionable authority for performing such a feat. In *A Letter to Dr. Coke, Mr. Asbury, and Our Brethren in North America*, dated September 4, 1784, Wesley stated, "Lord King's 'Account of the Primitive Church' convinced me many years ago, that Bishops and Presbyters are the

---

28. Wesley, *Works* (Jackson), 4.288. This reference only shows that Whatcoat and Vasey were "appointed" for America. However, Wesley's diary says for the same entry they were ordained. It also explicitly states for September 2, "ordained Dr. Coke!" This shows that when Wesley wrote in his journal for the same day, "I added to them three more," he was speaking of ordinations, not people, as Whatcoat and Vasey were ordained presbyters and Coke was ordained superintendent on that day. See Wesley, *Works*, 23.497.

29. Wesley, *Ordination Certificate of Thomas Coke*.

same order, and consequently have the same right to ordain."[30] This, then, is his justification for taking such an unusual step of ordaining two of his lay traveling preachers, and also ordaining Coke as a Superintendent/Bishop. However, the historicity of this statement by Wesley is not as clear in his *Journal*. The occurrence to which Wesley referred was on January 20, 1746. On that date Wesley recorded, "I set out for Bristol. On the road I read over Lord King's Account of the Primitive Church. In spite of the vehement prejudice of my education, I was ready to believe that this was a fair and impartial draught; but if so, it would follow that Bishops and Presbyters are (essentially) of one order; and that originally every Christian congregation was a Church independent on all others!"[31]

It would seem that Wesley eventually became convinced that King was correct in his assessment of the orders of ordained ministry, yet Wesley rejected the practical implication of such a situation, namely the independence of every congregation on earth and the superfluity of ecclesial structures to the contrary. Wesley selectively chose what to accept out of his reading for justification of his actions. Not only was the justification of the action questionable, but also there was little support for such a step among the Methodists Wesley consulted. Richard Heitzenrater has noted that at the time of the 1784 Methodist Conference in Leeds, "Wesley discussed the possibility of ordinations with only his senior advisors, or cabinet. According to one of them, John Pawson, the group advised against the idea but could tell that Wesley had made up his mind. Wesley consulted Fletcher, who was against it; a group of clergy in Leeds, who were against it; James Creighton, a new clergy assistant from Ireland, who was against it. Charles Wesley was not consulted at all."[32]

It is not surprising that, given the difficulty in justifying this decision, John kept his actions hidden from his brother Charles until after the newly ordained leaders had departed for America. Upon hearing what his brother had done, Charles penned a poem that was never published in a Methodist hymnal, for obvious reasons:

> So easily are Bishops made
> By man's or woman's whim?
> W— his hands on C— hath laid,
> But who laid hands on Him?
>
> Hands on himself he laid, and *took*

---

30. Wesley, *Works* (Jackson), 13.251.
31. Wesley, *Works*, 20.112.
32. Heitzenrater, *Wesley*, 287.

An Apostolic Chair;
And then ordain'd his Creature C—
His Heir and Successor.

Episcopalians, now no more
With Presbyterians fight,
But give your needless Contest o're,
"Whose Ordination's right?"

It matter not, if Both are One,
Or different in degree,
For lo! ye see contain'd in Prelate John
The whole Presbytery!³³

Charles also did not hide his distaste over Coke's ordination of Asbury nearly four months later. He wrote

A Roman emperor, 'tis said,
His favourite horse a consul made;
But Coke brings other things to pass,
He makes a bishop of an ass.³⁴

Nevertheless, despite Charles' objections to the course of action John chose to initiate, the separation of the American Methodists from the Church of England was underway.

To effect this separation, along with Coke, Whatcoat, and Vasey, Wesley sent to America in their custody the *Letter to Dr. Coke, Mr. Asbury, and Our Brethren in North America*, which not only detailed why Wesley decided to do what he did, as shown above, but also how he foresaw the American Methodists proceeding in the future; instructions for how to establish this new Church (which unfortunately are lost to history); a *Collection of Psalms and Hymns for the Lord's Day*; and an abbreviated version of the *Book of Common Prayer* known as the *Sunday Service of the Methodists in North America* (which he instructed the elders to use every Lord's Day). These people and documents were to form a Church where none existed to give access to the sacraments where none was provided. Wesley's major motivation was to provide his spiritual children in America with access to the sacraments for their continued growth in holiness. They all departed on September 18, 1784 at ten o'clock in the morning.³⁵ When they arrived in

---

33. Baker, *Representative Verse*, 368.
34. Heitzenrater, *Wesley*, 288.
35. Coke, *Journals*, 25.

the New World, it was to a new country to create a new Church. It was only fitting that they landed in New York.[36]

---

36. Ibid.

Section IV

# American Methodism: Indigenous Church

## Chapter 10

# 1784 and the Indigenous Church

### THE CHRISTMAS CONFERENCE

THOMAS COKE, RICHARD WHATCOAT and Thomas Vasey landed in New York on November 3, 1784. John Dickins, one of the main movers of the Flauvanna Schism and the same itinerant with which Francis Asbury recorded a conversation on his way to Manakintown to try and solve that schism brought about from Flauvanna, was appointed to the Johns Street Chapel in New York; and it is to him that Coke first showed John Wesley's solution to the sacramental question.[1] Coke recorded Dickins' reaction by saying, "he highly approves of it, [and] says that all the Preachers most earnestly long for such a regulation, and that Mr. Asbury he is sure will agree to it."[2] From there the newly ordained crew began their trip to Delaware in order to meet up with Francis Asbury, passing through Philadelphia on the way to their rendezvous.[3] Once in Delaware, both Coke and Asbury recorded their first meeting in their respective journals. Coke recorded

> In this chapel [Barratt's Chapel], in the midst of a forest, I had a noble congregation, to which I endeavoured to set forth our blessed Redeemer, as our wisdom, righteousness, sanctification, and redemption. After the sermon, a plain, robust man came up to me in the pulpit, and kissed me: I thought it could be no other than Mr. Asbury, and I was not deceived. I administered

1. Coke, *Journals*, 31.
2. Ibid.
3. Bangs, *History*, 155.

the sacrament after preaching, to, I think, five or six hundred communicants, and afterwards we held a love-feast. It was the best season I ever knew, except one in Charlemont, in Ireland.[4]

Asbury recorded the same event, "I came to Barratt's Chapel: here, to my great joy, I met these dear men of God, Dr. Coke, and Richard Whatcoat, we were greatly comforted together. The doctor preached on 'Christ our wisdom, righteousness, sanctification, and redemption.' Having had no opportunity of conversing with them before public worship, I was greatly surprised to see brother Whatcoat assist by taking the cup in the administration of the sacrament."[5]

Immediately following this meeting, Coke informed Asbury of his purpose in America. Of this revelation, Asbury simply stated, "I was shocked when first informed of the intention of these my brethren in coming to this country: it may be of God."[6] Freeborn Garrettson's response was similar. "I was somewhat surprised when I heard Mr. Wesley's new plan opened . . . [but] thought I would sit in silence."[7] It is no wonder these two reacted the way they did; they had spent the better part of 1780–82 convincing the southern societies not to pursue ordination and separation from the Established Church, and here was Wesley's plan—exactly what they had been arguing against!

The difference between Asbury's former opinion and the current situation brought forth by Coke, Whatcoat and Vasey was that now it was at the direction of John Wesley himself that the American Methodists take this extraordinary step of ordination and creation of a separate Church. As a point of fact, if Wesley were correct in his assessment that there was no difference between a bishop and a presbyter (the argument to which he had recourse in justifying his ordinations), then there was no reason for Coke to have been ordained, or even set apart, by Wesley as Superintendent since Coke was already an ordained presbyter in the Church of England. This would mean that Coke was on equal footing with Wesley with regards to the authority of ordaining a layman to holy orders, be they deacon or presbyter. The only reason for Coke to have had Wesley's hands laid upon him in whatever capacity they were was so that he would have the authority and backing of Wesley for this new venture, the very thing which Flauvanna was lacking. To this, Asbury simply stated, "My answer then was, if the preachers unanimously choose me, I shall not act in the capacity I have hitherto done

---

4. Coke, *Journals*, 34.
5. *JLFA*, 1.471.
6. Ibid.
7. Garrettson, *American Methodist Pioneer*, 243.

by Mr. Wesley's appointment. The design of organizing the Methodists into an Independent Episcopal Church was opened to the preachers present, and it was agreed to call a general conference, to meet at Baltimore the ensuing Christmas; as also that brother Garrettson go off to Virginia to give notice thereof to our brethren in the south."[8]

The "preachers present" were a group of itinerants that Asbury had gathered together to hear the news that Coke brought to them from Wesley. Coke recorded that, after he had spoken with Asbury concerning his mission, "They [the preachers] were accordingly sent for, and after debate, were unanimously of that opinion."[9] The opinion was to call a conference where the entire body of the traveling preachers could vote on the matter of creating a new, "Independent Episcopal Church."

Because of the unanimous opinion, Freeborn Garrettson was sent out "like an arrow"[10] to call as many as possible of the preachers together in Baltimore for a conference to begin on Christmas Eve. Sixty of the eighty-three traveling preachers attended and the scope of what Wesley envisioned was presented.[11] Jesse Lee succinctly explained the reason for the absence of twenty-one preachers. "But being fond of preaching by the way, and thinking he [Garrettson] could do the business by writing, he did not give timely notice to the preachers who were in the extremities of the work; and of course several of them were not at that conference."[12] The brevity of this statement may have much to do with politics and hurt feelings. Herbert Asbury, in his book *A Methodist Saint*, wrote

> Sixty of the eighty-three [itinerants] received the notice [for the Christmas Conference], and of those who did not the majority were preachers who had fought Asbury's policies and consistently opposed his rule. Among them was Jesse Lee, the first historian of the Church and for many years one of its most notable figures, with whom Asbury had many controversies. Lee knew nothing of the proposed conference until the Methodist Episcopal Church had been organized and both Asbury and Dr. Coke elected superintendents.[13]

---

8. *JLFA*, 1.471–72.
9. Coke, *Journals*, 35.
10. Ibid.
11. Bangs, *History*, 157.
12. Lee, *A Short History*, 94.
13. Asbury, *Methodist Saint*, 159.

Nevertheless, once the plan was presented to all in attendance, "the first act of the conference was, by a unanimous vote, to elect Dr. Coke and Francis Asbury as general superintendents."[14]

Despite never wanting to separate from the Church of England, Wesley believed very strongly in orderly Church governance, and fully believed in the Episcopal form of governance. In his letter to the American Methodists, he stated his opinion of the Church of England when he wrote, "I think, [it is] the best constituted national Church in the world."[15] Wesley could not abide laity administering sacraments, so he invested Coke, an ordained presbyter in the Church of England, with the authority to ordain others. He also sent instructions for Asbury to be ordained to the same position and authority. To this new position, Asbury reflected, "I observed this day as a day of fasting and prayer, that I might know the will of God in the matter that is shortly to come before our conference; the preachers and people seem to be much pleased with the projected plan; I myself am led to think it is of the Lord. I am not tickled with the honour to be gained—I see danger in the way. My soul waits upon God. O that he may lead us in the way we should go!"[16] As far as the American Methodists were concerned, God had led them to the creation of the Methodist Episcopal Church, complete with ordained orders of ministry and sacramental authority.

The response of the Methodists was near unanimous to the outcome that was produced at the Christmas Conference. Jesse Lee wrote, "The Methodists were pretty generally pleased at our becoming a church, and heartily united together in the plan which the conference had adopted."[17] William Watters noted in his autobiography, "It was adopted, and unanimously agreed to with great satisfaction, and we became instead of a religious society, a separate church under the name of the Methodist Episcopal Church."[18] Ezekiel Cooper, an early itinerant, commented, "This step met with general approbation both among the preachers and members. Perhaps we shall seldom find such unanimity of sentiment upon any question of such magnitude."[19]

Out of the traveling preachers, the sixty that attended the Christmas Conference elected thirteen to be elders, and eleven were ordained.[20] The

---

14. Bangs, *History*, 157.
15. Wesley, *Works* (Jackson), 13.252.
16. *JLFA*, 1.472–73.
17. Lee, *A Short History*, 107.
18. Watters, *Short Account*, 51.
19. Bangs, *History*, 166.
20. Ibid., 158. The eleven elders were Freeborn Garrettson, William Gill, Le Roy

other two were ordained shortly after the conference, since they were not in attendance.[21] In addition to the ordination of elders, three men were ordained as deacons.[22] These ordinations gave these elders the sacramental authority that had been such a point of contention five years earlier at Flauvanna. While there are no extant minutes of the Christmas Conference (aside from the *1785 Discipline*, which is entitled *Minutes*) and thus no record of how these men were chosen, it is important to note that all of them had experience as an Assistant.[23] Lester Ruth noted, "Of the thirteen elders ordained at the Christmas Conference, all had been Assistants before and twelve were currently serving as Assistants, having been appointed to that capacity during the annual conferences in the previous Spring . . . Thus, a strong continuity existed between those already serving in a specialized role among the itinerants and those who gained authority to administer the sacraments."[24] Out of these thirteen elders, two of them were sent to Canada to minister to the Methodists that had fled the Revolution, and one of them was sent to Antigua to spread Methodism in that British holding.[25] This left a grand total of fourteen ordained men with sacramental authority (Coke and Asbury as superintendents, and Whatcoat and Vasey and the remaining ten elders ordained at the conference) for the entirety of the new United States of America, an area that spanned the entire eastern seaboard from Georgia to (present day) Maine.

As the governing document and *constitution* of this new Church, the American Methodists approved an amended version of the *Large Minutes*.[26] There were several changes that had to be made to the *Large Minutes*

---

Cole, John Hagerty, James O. Cromwell, John Tunnel, Nelson Reed, Jeremiah Lambert, Reuben Ellis, James O'Kelly, and Richard Ivey.

21. Ibid. The remaining two were Beverly Allen and Henry Willis.

22. Stevens, *History of the Methodist Episcopal Church*, 2.189. These were John Dickins, Ignatius Pigman, and Caleb Boyer.

23. Jesse Lee noted "In this country they [the preachers] formerly stood in three grades, 1, Helpers, 2, Assistants, 3, General Assistants. The Helper, was the young preacher in each circuit where there were generally two preachers in a circuit. The Assistant, was the oldest preacher in the circuit, who had the charge of the young preacher, and of the business of the circuit. The General Assistant, was the preacher who had the particular charge of all the circuits, and of all the preachers, and appointed all the preachers to their several circuits, and changed them as he judged to be necessary, for the good of the preachers, or the benefit of the people" (Lee, *A Short History*, 41).

24. Ruth, "Reconsideration of the Frequency," 54. Jeremiah Lambert was the only person not currently serving in the position of Assistant, but had most recently held the position only one year prior to this.

25. Lee, *A Short History*, 94.

26. Jessie Shuman Larkins has recently argued "Almost simultaneously, the Christmas Conference of 1784 marked the American Methodists' own declaration of

for it to fit the American context and make any reasonable amount of sense as a governing document for a new, independent denomination within North America. The first change in the body of the *Minutes/Discipline*[27] (as the very first change was the names of Thomas Coke and Francis Asbury replacing John Wesley as the person with whom these conversations took place) was an inclusion of a declaration of submission and fealty to John Wesley for the rest of his life as the father of Methodism and they his "Sons in the Gospel."[28] The next addition was to state that this new Church would be Episcopal in nature, being governed by "Superintendents, Elders, Deacons, and Helpers."[29] These additions put this new document within the American Methodist context. The next change further explicates the change between the Methodists in England still under the sole authority of Wesley and the Methodists in America who were now independent. In the *Large Minutes* the question is asked and answered

> Q. 3. What may we reasonably believe to be God's design in raising up the Preachers called Methodists?
>
> A. Not to form any new sect; but to reform the nation, particularly the Church; and to spread scriptural holiness over the land.[30]

This same question and a different answer are found in the *Discipline*:

> Q. 4. What may we reasonably believe to be God's design in raising up the Preachers called Methodists?
>
> A. To reform the Continent, and to spread scriptural holiness over these lands.[31]

Again, this puts a document that was originally written for one context decidedly in an altogether different context. Now the call to stay within the Established Church and reform it has been dropped, and a new emphasis is on, not the singular nation in which this new Church finds itself, but

---

independence from the authority of the Church of England" ("John Wesley Among the Colonies," 242). In actuality, the declaration of independence came at Flauvanna when the oversight committee was beholden to Scripture and not the Methodist Discipline. To use Revolutionary metaphors, the Christmas Conference is more accurately the constitutional convention of the American Methodists.

27. *Discipline* from this point forward.
28. *Methodist Disciplines 1785–1789*, 1785.3. Hereafter *Disciplines*.
29. Ibid.
30. Wesley, *Works* (Jackson), 8.299.
31. *Disciplines*, 1785.4.

rather the entire continent on which it resides and all nations upon it. This point of "lands" instead of "land" and "continent" instead of "nation" would presumably have included not only the United States but also Canada since two elders were appointed to Nova Scotia, and it would also most likely have had an eye towards the West and the Indian nations beyond the Allegheny Mountains.

Most other changes between the *Large Minutes* and the *Discipline* follow along with the obvious change in context. All references to the Kingswood School were dropped, as well as the lengthy expositions concerning John Wesley's sole authority over the Methodists and the exhortation to remain within the Established Church.[32] In their place were written sections that delineate the new Church's understanding of ordained ministry, salaries for ordained ministers, its position relative to the problem of slavery, and its understanding of worship and sacraments.[33] Of interest to this study are the statements concerning the Lord's Supper. First and foremost, the responsibility for administration of the Lord's Supper is lodged fully within the office of Elder (presbyter or priest in the Church of England). "What is the Office of an Elder? To administer the Sacraments of Baptism and the Lord's Supper, and to perform all the other Rites prescribed by our Liturgy."[34] Here the reason for the creation of the office of Elder is expressed for the administration of the sacraments. This is further reinforced when the directions for Deacons are considered:

> What is the Office of a Deacon?
>
> To baptize in the absence of an Elder, *to assist the Elder in the Administration of the Lord's Supper*, to marry, bury the Dead, and read the Liturgy to the People as prescribed, *except what relates to the Administration of the Lord's Supper*.[35]
>
> N. B. No Helper, or even Deacon, shall on any Pretense at any Time whatsoever administer the Lord's Supper.[36]

In addition to these is the declaration of who is allowed to receive the Lord's Supper and how they are to be identified:

> Let no Person who is not a Member of the Society, be admitted to the Communion without a Sacrament-Ticket, which Ticket

---

32. Wesley, *Works* (Jackson), 8.310–14, 320–22.
33. *Disciplines*, 1785.11–12, 1785.14–18.
34. Ibid., 1785.12.
35. Ibid., emphasis added.
36. Ibid., 1785.14.

must be changed every Quarter. *And we empower the Elder or Assistant, and no others, to deliver these Tickets.*[37]

Here again the circumstances surrounding Lord's Supper was reserved for the particular office of Elder. In this case it is with the distribution of tickets for the sacrament, a practice most likely carried over from tickets for admittance to love feasts prior to the creation of the MEC. The admittance of Assistants in this section is not problematic since it was out of the Assistants that the Elders were chosen. This inclusion of Assistants also illustrated the fact that this new Church was still coming to the realization that it was indeed a separate ecclesial structure, and with the difficulty of this realization came the reality that much of their former ways of speaking concerning Society was retained, at least for the short-term. Russell Richey stated as such when, writing specifically about conferences, he noted, "The definition of conference American Methodists took straight from Wesley, incorporating 'The Large Minutes' into the first *Discipline* of the new church with modest change."[38] The title "Assistant" was dropped from the *Discipline* by 1787.

One final inclusion in the *Discipline*, above and beyond what was contained in the *Large Minutes*, is worth noting. The new Church inserted a question immediately following the question regarding how often a stranger may be admitted to a Society meeting. Strangers may be admitted at "every other meeting of the society," provided it is "the same person not above twice or thrice."[39] After this question, which was taken verbatim from the *Large Minutes*, the *Discipline* added

> Q. 12. How often shall we permit Strangers to be present at our Love-Feasts?
>
> A. Let them be admitted with the utmost Caution; and the same Person on no account above twice, unless he becomes a Member.[40]

This is important to note insofar as it shows a concerted effort on the part of the new Church to fence off its activities and fellowship in as many aspects of its life in which it saw fit to so do. Whether this rule was followed or not, the Church body felt it necessary to have some stipulation as to how often outsiders could participate in the life of the Church. And it is further important to note that this rule had been discussed in previous meetings of the American Methodists. The first General Conference the Methodists held in

---

37. Ibid., 1785.17.
38. Richey, *Early American Methodists*, 75.
39. *Disciplines*, 1785.5 and Wesley, *Works* (Jackson), 8.301.
40. Ibid.

America in 1773 contained the same stipulation of restricting admission to the Love Feast. This will be dealt with more fully below. For now, it is simply important to note the opinion of the new Church on the issue.

## CHURCH LIFE AFTER THE CONFERENCE

In January of 1785, the Methodist Episcopal Church (MEC) finally had all the pieces in place to be the full Church it wanted to be. Following in direct line with John Wesley's understanding of proper church polity, ordination was essential to the administration of sacraments. There was no self-appointed layman the likes of Robert Strawbridge making decisions on his own concerning the sacraments. There was not even a self-appointed and self-ordained presbytery the likes of the Flauvanna Conference to administer the sacraments. The MEC now had its own ordained "priests" and two individuals, Thomas Coke and Francis Asbury, who had the authority to ordain even more people. These ordinations derived their authority from the fact that it was a presbytery of three ordained presbyters of the Church of England, John Wesley, James Creighton, and Thomas Coke, which had ordained Richard Whatcoat and Thomas Vasey. And it was then in turn that very same presbytery that consecrated Coke for the position of Superintendent.[41]

With such a monumental change in the organizational status of Methodists in America, it is necessary to investigate exactly how the MEC adapted or continued its religious charge after receiving the added authority of ordination. This will help shed light on the situation at hand and help in determining what the Methodist Eucharistic piety was at the time. The simple answer to this inquiry is that nothing changed much at all. The American Methodists went to the Christmas Conference as a religious society that was determined to change the world, and they left the Christmas Conference as a Church that was determined to change the world. Sacramental authority was added to the role of an Assistant, now styled an Elder, and Methodist life continued much as it had before. Robert Tuttle wrote in *On Giant's Shoulders*, "Most scholars agree that the Christmas Conference was called specifically to ordain preachers. Ordination, however, simply provided the preacher/evangelist with credentials necessary to fulfill all of the pastoral

---

41. There has been much debate over whether or not Wesley actually had the authority to perform such a consecration (ordination, as Wesley recorded in his private diary). Whether or not such authority actually existed, the fact remains that Wesley had convinced himself that he had such authority, and therefore exercised it believing he was well within his right. This, for Wesley, Coke, and the American Methodists, was all that was needed for the ordinations to be proper in all respects.

offices. Nothing else changed."[42] One of those scholars to whom Tuttle is likely referring is Frederick Norwood. He wrote

> Thomas Coke and Francis Asbury continued their customary forms of activity in leadership. Itinerants attended the same Annual Conferences and answered the same disciplinary questions. People attended the same meetings and worshiped in the same way. Certain changes which in principle should mark a thorough transformation, especially the introduction of the rite of ordination and the observance of the Lord's Supper, were received with scarcely a ripple of significance. Almost everything remained as it had been. Separated from its historical context, 1784 was a date, nothing more.[43]

For an eyewitness account, Thomas Ware, an itinerant minister whose name first appears in the minutes of a Methodist conference in 1784, attended the Christmas Conference. In writing several years later about what transpired there, he said

> We were *itinerants*; and he whose servants we were knoweth that we were influenced by a desire to spread scriptural holiness through the land, and to preserve the ministry and membership pure from error and sin. The plan of a general superintendency had not only been submitted to, but was universally approved by both preachers and people. The system was simple and familiar to us all. *Every thing* [sic] *went on as it had before our organization*, with this advantage, that in our church capacity the delightful privilege was furnished us of bringing our children to be dedicated in baptism at our own altars, and of receiving the sacrament of the Lord's supper at the hand of our own ministers. *Ordination was the only thing we had seemed to lack; and this lack was now supplied.*[44]

The implication is clear that, at least for this attendee, nothing really changed as a result of the Christmas Conference. Ruth stated, "The 1784 conference did not create Methodism as a church out of nothing but fulfilled in Methodists' eyes the best aspects of their previous ecclesiological experience by adding marks of organization and sacrament."[45] To use Methodistic language, the American Methodists saw themselves as having the power of godliness, but lacking the form. The Christmas Conference gave them the form.

42. Tuttle, *Shoulders*, 51.
43. Norwood, *American Methodism*, 101.
44. Ware, *Sketches*, 245, emphasis added.
45. Ruth, *A Little Heaven Below*, 160.

This is not to say that change was not tried. Some of the newly ordained elders and the superintendents wore clerical robes and neck bands during the services in an attempt to look more like the ordained priests of the Church of England, but this innovation did not last. Jesse Lee recorded, "The Superintendents, and some of the Elders, introduced the custom of wearing gowns and bands, but it was opposed by many of the preachers, as well as private members, who looked upon it as needless and *superfluous*. Having made a stand against it, after a few years it was given up, and has never been introduced among us since."[46] Nathan Bangs also addressed this issue, most likely using Lee as one of his sources, but also included the Methodist response to Wesley's *Sunday Service*. Bangs wrote

> It has been already stated that Mr. Wesley made an abridgment of the Book of Common Prayer, as used in the Church of England, and recommended that it should be used by the preachers and people in this country. This accordingly was done in some of the larger towns and cities; but this practice, as well as that of wearing gowns, which the superintendents and some of the elders did for a season, was soon laid aside, on account of the opposition which was generally manifested against it, with the exception of the ordinations and sacramental services, which are retained and used at the present time.[47]

In his classically concise manner, Jesse Lee reported why Methodists ultimately decided not to follow the *Sunday Service*, despite Wesley's instructions to so do. The preachers, "being fully satisfied that they could pray better, and with more devotion while their eyes were shut, than they could with their eyes open,"[48] did not read the prayers. "After a few years the prayer book was laid aside, and has never been used since in public worship."[49]

---

46. Lee, *A Short History*, 107.
47. Bangs, *History*, 167.
48. Lee, *A Short History*, 107.
49. Ibid.

Chapter 11

# 1784 and the Sacraments

### SACRAMENTAL LIFE AFTER THE CONFERENCE

WHAT IS MOST INTERESTING for this study at this point is how this newly formed Church addressed the issue for which it was created, namely providing for the administration of the sacraments to the people. Many saw complete continuity in the life of American Methodists prior to the Christmas Conference and subsequent to it. Some innovations were introduced, but as Nathan Bangs was quoted above as saying, every innovation was dropped from the life of the Church except ordination and the sacraments. The question that naturally arises, then, is how the sacramental life of the MEC was lived out as a result of the authority now given it by virtue of these ordinations. That is the issue to which we now turn.

Ordination, for Methodists, was essential to the administration of the sacraments, and yet the very limited amount of ordinations at the Christmas Conference insured that the reception of the sacrament would be very infrequent. John Wesley wished for all the ordained elders to administer the Lord's Supper on every Sunday. This can be most clearly seen in his letter to the American Methodists. "And I have prepared a Liturgy little differing form that of the Church of England (I think, the best constituted national Church in the world), which I advise all the travelling preachers to use on the Lord's Day in all the congregations, reading the Litany only on Wednesdays and Fridays and praying extempore on all other days. *I also advise the elders to administer the Supper of the Lord on every Lord's Day.*"[1]

---

1. Wesley, *Works* (Jackson), 13.252, emphasis added.

Yet, even if the elders followed through with that injunction, there were only the ten elders ordained that remained in the United States, along with Coke, Asbury, Whatcoat and Vasey. This leaves a grand total of fourteen people (thirteen if one considers the fact that Coke was rarely in America) with the authority to administer the Eucharist for the entire Church. The simple fact of these limited ordinations and the core facet of Methodism being itinerancy, meant that reception of the Eucharist would necessarily be infrequent for the average Methodist.

Again, Ruth illustrated this point well in an article entitled "A Reconsideration of the Frequency of the Eucharist." In this article, he challenged the point made by William Nash Wade that weekly reception of the Eucharist was Wesley's intended outcome of the Christmas Conference and the creation of the MEC. Wade's argument was that

> Wesley had introduced in his 1784 *Sunday Service* a fundamental reform when he, in accordance with the practice he believed to be that of the early Christian Church of the Apostolic Age, demanded that not only a service of the Word as founding Morning and Evening Prayer but also a weekly eucharist be *normative* for American Methodist worship. From 1784 until 1792 such was the official normative standard, if not in fact the actual worship practice of American Methodists. In 1792 this central element of sacramental worship, so important to John Wesley and the early English Methodists, officially ceased to be a weekly event and an integral element of common Sunday worship for American Methodists.[2]

The problem with this statement is that it is not based on historical fact, but rather speculation on the part of Wade. Ruth rightly responded, "Because elders by polity were travelling preachers, the average lay Methodist in a society would not have had the opportunity for weekly reception of the eucharist. This would have been so even if the elders followed to the letter Wesley's instruction to administer the eucharist 'every Lord's day.' Itinerancy means absence, the absence of the ordained itinerant, and thus, for the average Methodist in early America, less than a weekly opportunity to receive the eucharist."[3] Part of the proof that Ruth is correct on this point can be seen in the average lay Methodist's reaction to the ecclesial structure created at the Christmas Conference regarding the Eucharist.

What does not resurface after the Christmas Conference is a call for increased sacramental life, by laity or clergy. This issue, access to the

---

2. Wade, "History of Public Worship," 115–16, emphasis included.
3. Ruth, "Reconsideration of the Frequency," 52.

sacraments, which was so hotly contested and debated prior to the formation of the MEC, was never mentioned again after the Christmas Conference. There were no more instances of lay administration. There were no more self-appointed presbyteries to ordain ministers. There were no more instances of local preachers administering the sacraments. None of the disagreements that plagued the American Methodists prior to the Christmas Conference surfaced again after the creation of the MEC. This would seem to indicate that the American Methodists were content with the ecclesial structure with which they were presented at the Christmas Conference and its resultant outcome of limited ordinations and infrequent reception of the Lord's Supper, usually relegated to Quarterly Conferences. Many scholars have said as much concerning this issue. In fact, Ruth has gone so far as to say that the "intent appears to have been for them [the elders] to exercise their new sacramental authority in the context of quarterly meetings."[4] Obviously, Ruth must be insinuating the intent of the Christmas Conference here, not of John Wesley. Wesley made his intent plain in his letter. Elders were to use their sacramental authority on every Lord's Day, not just quarterly meetings.[5] It is unclear how Ruth could divine such intent when even Francis Asbury's journal (which is famous for leaving out many details of actual events) records numerous instances of administering the Eucharist on occasions that do not coincide with a quarterly meeting.[6]

One possibility for Ruth's assertion that the Lord's Supper be administered within a quarterly meeting could come from Nathan Bangs in his *History of the Methodist Episcopal Church*. In this, Bangs wrote,

> The origin of the presiding elder's office may be traced to this year [1785], though those who had charge of several circuits were not so denominated in the minutes until 1789. The office originated in this way: at the organization of the Church in 1784, but twelve out of the whole number of preachers were elected and ordained elders, and hence many of the circuits were destitute of any officer who was authorized to administer the ordinances, as a deacon could only assist at the celebration of the Lord's

---

4. Ruth, *A Little Heaven Below*, 119.

5. Interestingly enough, when Jesse Lee printed the text of Wesley's letter in his *A Short History of the Methodists* in 1810 (and Nathan Bangs printed his *History of the Methodist Episcopal Church* in 1838), he completely omitted the section of the letter concerning the liturgy Wesley created and the injunction to administer the Eucharist every Sunday. While Lee's intentions cannot be proved, it may be that this omission was a subtle acknowledgement of the reality of life in the MEC by that point in history. It had stopped using the *Sunday Service* and the Eucharist had become a quarterly event.

6. See Appendix C.

supper. To remedy this defect, and to supply the people with the ordinances regularly, several circuits were linked together, and put under the charge of an elder, whose duty it was to visit each circuit quarterly, preach to the people, hold love-feasts, and administer the sacrament of the Lord's supper.[7]

On first reading, this seems to confirm Ruth's assertion, yet there is a problem with Bangs' statement. First, it is implied by this passage that there were a significant number of deacons available to the MEC in this first year, and it is only because they did not have full sacramental authority that the few elders were required to preside over several circuits together. In actuality, as was noted above, there were only three deacons in the entire MEC at this point in history. Bangs' statement concerning the presence of deacons apparently is an anachronistic reading of the situation in 1785. This becomes clear from the fact that, when he included the *1785 Discipline* in this section of his work, with the expressed intention of illuminating the proceedings of the Christmas Conference and how the MEC evolved over time to the present (1838 when the work was written), Bangs wrote, "That the reader may have an entire view of the doings of this conference, I think it expedient to give him the rules as they were then adopted, noticing, as we proceed in our history, such alterations or new rules as have been incorporated into the Discipline from time to time."[8]

The problem with this statement is that it is not the *1785 Discipline* that is then given. Bangs reprinted the *1789 Discipline* and called it the *1785 Discipline*.[9] In Bangs' quotation, the elders have specific charge over their districts, but in 1785 there was no such stipulation in the *Discipline*.[10] Perhaps the later *Discipline* merely recorded what was actually happening in the life of the MEC (as this language was included for the first time in 1787), or perhaps it created this role because of a perceived need. Abel Stevens, in dealing with the issue of bishops assigning appointments, noted, "He [the bishop] had no 'cabinet' of presiding elders, for this office was yet unknown in the Church; as the new elders, ordained at the Christmas Conference, were *appointed only to administer the sacraments*."[11] And again, Stevens wrote, "These [elders] were designed to supply the sacraments to the Societ-

---

7. Bangs, *History*, 244–45.
8. Bangs, *History*, 175. The *Discipline* then appears on pages 175–218.
9. This can be clearly seen with regards to the *Discipline* being composed in sections, an occurance that did not occur until 1787, and specifically Section XXXIII of the *Discipline* (page 210 in Bangs and 45 in *1789 Discipline*), where the wording is identical. The first year this section was worded as such was 1789.
10. *Disciplines*, 1785.12, 1787.7–8.
11. Stevens, *History of the Methodist Episcopal Church*, 2.222.

ies, as far as practicable; subsequently the elders were placed in charge of districts comprehending several circuits, and thence arose the permanent office of presiding elder, not for the administration of the sacraments, but for many and important executive functions."[12]

Either Stevens is correct and the districts were added for "executive functions" at a later date thereby changing the ecclesial make-up of the MEC, or Bangs is correct and elders always presided over districts for sacramental reasons and later *Disciplines* recognized the reality of life in the MEC, but ultimately the reason for the inclusion of the district language in the *Discipline* is unknown (or neither may be completely correct, as seen below when this study analyzes the *1798 Discipline*). Nevertheless, to make an argument that something was necessarily done to serve a need that was not stated until two years later is questionable in the extreme. Since Bangs' faithful recording of history on this point is questionable, possibly tainted by an anachronistic reading of 1784 and replacing the original *Discipline* with one that already had numerous additions four years later, so too is Ruth's assertion that the intention of the Christmas Conference was to place the Lord's Supper in quarterly district meetings. It may be reality, but it cannot be proved by extant evidence, and rests only on conjecture at this point. To make definitive pronouncements on such slender evidence, and use that statement as the basis for a scholarly opinion concerning the early American Methodists' Eucharistic piety and frequency of reception is not good practice.

## THE QUESTION OF FREQUENCY

Part of the reason for the perceived truthfulness of the above conjectural argument, that the Christmas Conference designed the Lord's Supper to be administered in quarterly meetings, is a common claim among scholars that it was not possible for the average eighteenth-century Protestant Christian to conceive of frequent communion, primarily due to the lack of opportunity to receive it, and to try and find such an idea in the eighteenth century is an anachronistic projection back onto those Christians of today's Eucharistic piety. Richard Bowmer succinctly stated, "That the Sacrament of the Lord's Supper was infrequently administered and indifferently regarded by large numbers of both clergy and laity, we cannot deny."[13] Karen Westerfield Tucker echoed this sentiment when she wrote of American Methodist quarterly reception of the Eucharist, "Methodists at least partook more frequent-

---

12. Ibid., 2.224.
13. Bowmer, *Sacrament*, 3.

ly than had been the custom in the great majority of Anglican parishes."[14] While the idea that regular reception of the Eucharist was not a common thought in the eighteenth century may be true of many (if not most) nominal members of established Churches of the time, this conclusion does not take into account how the eighteenth-century Methodists themselves wrote about the Eucharist, a point that must be investigated in order to understand and appreciate early Methodist Eucharistic piety more fully. And in order to see Methodist Eucharistic piety in the American context, it is necessary to start with John Wesley's instructions to Methodists in general, how those Methodists understood his instructions, put them into practice, and then see how their resultant piety bore congruence or incongruence with Wesley and his other spiritual children, English and American.

While the material concerning John Wesley has been dealt with more fully above, it will suffice to make reference to it here. Wesley himself wrote in numerous places that Christians ought to receive the sacrament on a regular basis. The rules for being a Band member included an injunction to receive the Lord's Supper every week.[15] One of the questions asked of one who desired to be a Helper was, "Do you constantly attend the church and sacrament?"[16] According to a passage in *An Earnest Appeal to Men of Reason and Religion,* Wesley notes that one of the objections to the Methodists is that they were jumping parish boundaries to receive communion any time it was offered.[17] The Bristol society convinced John and Charles Wesley to agree to administer the Lord's Supper every other week in 1770,[18] and then in 1787 Wesley proclaimed in one of his sermons, *On God's Vineyard,* that the service times for society meetings change on Sundays so the Methodists can receive the sacrament in their own service. "Their [Methodists'] public service is at five in the morning, and six of seven in the evening, that their temporal business may not be hindered. Only on Sunday it begins between nine and ten, and concludes with the Lord's Supper."[19] Obviously eighteenth-century Methodists could conceive of frequent reception of the Eucharist.

---

14. Tucker, *Worship*, 125.
15. Wesley, *Works*, 9.79.
16. Wesley, *Works* (Jackson), 8.325.
17. Wesley, *Works*, 11.185.
18. Ibid., 22.254–55.
19. Ibid., 3.512.

## The English Methodist Answer

After John Wesley died in 1791, the English Methodists took a very different route to address this very same issue of providing the sacraments to their people than their American brethren did. Prior to his death, Wesley ordained Alexander Mather for ministry in England in 1787. Jonathan Crowther, an itinerant preacher who joined the Methodist Connexion in England in 1784, wrote, "It seems as if he came at last to this settled opinion, that from the great variety of opinion among both preachers and people, as well as from the behaviour of many of the clergy, it would be expedient as well as lawful, that the ordinances should be administered to them who desired them."[20] Again, Wesley's concern in ordaining people was access to the sacraments, the soteriological dimension of the sacrament being in the fore on the issue. However, the unintended consequence of ordaining a few of the preachers, and no plan of continued ordination, was that the English Methodists debated the relationship of ordination and full connection, with respect to administering the ordinances, and it was a debate that was long and drawn out. It erupted at the first conference after Wesley had died. Of that 1792 Conference, Crowther recorded, "At this time there was much uneasiness in the connexion, occasioned by contentions about the propriety or impropriety of having the service in church-hours, and the Lord's supper administered among us in some places."[21]

This debate continued for the next five years. By the end of the Conference in 1797 the English Methodists had agreed to a Plan of Pacification (drawn up in 1795) that specified any Methodist Society having a majority of its trustees vote in favor of administering the sacraments, and the preacher in full connection amenable to administering them, then that said Society could receive the sacraments from its preacher.[22] A.B. Hyde wrote of this

> At last, in 1797, the adjustment between the Conference and the trustees of the chapels, as met in convention, was complete. To the Conference remained its right of appointing the preachers and controlling the pulpits; a majority of the Quarterly Conference having the right to demand at any time the trial of any preacher by the clerical officers of the circuit by whom he might be suspended until the next Conference. The sacraments also

---

20. Crowther, *Portraiture*, 64.
21. Ibid., 81.
22. Ibid., 81–84.

were to be administered in the chapels, and many other concessions were granted to the societies—i.e., to the laity.[23]

The English Methodists moved that any society that wished to receive the sacrament could do so by the full connection preacher that was sent to them. Being a traveling preacher in full connection was equal with being ordained, and thus admittance to the connection gave one the authority to provide the sacraments to all who wished to receive them.

Jonathan Crowther recorded the official position of the English Methodists with respect to the sacraments as such:

> 1. The sacrament of the Lord's supper shall not be administered in any chapel, except a majority of the trustees of that chapel on the one hand, and the majority of stewards and leaders belonging to that chapel, (as the best qualified to give the sense of the people,) on the other, allow it. Nevertheless, in all cases the consent of conference shall be first obtained before this ordinance shall be administered.
>
> 2. Where there is a society but no chapel, if the majority of the stewards and leaders of that society testify, in writing, to the conference, that it is the wish of the people that the Lord's supper should be administered among them, and that no separation will be made thereby, their desire shall be granted.
>
> 3. The sacrament of the Lord's supper shall not be administered to a society in a private house, within two miles of a Methodist chapel.
>
> 4. The Lord's supper shall be administered by the superintendent only, or such of his helpers as are in full connexion, and as he shall appoint; provided that no preacher be required to give it against his own inclination; and would it be granted to any place where the preachers on the circuit are all unwilling to give it, the superintendent shall, in that case, invite a neighbouring preacher who is properly qualified to give it.
>
> 5. It shall be administered at such times and in such manner as the conference shall appoint. And the conference agree that the Lord's supper shall be administered among us on Sunday evenings only; except the majority of the stewards and leaders desire it in church hours; or where it has already been administered

---

23. Hyde, *Story*, 285–86.

in those hours. Nevertheless, it shall never be administered on those Sundays on which it is administered in the parish church.

6. The Lord's supper shall always be administered in England according to the form of the established church: but the person who administers shall have liberty to give out hymns, to use exhortations and extemporary prayer.

7. Wherever the Lord's supper shall be administered according to the above-mentioned regulations, it shall always be continued, except the conference order otherwise.[24]

While this is a lengthy quotation, it is necessary to see how the English Methodists resolved the issue of the sacraments among them. Of special importance is to note that according to these rules, a majority vote was enough to allow the sacrament to be administered. In addition, section number five above implies that the Methodists were celebrating the sacrament on more Sundays than the Established Church, as the Methodists are required to desist from administering the sacrament on those days when the Established parish administers it. Finally, section number seven allows that, once the Lord's Supper was voted to be celebrated in a specific Methodist congregation, it ought to have remained as such, except under direct repeal of the Conference. The English Methodists gave the opportunity to receive the sacrament to any Methodist society that desired it by the traveling preacher of that circuit, as often as they desired to celebrate it.

### The American Methodist Answer

In America, however, this was not the case. Whether or not one was a traveling preacher, ordination was still the necessary requirement to administer the sacraments. William Ormond, an itinerant preacher, perhaps with an eye to the developments in England, at the General Conference of 1796 introduced a measure to ordain all the local preachers, thereby increasing the number of ordained preachers drastically. Ormond wrote in his journal

> 1796 [Friday 28th] Conference . . . I moved that the Conference should open a door for our juditious [sic] Local Preachers to be Ordained Elders in the Church, the Matter was put off & we Adjourned, we met in the Evening. I spoke to the subject concerning the Local Preachers—many talked upon both sides, & at last, the substance of their Argument, who opposed us, was if they were Ordained, they would draw the People, Money, &

---

24. Crowther, *Portraiture*, 210–11.

Power from Itinerant Preachers. It was put to vote. They carryed [sic] their point by a Majority of two Members.[25]

Unfortunately, the official Minutes for the 1796 General Conference did not record this motion, debate, or outcome. Instead, there is a reiteration of how long a prospective Elder must be in each successive station within the MEC before being considered for ordination.[26] Perhaps as an explanation of this decision and an accommodation to this motion, however, is the following:

> Ques. 4. What shall be the time of probation of a travelling deacon for the office of an elder?
>
> Ans. Every travelling deacon shall exercise that office for two years, before he be eligible to the office of an elder; except in the case of missions, when the yearly conferences shall have authority to elect for the elder's office sooner, if they judge it expedient.
>
> N.B. We would wish to show the utmost attention to the order of elders, and to have the fullest proof of the abilities, grace, and usefulness of those who shall be from time to time proposed for so important an office as that of a presbyter in the Church of God. And we judge that the man who has proved himself a worthy member of our society, and a useful class-leader, exhorter, and local preacher, who has been approved of for two years as a travelling preacher on trial, and has faithfully served in the office of a travelling deacon for at least two years more, has offered such proofs of fidelity and piety as must satisfy every reasonable mind. But as this continent is exceedingly large, and will continually open to our conferences new missions for the spread of the gospel, (perhaps for ages to come,) we have in the case of missions given a discretionary power to the yearly conferences.[27]

Whatever Ormond's motives for this motion, had it passed it would have opened the possibility of many more people administering the Eucharist "every Lord's day," if they followed Wesley's directive on the matter. This matter did not rest after the 1796 Conference. It was brought back again at the 1800 General Conference. The Minutes of that conference record:

> Wednesday, May 7: Brother Mansfield moved, that the local preachers be made eligible to the eldership. Withdrawn

---

25. Ormond, *Papers*.
26. *Journals of the General Conferences*, 25–26.
27. Ibid., 16.

> Thursday, May 15: Brother Mansfield's motion, to make local preachers eligible to the eldership, was carried in the affirmative. Vote to be reconsidered, and obtained leave to be withdrawn.
>
> Friday, May 16: Brother Ormond moved, that the bishops have liberty, by the suffrage of this General Conference, to ordain local deacons to the office of elders—those who have been travelling after a probation of four years, and other local deacons after a probation of eight years: provided, such deacons be approved and recommended by a majority of the quarterly conference of the circuit in which they live, and be elected by a majority of the annual conference. Negatived [sic].
>
> Saturday, May 17: Brother Ormond's motion to make local deacons eligible to the elder's office was negatived [sic]. Ayes 36, noes 47.[28]

With this, the issue of increasing the ranks of Elders outside of the normal channels of probation and ordination was effectively put to rest, and no further attempts were made to equate the rank of Elder with any time served in connection with the MEC in any other capacity. Ormond wrote in his Journal, "Tuesday, 20th May [1800]—The Conference arose. I have attended close by, have tried to do something for the Cause, but fear it is very little; some mighty Matters were brought in by myself & others but they were cast out."[29]

Even though Ormond's motions for increasing the rank of elders failed, more people were ordained over the years, but the geographic scope and populace of the MEC continued to grow as well. There never seemed to be quite enough ordained preachers to go around. From 1785 to 1792 the ratio of members to ordained ministers capable of administering the sacrament (elders and bishops) climbed from 82:1 to 825:1 with a high of 1556:1 in 1789.[30] It was during these years that Methodism spread into Georgia in 1785, Kentucky in 1786, New England in 1789, and Tennessee in 1792.[31] With the increase of members and the increase of sheer size of the MEC's territory, it was absolutely impossible for an average Methodist to receive the Eucharist on anything remotely similar to a regular schedule given the number of ordained clergy available for such a task. To give some idea of the scope of the work in these early days, when the MEC was expanding so greatly, Peter Cartwright recorded in his *Autobiography* the type

---

28. Ibid., 34, 40, 42.
29. Ormond, Ms. Journal.
30. Hitt and Ware, *Minutes*, 51–118.
31. Lee, *A Short History*, 119–42, and Bangs, *History*, 339.

of itinerancy in Kentucky in 1801. He wrote, "This year, 1801, the Western Conference existed, and I think there was but one presiding elder's district in it, called the Kentucky District. William M'Kendree (afterward bishop) was appointed to the Kentucky District. Cumberland Circuit, which, perhaps, was six hundred miles round, and lying partly in Kentucky and partly in Tennessee, was one of the circuits of this district. John Page and Thomas Wilkerson were appointed to this circuit."[32]

It was not the case that eighteenth-century Methodists could not comprehend frequent communion, but the two branches (English and American) had different opinions on the issue. The English had a high sacramental piety that was soteriological in nature that superseded the ecclesial union they had with the Church of England. For the Americans, ecclesiology, in this case itinerancy, superseded a high sacramental piety that was soteriological in nature. Reception of the Lord's Supper was subordinated to the reality of itinerancy of the ordained elders in the MEC, which necessarily limited the possibility of reception of the Lord's Supper. This is the argument Wade made in his thesis. He understood that the MEC allowed itinerancy to supersede sacramental piety and, because of this fact, calls Asbury an anti-sacramentalist because of the resultant outcome in American Methodism, of what he believed to be a virtually non-existent sacramental piety. He then bolstered his position by highlighting the 1792 revisions to the liturgy, placing the blame for these developments most squarely upon Asbury. Not only did Wade fault Asbury for what he saw as the MEC rejecting a vital sacramental piety, but he also accused Asbury of abandoning Wesleyan Methodism all together. Wade argued, "Asbury did, in fact, depart from Wesley's form of Methodism which, as we have seen in the first chapter, sought to balance both liturgical and *ex tempore* prayer in worship, both word and sacrament, both experience and rational orderliness, both Scripture and the tradition of the early Church, and which saw the sacramental means of grace, especially the Lord's Supper, as essential to achievement of true Christian perfection and holiness, not a hindrance and a stumbling block."[33] Again, this is a misreading of Wesley, Asbury, and the American Methodist situation. Wade, as demonstrated above, did not understand the multi-dimensional aspect of Wesley's Eucharistic theology, and consequently, did not realize that early American Eucharistic piety was actually working in conjunction with the MEC's polity at this point in history.

---

32. Cartwright, *Autobiography*, 36.
33. Wade, "History of Public Worship," 182.

## 1792 LITURGICAL REVISIONS

In 1792, the year immediately following the death of John Wesley, the MEC had its first General Conference since its creation in 1784. For the intervening years, the MEC functioned under a series of annual conferences and a short-lived Council to direct its life, both of which proved untenable as the Church grew in membership and geography. During the 1792 Conference two items of particular interest for this study took place: liturgical revision and a schism. The schism will be dealt with below. The liturgical revision is of interest here because of what it entailed and what that said about life in the MEC at that point in history.

When a short examination of the *Discipline* editions from 1785–1789 is made, one word is systematically eliminated: liturgy. In 1785, the (very few) duties of an elder included, in addition to administering the sacraments, "to perform all the other Rites prescribed by our Liturgy."[34] By 1789 the responsibility was reworded to read, "to perform all parts of divine service."[35] In 1785 deacons were responsible for "read[ing] the Liturgy to the People as prescribed, except what relates to the Administration of the Lord's Supper."[36] By 1789 this direction was completely dropped out of the *Discipline*. References to reading services or prayers and the Liturgy became fewer and fewer as time progressed. In 1792 these were completely removed from the *Discipline*. This change in 1792 was not imposed from the General Conference upon the people of the MEC, but rather was an official alteration of the MEC's worship format to reflect the reality of life in the Church. Not only was the word *liturgy* removed, but also the liturgy itself was seriously truncated.

> The attitude of the ministers and the churches was expressed in the General Conference of 1792, which radically altered Wesley's *Sunday Service*... The changes were not made haphazardly, but with a view to meeting the needs of the people... Gone were morning and evening prayer, the psalms, the litany and collects, Epistles and Gospels. Wesley's liturgical year was completely eliminated and the word *liturgy* was deliberately and purposely dropped. In short, there was no longer in American Methodism a book of worship as ordered by Wesley, but a brief section on "Sacramental Services," later called "The Ritual," placed at the back of the Book of Discipline. Here, retained in altered form,

---

34. *Disciplines*, 1785.12.
35. Ibid., 1789.6.
36. Ibid., 1785.12.

were orders for communion, baptism, weddings, funerals, and the ordaining of ministers.[37]

These liturgical revisions must be seen in light of how the MEC functioned in its worship life. Karen Westerfield Tucker wrote thus, "The separation of the Eucharist from the pattern for regular Sunday morning worship and the transformation of the Sunday liturgy into largely an extempore service undoubtedly reflected the practice of Sunday worship for almost all Methodists."[38] This opinion seems to be sustained by recorded opinions made by Methodists in attendance at this conference. A primary example is Ezekiel Cooper, who recorded, "During Conference we had much debating upon various subjects but still love continued. We spoke plainly and freely what was in our minds; made several alterations and improvements in our form of Discipline."[39] There is no sense that the changes at this conference were monumental at all, but merely that the business of the conference happened, and then the conference adjourned. In fact, this is exactly what Thomas Coke recorded. His only entry for the duration of this conference was focused on how the Americans surprised him with their skill and humility in debate. None of the debates were recorded, nor even the topics debated.[40] It was, therefore, not the case that some Wesleyan ideal for weekly reception of the Lord's Supper was nefariously thwarted by an anti-sacramental Asbury, as Wade argued; nor was it the case that the MEC retained a high soteriological Eucharistic piety, and thereby proved such by limiting reception of the sacrament to a quarterly occurrence, as Ruth argued. Rather, the MEC understood the Eucharist primarily in Wesley's ecclesiological dimension of Eucharistic theology: they had received the authority to administer the sacraments at the Christmas Conference, so now there could be no debate as to whether or not they were a legitimate Church. The 1792 revisions merely reinforced this ecclesiological Eucharistic piety and burgeoning theology within the life of the MEC. However, it would take the second major event of the 1792 General Conference, the schism, for the MEC to explain this understanding theologically and scripturally, and it is to that circumstance that we now turn.

---

37. McEllhenney, *United Methodism*, 46.
38. Tucker, *Worship*, 9.
39. Phoebus, *Beams of Light*, 153.
40. Coke, *Journals*, 174–75.

## Chapter 12

# On the Defensive

**SCHISM**

LITURGICAL REVISION WAS NOT the only major development in the life of the MEC in 1792. In that year, one of the Presiding Elders, James O'Kelly, led a group of preachers and congregations out of the MEC and created the Republican Methodist Church.[1] While this may not seem to have any bearing upon the issue of the sacraments, the MEC's response to O'Kelly gave posterity an illuminating look at its Eucharistic piety. Therefore, to more fully understand what brought the MEC to the point where it created the unique *1798 Discipline*, it is necessary to understand O'Kelly's schism as a precursor to the situation. O'Kelly had begun preaching among the American Methodists in 1778, when he was admitted on trial as a traveling preacher.[2] He was one of the primary architects behind the Flauvanna Schism in 1779,[3] and he was one of the first men ordained at the Christmas Conference in 1784.[4] When the role of *Presiding Elder* was officially created in 1789, O'Kelly was one of the first appointed to that position.[5] As a result of his being appointed a presiding elder, O'Kelly was a part of the short-lived Council that had been created in 1789 for the general oversight

---

1. Bangs, *History*, 344.
2. Hitt and Ware, *Minutes*, 16.
3. Lee, *A Short History*, 73.
4. Hitt and Ware, *Minutes*, 51.
5. Bangs, *History*, 305 and Hitt and Ware, *Minutes*, 82.

of the MEC.⁶ Bangs recorded that, as of 1792, O'Kelly was "a very popular preacher in the state of Virginia, who had acted as a presiding elder in that district for several years."⁷

It is unclear exactly what O'Kelly's motives were for deciding to separate from the MEC. There were some accusations of heresy, that O'Kelly denied the Trinity, and left the connection before he could be brought up on charges.⁸ Francis Asbury, in a letter to Thomas Morrell just after the General Conference in 1792 when O'Kelly left, suggested it was an issue of pride. "I believe now nothing short of being an episcopos was his first aim. His second was to make the Council independent of the Bishop and General Conference, if they would canonize his writings."⁹ The "Council" to which Asbury referred was created in 1789 to preside over the MEC. It was made up of the bishops (although in actual practice this meant only Asbury, since Coke was mostly out of the country) and the presiding elders, who were elders that were appointed by the bishop to serve in an oversight capacity over several circuits together. After trying to make the Council work as an administrative entity, it was universally decried a failure and was replaced with a General Conference to meet quadrennially (the first of which was in 1792). If Asbury were correct in his assessment of O'Kelly, then it would seem that O'Kelly took his position on the Council with the expectation that he would be appointed bishop shortly thereafter. When this did not happen, O'Kelly became embittered and took out his frustration on the MEC in general, and Asbury in particular.

This frustration manifested itself in the 1792 General Conference, when James O'Kelly moved that a preacher stationed by the bishop ought to have a "Right of Appeal" if he thought the appointment was not fair.¹⁰ The actual motion, recorded by Jesse Lee was, "After the bishop appoints the preachers at conference to their several circuits, if anyone think himself injured by the appointment, he shall have liberty to appeal to the conference and state his objections; and if the conference approve his objections, the bishop shall appoint him to another circuit."¹¹ Both Lee and Asbury recorded that the debate on this motion lasted for days. According to Robert Paine, in his biography of William McKendree, "After three days' animated

---

6. Ibid.
7. Bangs, *History*, 344.
8. Lee, *A Short History*, 180.
9. *JLFA*, 3.113.
10. Ibid., 1.733n.
11. Lee, *A Short History*, 178.

discussion, the resolution was lost by a large majority."[12] Ultimately, when the motion failed, O'Kelly left the fellowship of the MEC, citing its failure as the result. Thomas Ware stated that the defeat of the motion was not a foregone conclusion at the beginning of the debate. He wrote, "Had Mr. O'Kelly's proposition been differently managed it might possibly have been carried. For myself, at first I did not see any thing very objectionable in it. But when it came to be debated, I very much disliked the spirit of those who advocated it, and wondered at the severity in which the movers and others who spoke in favour of it indulged in the course of their remarks."[13] Ware was not the only preacher in attendance who initially thought of approving O'Kelly's motion. Jesse Lee recorded, "A large majority of them [the preachers] appeared at first to be in favour of the motion."[14]

The remarks that ultimately swayed Ware were preserved in O'Kelly's *Apology*, which was reprinted in the *Methodist Review* in July 1887 in an article entitled *Origin of Presiding Elders*. It was here that one could see the vitriol that so offended Thomas Ware. "Hope Hull, a worthy elder, sounded a proper alarm. He exceeded himself by far. I could wish his words were written in a book. He spake after this manner: 'O heavens, are we not Americans? Did not our fathers bleed to free their sons from the British yoke? And shall we be slaves to ecclesiastical oppression?' He lifted up his voice and cried, 'What! No appeal for an injured brother? Are these things so? Am I in my senses? . . . 'We are far gone into popery.'"[15]

Ware corroborated this in his autobiography by stating, "Some of them said that is was a shame for a man to *accept* of such a lordship, much more to *claim* it; and that they who would submit to this absolute dominion must forfeit all claims to freedom."[16] When the vote finally came, fortunes and opinions had changed tremendously. Lee recorded, "We were kept on that subject called the *Appeal*, for two or three days. On Monday we began the debate afresh, and continued it through the day; and at night we went to Mr. Otterbein's church, and again continued it till near bed time, when the vote was taken, and the motion was lost by a large majority."[17] Asbury confirmed this in his succinct manner by recording, "My power to station the preachers without an appeal was much debated, but finally carried by a very large

---

12. Paine, *Life and Times*, 61.
13. Ware, *Sketches*, 220.
14. Lee, *A Short History*, 179.
15. *Methodist Review*, 541.
16. Ware, *Sketches*, 221, emphasis included.
17. Lee, *A Short History*, 179.

majority."[18] There is a hint, though to the hurt this issue caused him, as he also wrote, "Perhaps a new bishop, new conference, and new laws would have better pleased some."[19]

The reason O'Kelly placed so much emphasis and importance upon this issue so as to leave a connection in which he had been a leading figure for almost fourteen years is spelled out in a letter he wrote to a local preacher, Jesse Nicholson, after the General Conference. In it O'Kelly wrote, "What have I done? Overturned government? What? the Council—not Methodism. I only say no man among us ought to get into the Apostle's chair with the Keys, and stretch a lordly power over the ministers and Kingdom of Christ . . . We have published that we believe a General Conference to be injurious to the Church. District Conferences have lost their suffrages . . . I am a friend to Christ; to his Church, but not to prelatick [sic] government."[20] O'Kelly, by his own admission, had a problem with the Council, the General Conference that replaced the Council, and Francis Asbury, whom he insinuated was attempting to be a pope of sorts for the MEC.

Jesse Lee recorded a charge that would have come against O'Kelly if he had continued with the MEC. He wrote,

> The preacher [to whom he was speaking] then informed me, that Mr. O'Kelly denied the doctrine of the Trinity, and preached against it, by saying, that Father, Son and Holy Ghost were characters, and not persons: and that these characters all belonged to Jesus Christ. That Jesus Christ was the Father, the Son and the Holy Ghost. The preacher further said, that it was his intention to have had O'Kelly tried at that conference for the false doctrines which he had been preaching; and he believed that his leaving the conference was more out of fear of being brought to trial, than on account of the appeal.[21]

Concerning O'Kelly's exodus from the General Conference and the MEC to form his own Church, Bangs agreed with Asbury's assessment of the root cause being pride. Bangs wrote that O'Kelly's new Church, the Republican Methodist Church "began in the obstinate attachment of a vain man to his favorite theory."[22] This "favorite theory" of O'Kelly's was his insistence that he was following the injunctions of Scripture solely in his motives and actions. This can be best explained by an interaction between O'Kelly and a

18. *JLFA*, 1.734.
19. Ibid.
20. Ibid., 3.114.
21. Lee, *A Short History*, 180.
22. Bangs, *History*, 355.

woman as retold by Asbury. "Brother James O'Kelly answered a woman who asked the difference between me and him. He gave her the powerful return. 'Suppose,' said he, 'I were to show you the Bible and a form of discipline made by the General Conference, would you not know the difference?'"[23]

It is most likely that pride and perceived scriptural authority were the cause of O'Kelly's schism rather than any unsubstantiated innuendo of heresy as Jesse Lee recounted. The reason for this is that O'Kelly was not content to disappear from the scene or simply begin anew in a new denomination fashioned after his own prerogatives. Rather, he continued to attack the MEC in general and Francis Asbury in particular. There were many heated exchanges through competing pamphlets and reports pointing to the theological defects of each Church and the character defects of those leading each Church. By 1796 it was clear that O'Kelly was not simply going to go away. Realizing this fact, the General Conference of that year requested Bishops Coke and Asbury to add explanatory notes to the next edition of the *Discipline* to delineate the theological reasoning behind the doctrines and polity of the MEC. Frederick Norwood stated that the bishops "diligently gathered two types of material: (1) biblical texts which defined Methodist polity on scriptural grounds, and (2) explanations of the importance or significance of particular standards and regulations."[24] This *Discipline* with notations was published in 1798 and to this day remains unique in the fact that there are explanations and scriptural notations for every entry within the book. Asbury wrote of this work

> We [Dr. Coke and Asbury] have written what will make about 100 printed pages, have bound our work with six or 700 printed scriptures. Our hearts, hands, heads, eyes, Bibles, and concordances have been employed. I hope the work will please, convince, and instruct. We are only sorry we did not ask the General Conference to give us leave to strike out the childish questions, and to lay the text as well as the notes properly together. I view the work of vast importance that hath cost us such application and thought for months and years ... For this cause [to counter O'Kelly's assertion that the MEC disregards Scripture] we have abounded in scripture, and when we consider the form is 70 pages, we have not been prolix in the notes. Every explanation

---

23. *JLFA*, 3.159. While it cannot be proven, this propensity for Scripture as the foundation for all decisions, and the fact that James O'Kelly was one of the primary instigators at Flauvanna, the case could be made that it was at the encouragement of O'Kelly that the authority of the oversight committee be rooted in Scripture rather than the Methodist Discipline.

24. Tuckniss, *Doctrines and Disciplines*. Hereafter *1798 Discipline*.

must be more than the text. We have guarded against weak arguments, and improper scripture, and against anything harsh and reflecting on others.[25]

To Ezekiel Cooper, who had the responsibility of publishing the *Discipline*, Asbury wrote, "I am sure I am right in my desire of printing the notes on the discipline. You in your annual distant station can hardly conceive the mischief and abuse we meet with from unchristian and illiberal minds. For many parts they raise a dust and escape on the clouds."[26] Interestingly, in this quotation Asbury stated that it was his own desire to have notes in the *Discipline*, and equally interesting is the fact that there is no decision recorded in the 1796 General Conference minutes that shows a request of the Conference for such an undertaking by the bishops.[27] Thomas Coke recorded the composition of these notes in his journal when he wrote, "I spent my leisure-hours for the last three months in writing annotations on all the parts of the Methodist Economy. Mr. Asbury had before drawn up his thoughts at large on the subject. I therefore endeavoured to unite our ideas; and think that if ever I drew up any useful publications for the press this was one of them, and perhaps the best."[28]

This issue may have been a personal grudge between Asbury and O'Kelly, who had questioned Asbury's intentions and motives, and Asbury suggested/requested that this work be done to defend himself and the MEC from such character attacks. Whatever the cause for its compilation and publication, though, the net effect was that the *1798 Discipline* essentially became the first attempt at a systematic theology for the Methodist Episcopal Church in America. This was done in a very thorough manner and gives the present reader a magnificent insight into the logic, piety, and burgeoning theology of those early days of Methodism in America.

25. *JLFA*, 3.159.

26. Ibid., 3.165. This portion is from the actual letter to Cooper, which was not published. What was published as the letter was merely Asbury's instructions concerning how to print the *Discipline*. The actual letter is a part of the Ezekiel Cooper Collection at Garrett Evangelical Theological Seminary.

27. *Journals of the General Conferences*, 7–29. Nor is there any record of such a decision in Lee's *Short History*. There is, however, a note within the first pages of the *1798 Discipline* itself that states, "The last General Conference desired the Bishops to draw up Annotations on the Form of Discipline, and to publish them with the present edition:—The Bishops have accordingly complied, and have proved or illustrated every thing by quotations from the Word of God, agreeably, also, to the advice of the Conference; and they sincerely pray that their labour of love may be made a blessing to many. 1797" (iv). This is the only reference to the 1796 General Conference requesting this work to be done.

28. Coke, *Journals*, 232.

## 1798 DISCIPLINE

The *1798 Discipline* is the closest work American Methodists created that can be construed as being theological in nature. The fact that the notes and commentary in it were the work of Bishops Coke and Asbury makes it doubly important. This theological work was produced by the leaders of the MEC, the ones who ultimately influenced the mission, emphasis, and priorities of the Church. In this *Discipline*, the bishops gave not only their immediate peers (supporters and detractors) rationale for the method of the Methodist system in America, but also gave posterity a valuable insight into the theological understanding and thinking of American Methodists prior to any significant influence from English Methodist theologians in the nineteenth century. Formal theological training for American Methodist preachers came in the Course of Study, which used British Methodist theologians for its texts, but it was not created until the 1816 General Conference.[29] The theology depicted in the *Discipline* came from the Americans without much British training.

The irony in that statement is that both Thomas Coke and Francis Asbury were English. However, what they included in the *1798 Discipline* had to pass the litmus test of the American Methodists themselves. Those Americans proved in their collective life as the MEC that they would and could assert their independence from the English. First, they removed the name of John Wesley from the *1787 Discipline*. This was done on account of Wesley directing the MEC to make Richard Whatcoat a new Superintendent in the Church. Because of this declaration, the MEC rescinded its rule from the Christmas Conference whereby they pledged themselves "During the Life of the Rev. Mr. Wesley, we acknowledge ourselves his Sons in the Gospel, ready in Matters belonging to Church-Government, to obey his Commands."[30] The second incident at this same conference occurred when they asserted themselves over and against their British brethren by forcing Coke essentially to abdicate his Episcopal authority over the Church. By bringing Wesley's command concerning Whatcoat, by changing the time and place for the conference, and by writing some letters to preachers that they deemed unwelcome, Coke became unwelcome in his position of authority. To pacify the situation, he had to make the following statement in writing,

> I do solemnly engage by this instrument, that I never will, by virtue of my office, as superintendant [sic] of the Methodist

---

29. Chiles, *Transition*, 32.
30. *Disciplines*, 1785.3. See also Ware, *Sketches*, 130–31.

> church, during my absence from the United States of America, exercise any government whatever in the said Methodist church during my absence from the United States. And I do also engage, that I will exercise no privilege in the said church when present in the United States, except that of ordaining according to the regulations and law, already existing or hereafter to be made in the said church, and that of presiding when present in conference, and lastly that of travelling at large.[31]

Both of these instances together show that the Americans would only allow those points in which they were in agreement to be published in this edition of the *Discipline*.

Thus, the *1798 Discipline* shows how the Americans theologically understood themselves, their Church, and ultimately their God; and this is prior to the camp meeting revivals that dominated several Protestant denominations and specifically characterized American Methodism in the nineteenth century. This work allows scholars to investigate American Methodist theology when it was truly American and as exclusively Methodist as it could be. It is for this reason that it is an invaluable tool for this present study. It is within the notes and commentary of this edition of the *Discipline* that the American Methodists show their theological understanding of the Eucharist at the dawn of the nineteenth century. This work is perhaps the most "American" of any theological work during the first nearly one hundred years of American Methodism. There are essentially two different sections to this work: the *Discipline* itself and the Notes that accompany it. It will be necessary to analyze both to fully understand the implications within this work.

The *Discipline* opens with the statement

> The preachers and members of our society in general, being convinced that there was a great deficiency of vital religion in the church of England in America, and being in many places destitute of the Christian sacraments, as several of the clergy had forsaken their churches, requested the late Rev. John Wesley to take such measures, in his wisdom and prudence, as would afford them suitable relief in their distress.[32]

This is the first paragraph on the first page (after the introduction) of the entire book, and here is the issue at hand. The American Methodists saw in the Established Church a lack of true piety and religion. This is the primary cause for the call by them to Wesley for "suitable relief." If there were any

---

31. Lee, *A Short History*, 125.
32. *1798 Discipline*, 5.

doubt as to the importance of the sacraments in light of this statement, the Note explains the situation clearly. "The two sacraments of baptism and the Lord's supper have been allowed to be essential to the formation of a Christian Church, by every party and denomination in every age and country of Christendom."[33]

This, from the hands of the bishops, states that the sacraments are necessary ingredients to the establishment of a Church. The ecclesiological dimension and understanding of the sacraments is the primary lens through which to view the issue of the Eucharist for the American Methodists of this era. As a result, this statement concerns what is necessary for a true Church to be in existence, not what is necessary for true growth in holiness in the life of a believer. And even given the possibility that the soteriological dimension of the Eucharistic theology could be implied within the "formation of a Christian Church," there is no indication on the part of the bishops that soteriology is even an issue here. Rather, the issue at hand is one of ecclesiology and what constitutes a valid denomination or Church. This statement can also be further illuminated when the bishops' statement for the presence of ordained elders, those with the authority to administer the sacraments, is taken into consideration. They stated, "We need not enlarge upon the necessity of an office, which every organized Christian church in the world, in all ages, has adopted."[34]

Both understandings are present within the Article of Religion that Wesley prepared for the MEC. Article XIII stated, "The visible Church of Christ is a congregation of faithful men, in which the pure word of God is preached, and the sacraments duly administered according to Christ's ordinance, in all those things that of necessity are requisite to the same."[35] This was copied by Wesley directly from the Article of Religion for the Church of England (Article XIX). Wesley also wrote Article XVI for the MEC (Article XXV for the Church of England), which stated, "Sacraments ordained of Christ, are not only badges or tokens of Christian men's profession; but rather they are certain signs of grace, and God's good will towards us, by the which he doth work invisibly in us, and doth not only quicken, but also strengthen and confirm our faith in him."[36]

This is the soteriological understanding of the sacraments, and it is one to which Wesley frequently referred, if not in so many words, when he spoke of the Lord's Supper as the supreme means of grace, the means of grace *par*

---

33. Ibid., 6.
34. Ibid., 54.
35. Ibid., 18.
36. Ibid., 20.

*excellence*. It was this understanding of the Eucharist that prompted Wesley to defend against the Stillness Controversy so strenuously in 1739-40. It was this understanding of the Eucharist that led to the inclusion of the necessity of receiving the Lord's Supper weekly to the *Rules for Bands*. It was also this understanding of the Eucharist that led to Methodists jumping parish lines to receive the sacrament wherever and whenever it was offered. And yet there are hardly any references in the Notes in this *Discipline* that shows the same understanding of the sacraments as this Article. In fact, there is only one Note that approaches this understanding. The bishops commented on the section entitled "Of the Duty of Preachers to God, themselves, and one another," which itself was copied from the *Large Minutes* and left essentially unchanged (except for a few minor revisions), concerning the reception of the Lord's Supper as one of the duties. They wrote, "Whenever we have opportunity to eat of the bread and drink of the cup of the Lord, we should not only as far as possible make it a blessing to others, but also to ourselves."[37] That is the extent of the description of the Eucharist as an event in the life of the Church with a soteriological dimension.

Even more informative than these sections of the Notes with respect to the Eucharist and the American Methodists' understanding of them are several passages in the Notes concerning the nature of the ordinances, none of which come from the sections that dealt directly with the issue of the sacraments themselves, for the sections on the sacraments are extremely short, and there is not much said concerning them, either in the *Discipline* itself or the Notes for those sections. Rather, one must look to the Notes in other sections to see how the bishops described the sacraments in relation to the life and piety of the MEC. Considering the soteriological dimension of the Eucharist, the bishops made an extraordinary claim when commenting on Chapter II, Section I: *The Nature, Design, and general Rules of the United Societies*, specifically on the third portion, which consisted of "attending upon all the ordinances of God" by stating,

> We have also spoken largely on all the ordinances of the gospel, and the necessity of being constant partakers of them; and have proved this by a great variety of scriptures. Although the ordinances are but means of grace, their end, which is the salvation of our souls, cannot be attained without them. Such is the order of God, except when unavoidable hindrances prevent our attending of them; in which case, God will himself be to the

---

37. Ibid., 93, and Wesley, *Works* (Jackson), 8.322-24.

sincere soul instead of all the ordinances, yea, will turn *the very hindrances themselves into the most profitable of all means.*[38]

Here the bishops defined and then reframed the definition of a means of grace. In this new framework, their concept was that God had an ordinary way of conveying grace, through the established means of grace, but in the (then) present situation with the MEC, since it was without the sacraments for so long and yet still apparently grew in grace, God used the very absence of the sacraments to grow the people spiritually and the Church numerically. In this understanding, the bishops actually claimed that the absence of the sacraments became, for the MEC, more grace filled than their presence would have been. While the bishops gave a nod to the soteriological dimension of the sacraments and the fact that "the salvation of our souls" could not be fulfilled without them, they proved in the end that this dimension of the faith was not located in the sacraments for either the MEC or the bishops themselves, but rather has been relocated by God somewhere else to compensate for the lack of the sacraments in the life of the societies, both before the Christmas Conference and after it. In other words, while the Eucharist is a wonderful way God has created to impart grace to his children, God has chosen in the life of the MEC to impart even more grace to the American Methodists apart from it.

This can likewise be seen in the call for members of the MEC to sacrifice the means of grace to be in service to the poor. In Chapter I, Section XVI: *On the Instruction of Children*, the bishops wrote, "If they [our people] would establish Sabbath-schools, wherever practicable, for the benefit of the children of the poor, and sacrifice a few public ordinances every Lord's-day to this charitable and useful exercise, *God would be to them instead of all the means they lose*; yea, they would find, to their present comfort and the increase of their eternal glory, the truth and sweetness of those words, 'Mercy is better than sacrifice,' Matt. ix.13 and xii.7. and Hos. vi.6."[39]

Again, here is the concept that God will replace the regular means of grace with something far greater for those who do not have access to them, either by circumstance, design, or choice. This second example is a radical departure from the soteriological dimension of the Eucharist that Wesley had, and the first example, while logically defensible in a theological debate, likewise is not consistent with Wesley's understanding of the means of grace in the sacraments. Speaking specifically of baptism, yet with an understanding that can also apply to the Eucharist, Wesley stated, "It is true the Second Adam hath found a remedy for the disease which came upon all

---

38. Ibid., 145, emphasis added.
39. Ibid., 105, emphasis added.

by the offence of the first. But the benefit of this is to be received through the means which he hath appointed; through baptism in particular, which is the ordinary means he hath appointed for that purpose; and to which God hath tied us, though he may not have tied himself. Indeed, where it cannot be had, the case is different, but *extraordinary cases do not make void a standing rule*."[40] In Wesley's language, the MEC's understanding was that its life, past and present, was one large extraordinary case, and thus God worked (and was working) in extraordinary means beyond the established means of grace. Directly contrary to Wesley's own theology, the MEC made its own extraordinary case into a new "standing rule" in which God's grace was available to them consistently apart from the means of grace.

This makes evident the concept that Wesley's understanding of the Eucharist as having a soteriological dimension was either not entirely present in the MEC as of 1798, or was deeply buried under the ecclesiological dimension of the Eucharist. In actuality, it seems that the soteriological dimension of the faith was now located outside of the Eucharist and was now located in another aspect of the MEC's life, both prior to its becoming a legitimate Church and subsequent to it. One example of this shift in emphasis can be seen in how the bishops discussed itinerancy. They wrote

> Our grand plan, in all its parts, leads to an itinerant ministry. Our bishops are travelling bishops. All the different orders which compose our conferences are employed in the travelling line; and our local preachers are, in some degree, travelling preachers. Every thing is kept moving as far as possible; and we will be bold to say, that, next to the grace of God, *there is nothing like this for keeping the whole body alive from the center to the circumference, and for the continual extension of that circumference on every hand.*[41]

This language is very similar in intent as the language in Article XVI (*Of the Sacraments*) concerning the quickening and strengthening of faith and grace through the sacraments. More compelling than this reference to growth through itinerancy, however, is the case that the bishops viewed the closed meeting as containing that soteriological dimension of the faith and means of grace. In their Notes on Chapter II, Section III: *Of the Band Societies*, the bishops wrote

> When bands can be formed on this plan (and on no other do we form them) they become one of the most profitable means

40. Wesley, *Works* (Jackson), 10.193, emphasis added.
41. *1798 Discipline*, 42, emphasis added.

of grace in the whole compass of Christian discipline. *There is nothing we know of, which so much quickens the soul* to a desire and expectation of the perfect love of God as this . . . Thus does our economy by its prudential ordinances, under the grace of God, tend to raise the members of our society from one degree of grace to another. And we have invariably observed, that where these meetings of the bands have been kept up in their life and power, the revival of the work of God has been manifest both in the addition of members to the society, and in the deepening of the life of God in general. We earnestly wish, that our elders, deacons, and preachers be peculiarly attentive to these blessed ordinances [band and class meetings] in their respective spheres of action.[42]

This is almost the exact language in Article XVI (*Of the Sacraments*), which stated, "Sacraments ordained by Christ . . . are certain signs of grace . . . by the which he doth work invisibly in us, and doth not only quicken, but also strengthen and confirm our faith in him;"[43] only here it was being used to describe the band meeting rather than a sacrament. By this analysis of the band meeting by the bishops, it would seem that the soteriological dimension of Wesley's Eucharistic theology had been transferred to the work of the band meetings by the American Methodists.

This difference in locus for the soteriological dimension of a Eucharistic theology can be especially seen if one contrasts the above statement with John Wesley's extract of Brevint and Charles Wesley's hymn on the same passage in their *Hymns on the Lord's Supper*. As noted above, John wrote, "Of these blessings Christ from above is pleased to bestow sometimes more, sometimes less, in the several ordinances of his Church, which as the stars of heaven, differ from each other in glory. *Fasting, prayer, hearing* his Word, are all good vessels, to draw water from this Well of Salvation. But they are not all equal. The Holy Communion when well used, exceeds as much in blessing, as it exceeds in danger of a curse, when wickedly and irreverently taken."[44] Charles wrote his poetic interpretation of this extracted passage in Hymn 42, which is in Section II: *As it is a Sign and a Means of Grace*:

> Glory to Him who freely spent
> His Blood that we might live,
> And through this choicest Instrument
> Doth all his Blessings give.

---

42. Ibid., 151–52, emphasis added.
43. Ibid., 20.
44. *HLS*, 15.

Fasting he doth and Hearing bless,
And Prayer can much avail,
Good Vessels all to draw the Grace
Out of Salvation's Well.

But none like this Mysterious Rite
Which dying Mercy gave
Can draw forth all his promis'd Might
And all his Will to save.

This is the richest Legacy
Thou hast on Man bestow'd,
Here chiefly, Lord, we feed on Thee,
And drink thy precious Blood.

Here all thy Blessings we receive,
Here all thy Gifts are given;
To those that would in Thee believe,
Pardon, and Grace, and Heaven.

Thus may we still in Thee be blest
'Till all from Earth remove,
And share with Thee the Marriage-feast,
And drink the Wine above.[45]

Between John's extract and Charles' hymn, it can be seen that the MEC had essentially the same soteriological dimension of a sacramental theology in place with regards to their band meetings. This is an important point, as it impacts how one understands why the MEC did not feel it necessary to ordain the local preachers and deacons to the position of elder as proposed by William Ormond in 1796 and 1800. It also sheds light on why the debate and discussion of the sacraments in 1779–80 during the Flauvanna schism used exclusively ecclesiological language when speaking of the sacraments. The soteriological dimension was already present in the life of the American Methodists apart from the actual sacrament of the Eucharist.

In addition to a difference of priority with respect to the means of grace between the MEC and John Wesley's theology, there was some confusion on the part of the American Methodists as in to which category of the means of grace, instituted or prudential, the meetings, band or class, resided. In the section on class meetings, the bishops noted, "But we must

---

45. Ibid., 31.

say, that those who entirely neglect this *divinely instituted* ordinance (however various the names given to it, or the modes of conducting it, may be) manifest, that they are either ashamed to acknowledge as their brethren, the true children of God or 'are enemies of the cross of Christ,' Phil. 3.18."[46] In one place the meetings are called prudential means of grace, in another they are highlighted as instituted. The difference here is significant. As John Wesley himself stated when delineating the difference between the instituted and prudential means of grace, "That with regard to these little prudential helps we are continually changing one thing after another, is not a weakness or fault, as you imagine, but a peculiar advantage which we enjoy. By this means we declare them all to be merely prudential, not essential, not of divine institution."[47] If this definition of instituted means of grace held constant from Wesley to the American Methodists, the bishops stated that class meetings were essential to salvation because Christ instituted them. The language used to describe the effects of these meetings on the Methodists themselves tends in that direction, as seen in the quotation above concerning the efficacy of the band meeting in the life of a believer as opposed to the instituted means of grace as Wesley delineated them (the sacraments), whose absence in the life of the Church the bishops justified in their Notes.

---

46. *1798 Discipline*, 147–48, emphasis included.
47. Wesley, *Works*, 9.262–63.

# Chapter 13

# Closed Doors

## SACRAMENTAL LANGUAGE

INTERESTINGLY, AND COMPLETELY CONTRARY to the evidence that the American Methodists had a different understanding of the Eucharist and its soteriological and ecclesiological dimensions in the life of the Church, Lester Ruth has made the statement, "There was a clear connection between American Eucharistic spirituality and that of British Methodism—particularly as found in John and Charles Wesley. Generally, the writings and sacramental hymns of Americans show a definite continuity with the Wesleys' thought, even if the sophistication and breadth of their thought are not as evident."[1] As evidence for this position, Ruth put forward the publication of an American edition of Robert Spence's *Pocket Hymn-Book* in 1786. This hymnal "added a new sacramental section containing nine hymns from the Wesleys' *Hymns on the Lord's Supper*."[2] In addition to these nine hymns, Ruth also pointed out that Philip Gatch's papers have "a manuscript sermon outline book in which fifteen Wesleyan Eucharistic hymns are written out by hand," and "some bear the hymns' numbers in a British edition of the Eucharistic hymnal."[3] Out of these fifteen hymns written in Gatch's papers and the nine in the American hymnal there is one duplicate hymn between them. This means there were twenty-three of the Wesleys' Eucharistic hymns known in America prior to 1800. Based upon these twenty-three

---

1. Ruth, *A Little Heaven Below*, 139–40.
2. Ibid.
3. Ibid.

hymns, out of a total of one hundred sixty-six Eucharistic hymns, Ruth made the claim that the American Methodists were "familiar with the entire corpus of Wesleyan Eucharistic hymnody."[4] How this conclusion is justified is completely unclear considering the evidence points to the American Methodists knowing nine of the hymns and one preacher knowing fourteen other hymns. Even if the entire MEC knew of these twenty-three different Eucharistic hymns, it is still a very large (and not very logical) leap to the conclusion that they necessarily knew all one hundred sixty-six. Rather, the evidence shows that not even fourteen percent of the Wesleys' Eucharistic hymns were known to the MEC (giving the manuscript ones the benefit of the doubt as to being known by more than just Philip Gatch), and only five percent were definitely known, having been printed in a hymnal for use in the MEC. Finally, in complete refutation of the idea that "there is evidence that American Methodists were otherwise familiar with the entire corpus of Wesleyan Eucharistic hymnody," the first time all one hundred sixty-six hymns were printed in America was in 1990 by the Order of St. Luke![5]

Nevertheless, Ruth used this point as a basis for his understanding that American Methodists had the same understanding of the Eucharist as John Wesley, if only not as theologically astute. Ruth stated, "If there is any discontinuity between Wesley's Eucharistic spirituality and that of early American Methodists, it is in hints that American thought did not possess the same breadth and complexity as Wesley's."[6] Ruth then supported this claim by showing that, of the hymns printed in America, none were from the sections dealing with sacrifice, "both the sacrifice of Christ and that of the believing community."[7] This, however, seems to be the only deficiency between the MEC and Wesley concerning the multifaceted nature of the sacrament as far as Ruth's analysis is concerned. Ruth then took great pains to prove American Methodists and Wesley emphasized similar and complementary thoughts concerning the sacrament. He noted that "there was fluidity in Wesleyan and American Methodist spirituality about what exactly constituted a 'sacramental' theme," by which Ruth meant, "Themes that appear in explicitly Eucharistic material in Wesley might appear elsewhere in American Methodism or, conversely, Wesleyan hymns like 'Arise, My Soul, Arise' could be labeled as 'sacramental' by American Methodists."[8]

---

4. Ibid.
5. *HLS*, xiii.
6. Ruth, *A Little Heaven Below*, 141.
7. Ibid.
8. Ibid., 142.

This statement gives a superficial nod to the fact that American Methodists did not share Wesley's sacramental understanding, but then proceeds to "prove" their congruence with Wesley by focusing on those elements that do overlap between the two. In other words, if Wesley spoke with sacramental language concerning item $x$, and the American Methodists used the same language for items $x$, $y$, and $z$, and neither $y$ nor $z$ relate to the sacraments at all, Ruth sees the overlap of $x$ as justification for stating Wesley and the American Methodists had the same sacramental understanding. This is not logical. While there was some congruence between them, the incongruence is too large to ignore by simply stating there was "fluidity."

Ruth proceeded to highlight three parallels between the MEC and Wesley to demonstrate their congruence with each other. First, Ruth wrote, "American Methodists frequently emphasized the visibility of the commemoration of Christ's passion, as did Wesley and other contemporaries,"[9] and he provided quotations from American Methodists and Charles Wesley's hymns that show the similarities of this dynamic. Second, Ruth illustrated with similar quotations, "as Wesleyan spirituality emphasized the bread and wine as effectual means of grace, American Methodists frequently spoke of experiencing the grace of God in their use."[10] Third, Ruth emphasized the eschatological aspect of American Methodists in conjunction with the same concept in the corpus of Wesleyan hymns.[11]

Throughout Ruth's analysis, most of the quotations he uses from the Americans as proof that their Eucharistic piety, or spirituality, was congruent with Wesley are quotations that could just as easily have been made about Methodist worship in general or a love feast in particular, without the presence of the Lord's Supper. In trying comprehensively to prove that Americans experienced the Lord's Supper in the same manner as Wesley theologically described it, Ruth neglected the fact that the American Methodists used the very same language for events other than the sacrament. Perhaps the best illustration of this would be the quotation from which Ruth took the title for his work, *A Little Heaven Below*. This was from William Watters who stated, "We sat together in heavenly places; and to express myself the words which I immediately wrote down, I was as in a little Heaven below, and believe Heaven above will differ more in quantity than in quality."[12] Following Ruth's analysis, it would be reasonable for this statement to have been in relation to the celebration of the Eucharist, but it was

---

9. Ibid.
10. Ibid., 143–44.
11. Ibid.
12. Watters, *Short Account*, 39.

not. This was written concerning a love feast on the Deer Creek circuit at its last quarterly meeting for the year 1779/80. The full quotation is

> Our love feast was one of the best I ever was in. We sat together in heavenly places; and to express myself the words which I immediately wrote down, I was as in a little Heaven below, and believe Heaven above will differ more in quantity than in quality. Never did I hear such experiences before. Our eyes overflowed with tears, and our hearts with love to God and each other. The holy fire, the heavenly flame, spread wider and wider, and rose higher and higher. O! happy people whose God is the Lord, may none of you ever weary in well doing. May we after having done the work allotted us, meet in our Father's Kingdom, to tell the wonders of redeeming love and part no more.[13]

In addition to this statement, there are other instances in the lives of American (and English) Methodists that use similar sacramental language for meetings and love feasts (which were conducted during society meetings). Asbury recorded in his *Journal* an experience that took place on March 25, 1776. In it he wrote, "My soul was greatly blessed in meeting sister Lambert Wilmer's class, and all present seemed to partake of the same blessing. 'The opening heavens around me shine/with beams of sacred bliss/if Jesus shows his mercy mine/and whispers I am his.'"[14] The poetry that Asbury included was a hymn written by Isaac Watts that was popular with Methodists. In fact, Hester Ann Rogers used the same hymn to describe her experience of union with Christ while walking through a church yard the same year, 1776, and this experience described in "sacramental language" was prompted, not by a sacrament or meeting, but by a sermon.[15] Thomas Rankin recorded in his Journal on May 22, 1774, "We concluded the evening with a general love-feast, in which meeting the Lord's presence was powerfully felt by many persons."[16]

Beyond these journals, there were also hymns composed that blurred the distinction between a sacramental event and a meeting or love feast. One prime example is a hymn describing a class meeting.

> This is the place where Jesus meets
> The purchase of his blood.
> Here, Lord, we sit in heavenly seats
> Beside the crimson flood.

13. Ibid.
14. *JLFA*, 1.182.
15. Rogers, *Experience of Hester Ann Rogers*, 99–100.
16. Wakely, *Lost Chapters*, 241.

> Rise, gather manna round the camp.
> Come, taste of angels' bread.
> Come, now supply your every want.
> Lift up your drooping head.
>
> Here, Lord, we drink the living stream.
> We long, we thirst for more.
> Come to the fountain, wash, be clean
> From sin or Satan's power.
>
> In holy love let us begin
> This day our heaven below.
> Renounce the world, the flesh, and sin.
> Lord, [give] life and light below.
> 'Tis heaven to meet our Jesus here,
> To praise redeeming love.
> Glory to God, we shall appear
> To praise in worlds above.
>
> With shining millions clothed in white,
> All prostrate at thy feet,
> In that blest world of love and light
> No more to part we meet.[17]

This hymn used the very same "sacramental" themes which Ruth lifted up as proof of American Methodists' continuity with the Wesleys in their sacramental piety, yet it was composed concerning a class meeting. The following hymn, from the same hymnal, detailed a love feast. It read,

> Come, Jesus, crown our feast of love.
> We come to meet thee here.
> Send down thy Spirit from above
> And drooping souls to cheer.
>
> We come from far to taste thy love
> And Brethren here to meet,
> To raise our notes to God above,
> To fall beneath his feet.
>
> Lord, thou will hear us when we pray
> And praise thy holy name.
> To us thy goodness, Lord, display.

---

17. Ruth, *Early Methodist Life*, 144–45.

Send down the sacred flame.

Here, Lord, thy children thou dost meet,
To feed the hungry child
The bread of life divinely sweet,
Through Jesus reconciled.

Here, Lord, on earth we speak thy praise.
Thy goodness we adore.
Lord, make us perfect in thy ways
That we may praise thee more.

Glory to God, come taste his love,
Brethren and sisters all.
In streams of blessing from above
From heaven now may it fall.

Here, Lord, we cast our burdens down
Beneath the Savior's cross,
In raptures all our sorrows drown,
Of sin consume the dross.

O wondrous grace, o boundless love,
Our tongues begin to sing,
But when we rise to worlds above
To praise our God and King,

A feast of love we then shall keep
Of perfect love professed,
At God's right hand then take a seat
And reign among the blest.[18]

Again, there is the theme of Jesus being present in the love feast in a real way, with the people meeting him through it and experiencing his grace through the encounter, all seen as proof by Ruth of the American Methodists' continuity with Wesley concerning Eucharistic theology. And yet these very themes are not found in relation to the sacrament, but rather other aspects of an American Methodist's life. Yet one more hymn on the class meeting illustrates the very same principle of God's presence among the people and receiving grace through the experience.

Ye children of the heavenly king

---

18. Ibid., 213–14.

Before your Father bow.
With humble souls your off'rings bring
And pay your solemn vow.

He loves to hear his children pray,
To hear their songs of praise.
Come, he will feed your souls today
To him your voices raise.

From heaven to earth he comes to see,
To meet his children here,
With blessings all divinely free
Their drooping souls to cheer.

Temptations, darkness, fear, or doubt
All flee before his face.
His presence drives the tempter out
From this devoted place.

Make known your want of every kind
By prayer unlock the store.
A balm for every wound you'll find,
Wine, oil for every sore.

Refreshing dews of heavenly love
Fall round this little camp.
Come Holy Spirit, heavenly Dove,
Nor let yours joys be damp.

Celestial fire, consume the dross
and take away the tin.
Then will our longing souls rejoice
And triumph over sin.

Holy desires and heavenly peace
And consolation flow.
While faith and home and love increase
Still more and more bestow.[19]

Just between these three hymns, two concerning a class meeting and one on a love feast, there is language of meeting God face to face, of being divinely fed, of receiving grace, and of heaven and earth meeting together. All this

---

19. Ibid., 266–67.

language could just as easily have been used for the Eucharist, as these are "sacramental" themes. Simply stating that the American Methodists had a similar vocabulary for the Eucharist as Wesley did is not enough to state they had a similar theology as Wesley did. It is obvious this language was used for much more in an American Methodist's life than for the sacrament. This shows that the soteriological dimension of Wesley's Eucharistic theology went beyond the confines of the sacrament itself in the MEC.

Another example of this "sacramental" vocabulary being used for both the Lord's Supper and other instances is the language of "melting," which Ruth uses to highlight the similarities between the American Methodist experience and Wesley's theological descriptions of the Eucharist.[20] While it is true that "melting" was a term that was used for the Eucharist within American Methodist vocabulary, it is also true that this idea of "melting," whether it was a heart, a soul, or some other manifestation, was used in Methodist descriptions of services and gatherings long before they were participating in the Lord's Supper, and continued to be used of various meetings and services after the American Methodists had access to the sacraments. Francis Asbury, not one to effuse with emotive language in his journal, nevertheless recorded instances of people "melting," or of having a "melting time," prior to the Christmas Conference and in reference to preaching or a love feast.[21] William Watters, likewise, used the language of "melting" to describe prayer meetings and even a time of simply speaking in a class meeting.[22] Abel Stevens recorded Nathan Bangs as using the same language of "melting" in reference to preaching and testimonials.[23] And Robert Paine also recorded William McKendree using the language of "melting" in reference to his own personal devotional time and times of preaching.[24]

## QUARTERLY RECEPTION?

The result of this is that, while Ruth was extremely thorough in analyzing primary sources for his research, he nevertheless read those sources through the lens of John Wesley's soteriological dimension of the Eucharist. In so doing, he was led to the conclusion that the language American Methodists used surrounding a celebration of the Lord's Supper was equal in essence, if not in actuality, with Wesley's theology concerning the same.

20. Ruth, *A Little Heaven Below*, 144.
21. *JLFA*, 1.243, 1.299, 1.445.
22. Watters, *Short Account*, 9, 34, 72.
23. Stevens, *Nathan Bangs*, 66, 95, 202.
24. Paine, *Life and Times*, 39, 84, 95, 240.

This predisposition to understand the MEC in light of Wesley's soteriological dimension also led to Ruth's assertion that, from the creation of the MEC in 1784, the Eucharist was designed to be celebrated in quarterly meetings only. As noted before, Ruth stated, "When the preachers met a month later in a specially called conference in Baltimore and some were ordained as elders, the intent appears to have been for them to exercise their new sacramental authority in the context of a quarterly meeting."[25] As proof of this statement, Ruth cited a passage from the Methodist Quarterly Review in 1832 in which Thomas Ware reported on the Christmas Conference. This passage was copied verbatim from Ware's own autobiography in which he stated, "After our organization, we proceeded to elect a sufficient number of elders to visit the quarterly meetings, and administer the ordinances; and this it was which gave rise to the office of presiding elders among us."[26] This statement of Ware's could be read in two different fashions. First, administering the ordinances could be one duty of the elders along with visiting the quarterly conferences, or, second, administering the ordinances could be subsumed within the duty of visiting the quarterly conferences. Ruth chose the latter understanding, which grammatically is not the most appropriate interpretation given the comma in the sentence, thereby delineating separate duties of administering the sacraments and also visiting quarterly meetings.

Further complicating this issue is the fact that Ware linked these elders, ordained in 1784, with the office of presiding elder. As noted above, there are two differing views on the origin of the office of presiding elder. One is typified by Nathan Bangs, who asserted that administering the sacraments was one of the presiding elder's duties and necessity for the position's creation; the other is typified by Abel Stevens who asserted that the office grew out of administrative concerns. Again, it is important to allow the MEC to speak for itself on this matter. In the *1798 Discipline*, under Chapter I, Section V: *Of the Presiding Elders, and of their Duty*, the fifth duty is "to be present, as far as practicable, at all the quarterly meetings: and to call together at each quarterly meeting all the travelling and local preachers, exhorters, stewards, and leaders of the circuit, to hear complaints, and to receive appeals."[27] There is no mention, however, concerning administering the sacraments as a part of the duties of a presiding elder at all. That could be construed as the position evolving over time to the present (1798) state

---

25. Ruth, *A Little Heaven Below*, 119.
26. Ware, *Sketches*, 106–7, and "The Christmas Conference," 98.
27. *1798 Discipline*, 46.

of administration only, however the Notes to this section do not corroborate that interpretation. They state,

> Mr. Wesley informs us in his works, that the whole plan of Methodism was introduced, step-by-step, by the interference and openings of divine Providence. This was the case in the present instance. When Mr. Wesley drew up a plan of government for our church in America, he desired that no more elders should be ordained in the first instance than were absolutely necessary, and that the work on the continent should be divided between them, in respect to the duties of their office. The general conference accordingly elected twelve elders for the above purposes. Bishop Asbury and the district conferences afterwards found that this order of men was so necessary, that they agreed to enlarge the number, and give them the name by which they are at present called, and which is perfectly scriptural, though not the word used in our translation: and this proceeding afterwards received the approbation of Mr. Wesley.[28]

Here, the justification of the office of presiding elder was put forth, and it referred to the administrative functions of the office alone. The Notes went on to further explain that in 1792 the office was made official by the General Conference of that year and presiding elders were empowered to assist the bishops "so to superintend the vast work on this continent as to keep every thing in order in the intervals of the conference."[29] The issue of sacramental authority was quietly dropped from the discussion of the duties of presiding elders or even in the creation of the office of elder itself. In highlighting this portion of the MEC's history, it is difficult to see how one could conceive that the MEC shared Wesley's soteriological dimension of his Eucharistic theology, and because they shared it, they necessarily created a scheme in which the sacrament could only be administered in a quarterly setting. That understanding is not logical.

Yet, by ceasing to read the American Methodists through this lens, it becomes obvious that they were using "sacramental" language for much more than the Eucharist. American Methodists spoke of almost all their services together, both with and without the Eucharist, in these sacramental terms. One cannot simply lift out by example this language about meetings where the Eucharist was celebrated and use that as proof of congruence between Wesleyan theological concepts and American Methodist experience with regards to the Eucharist. Likewise, one cannot with certainty declare

28. Ibid., 49.
29. Ibid.

that the intention at the foundation of the Church was for the MEC to celebrate the sacrament quarterly. On the contrary, the testimony of the early American Methodists shows that the scope of their "sacramental" understanding must be enlarged beyond the Eucharist itself and encompass the Methodists' gatherings themselves. Wesley's soteriological dimension of the Eucharist is found by American Methodists, not in the Eucharist, therefore, but in their meetings together. This can be seen in the bishops' statement regarding the band meetings, that, "There is nothing we know of, which so much quickens the soul to a desire and expectation of the perfect love of God as this."[30] This, then, was the understanding of the Eucharist at the dawn of the nineteenth century, and of camp meeting revivalism, for the American Methodists.

Yet one more position can be clarified with respect to early American Methodist Eucharistic piety by ceasing to read those Methodists through the soteriological dimension of Wesley's Eucharistic theology. Ruth, for all his insistence that the intention of the Christmas Conference was to celebrate the Lord's Supper quarterly, made the observation that "Despite the regularity with which it was included, for various reasons—most of which are obscure—the Lord's Supper was sometimes not administered at quarterly meetings."[31] If one does not look for Wesley's soteriological dimension of Eucharistic theology to be attached to American Methodist Eucharistic practice and piety, this problem solves itself. The Eucharist, for the American Methodists, was primarily ecclesiological in nature, showing they were a true Church. God's grace was experienced by those early Methodists apart from the sacrament in all its salvific qualities as definitively as it was for Wesley in the sacrament. It is no wonder, then, that the sacrament would be absent at times when one would expect it to be present. It is also no wonder, as Ruth has also noted, that the Love Feast retained preeminence in the life of the MEC during this period.[32] The Love Feast, in the closed meeting, was where the soteriological dimension of Wesley's Eucharistic theology was made manifest in the life of the American Methodists. The closed meetings were not to last long, however. On the horizon, a new and extremely open type of meeting was dawning: the Camp Meeting.

---

30. Ibid., 151.
31. Ruth, *A Little Heaven Below*, 120.
32. Ibid.

Chapter 14

# Open Fields

IT HAS BEEN SAID that, after the American Revolution, the Americans simply picked up and moved west, at an almost alarming rate. Nathan Hatch, in his *The Democratization of American Christianity*, noted, "After the Revolution, a single generation of Americans rushed to occupy more land than their forefathers had subdued during the entire colonial period. By 1790 counties that had been virtually unpopulated before the American Revolution claimed one third of the nation's population; ten years later, land unsettled before 1760 claimed over 40 percent of the nation's total, an increase of over 75 percent since 1790."[1] William Warren Sweet stated the situation in more blunt terms by writing, "For the first two generations following independence the American people might be accurately characterized as a society in motion, seemingly bent upon populating the vast empty continent west of the Alleghenies as quickly as possible."[2] This can be seen as well in the addition of preaching stations in areas labeled Kentucky, Tennessee, and Ohio for the MEC at the same time, and the relatively quick elevation of these areas as States in the new nation: Kentucky in 1792, Tennessee in 1796, and Ohio in 1803.

In addition to new preaching stations, districts, and whole conferences that appear in the West during this time, it can be seen in the life of the MEC that its own emphasis was moving west, mirroring that of the United States itself. Kentucky is first mentioned as a circuit in the 1787 minutes, where it was noted that there were ninety members there.[3] By the year 1792, when

---

1. Hatch, *Democratization*, 30.
2. Sweet, *Religion*, 129.
3. Hitt and Ware, *Minutes*, 28.

Kentucky was made a State, the Methodist membership was 1,808.[4] In the areas that made up Tennessee and Ohio, the growth was similar. When the MEC recognized the need for another bishop in 1804, it was William McKendree who was elected, an itinerant who, while having his start in Virginia, spent most of his ministry in the West. As the population moved west, the increasing demographics west of the Alleghenies proved to be an increasingly important locus of power and influence. All of this was beginning to coalesce in 1800.

At this point in history, though, that clout and importance were not yet realized. This is because, according to Sweet, "The great mass of these early settlers were too poor to acquire more than eighty acres, the minimum amount of land that could be purchased, while not a few could buy no land at all and became mere squatters."[5] The reasons for this increase in poorer citizens moving west are varied, but one of the primary motivators was that of the availability of land. While much of the States east of the Alleghenies had been settled, or parceled out to wealthy landowners, there was the lure of new land in the West for potential purchase. This concept of land ownership was a great factor in the westward movement. Ellen Eslinger explains in *Citizens of Zion*

> Land ownership constituted the single most important distinction among free white males in the rural world of early America. The difference between a man who owned no land and another who owned just one hundred acres was much greater than the difference between a man who owned one thousand acres and another who owned two thousand. Regardless of the quantity, men who owned land were what eighteenth-century Americans considered independent. Though often dependent on trade with the outside world for a wide range of goods and services, the man who farmed his own land enjoyed an unmistakable autonomy. He decided for himself how to spend his hours and what crops to plant... Cheap land on the edge of settlement therefore exerted a strong pull on landless citizens and small property owners who worried about providing land for their children.[6]

This explains, in part, why the clear majority of settlers were generally of lower socio-economic classes, and with those rougher elements of society making inroads into new territories, it gives an important insight into the type of person one would find at the forthcoming camp meetings.

4. Ibid., 47.
5. Ibid.
6. Eslinger, *Citizens of Zion*, 67–68.

## THE "FIRST" CAMP MEETING

To say that camp meetings began in Kentucky in 1800 or 1801 is becoming more and more of a caricature of the actual events of religious history leading up to the camp meeting. Recent scholarship is proving that the events in eastern Kentucky at the beginning of the nineteenth century were more or less present in other locales prior to this time. What set the Kentucky revival apart from its historical antecedents was the fact that it was ecumenical in nature and larger in scope than previous events. However, to fully understand what happened in Kentucky, it is necessary to see how this revivalism was congruent with previous religious events.

Owing to the fact that the primary participants of the first camp meetings were Presbyterians, it is necessary to investigate the genesis of the idea of the camp meeting from their own history. To this end, Leigh Eric Schmidt has compiled priceless research in his *Holy Fairs*. In it, Schmidt illuminated the correlation between Scottish sacramental fairs and earlier Roman Catholic festivals. Beginning with the early days of the Scottish Reformation, Schmidt noted, "What the Reformed Church offered in the place of the old calendar and traditional festivals was a spiritual life of sustained discipline and devotion."[7] The problem with this transformation was, according to Schmidt, that while the cycle of festivals was eliminated in the Reformed calendar, nothing was created to take its place. "Day-in, day-out, Sabbath after Sabbath, the Reformed saints were to strive after joyful, harmonious communion with their God and their fellow Christians. Demanding great steadfastness and perseverance, this ideal, grand as it was, often proved unrealistic."[8] While the cycle of mourning and feasting gave the average Catholic Christian something to celebrate, the Reformed alternative gave the average Scottish Protestant hard work with no reason to celebrate.

This was not acceptable to many Scottish Presbyterians. Schmidt noted, "By the early seventeenth century there were discernable signs that a growing group of fervent Presbyterians was ready to counter these oft-noted trends within the Reformed faith. These evangelicals seemed prepared to step into the breach created by the elimination of the high days of medieval Catholicism and offer in their stead a great public event centered on the celebration of the Reformed Lord's Supper."[9] The net effect of these "discernable signs" was the creation of a holy fair. It was a "rejuvenation

---

7. Schmidt, *Holy Fairs*, 17.
8. Ibid.
9. Ibid., 18.

and perpetuation of sacramental festivity."[10] Schmidt wrote, "As with [Roman Catholic celebrations of] Easter and Corpus Christi, the Presbyterian sacramental occasion was to attract great crowds and to evoke great public displays of piety."[11]

As Scots who grew in this setting emigrated from Scotland to the North American colonies, so too they brought this tradition of the holy fair with them. These Presbyterians began worshiping in the ways they knew best. "As early as 1724 at Londonderry, New Hampshire, only four years after the formation of a church there and only five after settlement of the town, over two hundred saints were said to have partaken at the 'communion season.' A decade later the number of communicants at a similar event had grown to seven hundred, many evidently flocking to Londonderry from other Presbyterian settlements."[12] Wherever the Presbyterians settled, they brought this mode of worship with them. Thus, there are accounts of sacramental festivals throughout the colonies prior to the American Revolution. Therefore, when the Presbyterians in Kentucky began to have sacramental festivals, it was merely a continuation of their worship practice for the past several generations.

Concurrent with the spread of these sacramental festivals, the American Methodist Quarterly Meeting was drawn out to last multiple days, usually involving the attendees to camp out at them, and culminating in a love feast. Per Lester Ruth, Methodist quarterly meetings underwent a transformation during the colonial period. He wrote, "By the spring of 1776 a new format for American quarterly meetings began to emerge. It involved two basic changes: the expansion of quarterly meetings from one-day to regular two-day events, and the move to hold the meetings on Saturdays and Sundays."[13] Prior to this development, the quarterly meeting was a one-day affair that dealt with the business of the circuit and culminated in a love feast, a setup that was imported from England as the traditional Wesleyan design for a quarterly meeting.

The change in America that accounted for the need of a multiple day meeting was revival. The specific quarterly meeting that Ruth pointed to as the first two-day event was held in conjunction with the revival that developed under the leadership of Deveraux Jarratt in Virginia.[14] This revival had been growing for months under Jarratt's leadership in his parish, Bath

10. Ibid., 19.
11. Ibid.
12. Ibid., 53.
13. Ruth, *A Little Heaven Below*, 25.
14. Ibid.

in Dinwiddie County, and when the members of the Methodist societies gathered for their quarterly meeting, the passions of revival came to a head. This resulted in the need for a longer period of worship and fellowship, thereby distancing the love feast from the business portion of the meeting.

It was not simply enough for the American Methodists to try some new plan or worship style; if it proved successful, they duplicated it. This was a trait the American Methodists inherited from John Wesley himself. The very concept of the class meeting was stumbled upon, seen to be a success, and reproduced throughout the entirety of Methodism. In fact, Wesley saw the adaptability of Methodism as one of its particular strengths. Regarding the class meeting format disseminated throughout the connection, Wesley wrote

> Some objected, "There were no such meetings [class meetings] when I came into the society first: And why should there now? I do not understand these things, and this changing one thing after another continually." It was easily answered: It is pity but they had been at first. But we knew not then either the need or the benefit of them. Why we use them, you will readily understand, if you read over the rules of the society. That with regard to these little prudential helps we are continually changing one thing after another, is not a weakness or fault, as you imagine, but a peculiar advantage which we enjoy.[15]

In keeping with this "peculiar advantage" of Methodism, the quarterly meeting was spread over two days throughout the colonies from 1776 onward. If it worked in one place, the Methodists transplanted it and used it in another place.

With the holy fairs and the multiple day format for the quarterly meeting, the groundwork was laid for the birth of the camp meeting as an entity in and of itself. The most likely reason something new came about out of these two ingredients was ecumenical cooperation of the Presbyterians and Methodists in Kentucky. That each participated together in the revivals that began in 1800 and 1801 almost ensured that something new would be created. The Methodists were introduced to the concept of a holy fair: that great numbers of people would come together to hear preaching and receive the sacrament. The Presbyterians were introduced to the universal scope of Methodist preaching and the passion with which its preachers delivered it. The large numbers, the passion, the universal call to salvation, and the sacrament all together created a movement in American revivalism that

---

15. Wesley, *Works*, 9.262–63.

Methodists, being true to their heritage, duplicated in every environment in which they could so do.

## CAMP MEETING PIETY AND AMERICAN CULTURE

While the camp meetings themselves were not without organizational precedent within Presbyterian and Methodist polity, neither was their resultant outcome without precedent. During the First Great Awakening, there were many different responses to the revivalism that swept throughout the colonies. These responses have been delineated earlier in this study, but one specific comparison will suffice to show continuity between these camp meeting revivals and the religious culture that had been formed through the revivalism of the First Great Awakening. The comparison that would be most beneficial for this study is that between two preachers, James Davenport of the First Great Awakening period and Lorenzo Dow of Post-Colonial Revivalism. Both were central to their respective revivals, and yet both were on the fringes of the established order. Both had similar styles, and both experienced similar results.

James Davenport was a revivalist who drew praise and condemnation, depending upon who was evaluating his ministry. He itinerated throughout the American Colonies preaching in churches and in fields. He was looked on favorably (at least initially) by George Whitefield and other eminent preachers of the day. And his ministry led to the reported conversions of hundreds, if not thousands of souls during this period. However, as the revival continued through the early 1740's, Davenport's methods, his preaching, and his expected results grew increasingly more uncomfortable for many religious leaders. Thomas Kidd, in his work *The Great Awakening*, wrote about the manifestations that accompanied many of the more radical revivalist preachers, Davenport included, when he noted that there were people "screaming out for mercy . . . [having] shaking, fits, and trances . . . visions."[16] He further explained, "The more such outbursts happened, the more likely they were to continue, and radicals no doubt encouraged these verbal responses from the congregation."[17]

As the responses to preaching increased, so, too, the reactions became more acute against such responses to radical revivalist preaching. Once ministers questioned the legitimacy of such revivalist outbursts, thereby questioning the legitimacy of the conversions purported to have come from such outbursts, Davenport began questioning the salvation of the

16. Kidd, *The Great Awakening*, 131.
17. Ibid.

questioning ministers. He even questioned the salvation of any ministers at all and began "calling out unconverted ministers by name."[18] The reaction to this development was expected: more and more pulpits were closed to Davenport. Without the moderating influence of others around him who did not share such a radical view of conversion and religious experience, Davenport's preferred responses became even more "enthusiastic," and his preaching was less supportive of established churches or their sacraments. His emphasis was on instantaneous conversion and instantaneous assurance of that conversion, as evidenced by shouts, fits, visions and other such demonstrations of such a spiritual state.

Lorenzo Dow, roughly sixty years later, saw similar reactions to his ministry and used them as evidence of the work of God through that ministry just as Davenport had done, and, like Davenport, it was apart from any ecclesial structure or sacrament.[19] Dow was a Methodist, but was not officially sponsored by the MEC to itinerate and preach.[20] "Crazy" Lorenzo Dow, as he was called, "openly claimed to be guided by dreams and visions and implied that he possessed visionary powers to know the secrets of the heart and to foretell the fate of individuals."[21] He wore his hair like that of women of the time and encouraged the same kind of response and behavior that James Davenport had done years earlier. Frederick Norwood wrote of Dow

> In and out of the scene came eccentric figures like Lorenzo Dow who, after hesitation by the annual conference, was admitted on trial in Massachusetts in 1798 and immediately began an industrious, spottily successful, frenetic ministry. He was never admitted in full connection. He disappeared from his appointment because of a 'divine impression'; that he must go to Ireland to proclaim the gospel. Back in the United States, he traveled extensively in the South and Southwest. Everywhere he went his eccentric appearance and manners made a startling impression.[22]

This "startling impression" led to shouts and convulsions among his hearers at camp meetings, and even the formation of the Primitive Methodist Connexion in England when he persuaded several Methodists to

---

18. Ibid., 146.

19. It should be noted that Davenport eventually left his more radical ways and repented of his excesses.

20. Andrews, *Methodists*, 228.

21. Hatch, *Democratization*, 36–37.

22. Norwood, *American Methodism*, 236.

implement the camp meeting format there. This division probably should not be construed as a fundamental difference in styles of preaching, but rather the difference between the cultural backgrounds of the hearers. Leland Scott, in his doctoral dissertation on Methodist theology wrote

> The American frontier did not solicit any new tendencies within the Methodist mind or practice, but simply sustained and underscored elements already characteristic of the Wesleyan heritage. Actually, it was the very "evangelical pragmatism" essential to the Wesleyan movement which so well fitted it for the peculiar demands of the frontier context. The English Methodist itinerant also preached experientially, made plain evangelical appeals, spoke to the emotional and religious hunger of spiritually isolated Welsh coal-miners and English textile workers. There was no extended theological reflection among the eighteenth century Wesleyan preachers in England; rather, there was a concern of practical, evangelical conduct, apart from "doubtful disputations." To compare the experiences, preaching, and doctrinal concerns of the English and American Methodist itinerants is to be struck by their basic identity.[23]

In this it can be seen that the social circumstances among the Methodist audiences on both sides of the Atlantic were similar; what was dissimilar, and dissimilar enough to allow for general acceptance of camp meetings in America and their general rejection in England, was the religious background of the First Great Awakening and radical preachers like Davenport.

The fact that Dow conducted himself in an extremely reminiscent manner to that of Davenport shows how the religious culture in America had not significantly altered in the intervening years from the 1740s to the 1800s. The religious authorities' responses were reminiscent as well. They tolerated Dow, and that was the limit of their acceptance of him. This toleration may be intimated by the fact that Asbury recorded only one reference to Dow in his *Journal*, and that entry (July 9, 1807) was only that he dined at Dow's home.[24] For one of the most popular "Methodist" preachers of the day, the lack of mention is notable. The masses of people loved Dow for his unusual ways of preaching. Both Davenport and Dow focused on the Final Judgment as a reason for and justification of their radical methods. With Dow, one of the more extreme preachers of the era, there can be seen a continuity within the religious culture of America from the revivals of the

---

23. Scott, "Methodist Theology," 23.
24. *JLFA*, 2.545.

colonial era, specifically under the leadership of James Davenport, and that of the early years of the new nation.

## CAMP MEETING CULTURE AND AMERICAN METHODIST PIETY

In America, the post-colonial revivalism that was typified by the camp meeting was not new, as was demonstrated above. Its roots in Presbyterian sacramental meetings and Methodist quarterly meetings are obvious. What is of interest to this study, however, is how those roots were congruent or incongruent with what would become one of the singularly defining characteristics of Methodist piety for at least the next fifty years.

Camp meetings very quickly became normative in the life of the MEC. One reason for this is that they found a champion in Francis Asbury. Asbury, like Wesley, was very pragmatic in his approach to ecclesiastical life. If a particular event or style of ministry worked in one place, his goal was to replicate it other places. Asbury wrote a letter to John Dickins' wife on September 12, 1801 in which he expressed awe at the reports of one of the first camp meetings in Kentucky, most likely the Cane Ridge meeting in 1801. He wrote, "The work of God is running like fire in Kentucky. It is reported that near fifteen if not twenty thousand were present at one Sacramental occasion of the Presbyterians; and one thousand if not fifteen hundred fell and felt the power of grace."[25] Five years later, Asbury's admiration for this mode of ministry had not diminished in the least. On November 7, 1806 Asbury wrote to Thornton Fleming, the presiding elder on the Monongahela District in the Baltimore Conference,[26] "Oh, my brother, when all our quarterly meetings become campmeetings [sic], and 1000 souls should be converted, our American millennium will begin."[27] This is exactly what was to happen: the camp meeting would eventually replace the quarterly meeting as the locus of Methodist piety and revival in America.

It is not difficult to see how this transition occurred, especially when someone such as Asbury was pressing for such a transition. Nevertheless, it would not have happened if there were not tangible results seen for the Methodists in the camp meeting. It was already a readily identifiable concept: a multi-day meeting where people camped overnight. As Lester Ruth pointed out, this had been happening in the life of the MEC for several years already. The difference was the scope of the camp meeting and the focus of

---

25. Ibid., 3.226
26. Hitt and Ware, *Minutes*, 140.
27. *JLFA*, 3.357.

it. No longer were these meetings designed primarily for the Methodists from a particular circuit; now they were designed to attract any and all, from hither and yon. John Totten published an apologia for camp meetings in 1810 in which he described the types of people who attended a typical camp meeting. He wrote

> There are many, who, for various reasons, seldom, and some perhaps never see the inside of a house of worship; some, because they have no relish for religious exercise; others, because they are irksome to them; not a few, because they cannot attire themselves in a manner judged suitable by their pride, to appear in a gay, modish congregation; and many more, because of their avowed enmity to Jesus Christ and his religion. But Camp-meetings attract the attention, and draw together some of all these, and many other characters and descriptions of men and women; as well as Christians of different sects and persuasions, from some motive or other; if not Christians, often curiosity; fondness or novelty; inquisitive speculations; philosophical, religious, or literary criticism; sectarian opposition; romantic disposition; and a propensity to trifle with, and ridicule sacred things.[28]

While much of the quarterly meeting was closed to non-Methodists, the entirety of the camp meeting was evangelistic in nature, specifically intending to reach those who were not yet Christian. It is because of this facet of design that American Methodism made yet another subtle change in their piety from the theology they inherited from Wesley. As demonstrated previously, the soteriological dimension of Wesley's Eucharistic theology was, consciously or not, transferred by the American Methodists to their meetings, both class and band. They saw God working in the same soteriological manner here as Wesley did through the Eucharist, and they used the same language to describe that work. The high point and culmination of these meetings was often the love feast, which explained why the American Methodists would use the same language for the love feasts as the sacrament in describing God's presence among them, and why the bishops would state the meetings "[became] one of the most profitable means of grace in the whole compass of Christian discipline"[29] precisely because God transformed "the very hindrances themselves [lack of access to the sacraments] into the most profitable of all means."[30]

28. Richey, Rowe, and Schmidt, *Methodist Experience*, 166.
29. *1798 Discipline*, 151.
30. Ibid., 145.

Because of these developments in American Methodist piety, bringing to ascendancy in their soteriological understanding the meeting and shifting emphasis away from the sacrament as the means of grace *par excellence*, the meetings of the society needed to be protected from impropriety. Thus, the bishops included a Note in the *1798 Discipline* to that effect on Chapter II, Section IV: *Of the Privileges granted to serious Persons who are not of the Society*, which dealt with how often a non-Methodist ought to be admitted to a meeting and/or love feast. The answer to the query was "not above twice or thrice,"[31] but the theological reasoning behind the answer is what is most illuminating for this study. The bishops noted,

> It is manifestly our duty to fence in our society, and to preserve it from intruders; otherwise we should soon become a desolate waste. God would write Ichabod upon us, and the glory would be departed from Israel. At the same time we should suffer those who are apparently sincere, if they request it, to see our order and discipline twice or thrice, that they themselves may judge, whether it will be for their spiritual advantage to cast in their lot among us. But we should by no means exceed the indulgence here allowed; otherwise we should make our valuable meetings for Christian fellowship cheap and contemptible, and bring a heavy burden on the minds of our brethren.[32]

The closed meeting was an important facet of American Methodist life and piety, with or without the presence of the sacrament at it. Ruth rightly pointed out that it was the testimonials given at such meetings, usually attached to the love feast, that were the impetus for closing the meetings. He wrote,

> The freedom to testify to Christian experience openly—and the concomitant Methodist understanding that God's presence was experienced anew in these testimonies—was closely tied to a more explicitly theological reason for restricting access to love feasts. Simply put, early Methodists considered that God was uniquely present and revealed in their midst when they gathered as God's distinct people. Mixture with unawakened outsiders voided the condition by which God was present and revealed. Methodists restricted admission to their worship because there they experienced the glorious presence of God.[33]

---

31. Ibid., 153.
32. Ibid., 154.
33. Ruth, *A Little Heaven Below*, 116.

This was not only true of the love feast, but also for the Eucharist. More often than not, during the period under discussion for this study, the Eucharist was administered in a closed setting. As the Notes in the *1798 Discipline* point out in Chapter I, Section XXIII: *Of the Lord's Supper*,

> We must also observe, that our elders should be very cautious how they admit to the communion persons who are not in our society. It would be highly injurious to our brethren, if we suffered any to partake of the Lord's supper with them, whom we would not readily admit into our society on application made to us. Those whom we judge unfit to partake of our profitable, prudential means of grace, we should most certainly think improper to be partakers of an ordinance which has been expressly instituted by Christ himself.[34]

While this does not mean that the Eucharist was solely administered in a closed meeting, which in fact it was not, it does expand the "fence" to which the bishops referred around not only the meetings of the societies, but also the Lord's table within the MEC. In practice, because of the Eucharist being administered within the context of a quarterly meeting, it was usually restricted to the Methodists at those meetings. Ruth himself only gives four instances for when it was not administered solely to Methodists in his analysis of early Methodism. Two of the incidents are beyond the scope of this study (occurring after the camp meetings had begun), but the two that are pertinent for us are from Bishops Coke and Asbury. The incident with Coke occurred in George-town, South Carolina in March of 1789. Coke "gave permission to any serious persons of the congregation who desired it, to communicate with us."[35] Ruth used this as an example of a less stringent fencing of the Eucharistic table than the love feast. The problem with this interpretation of this instance is that, according to Coke, there were no Methodists in George-town at this time. He was preaching at the courthouse and was asked to administer the Lord's Supper by the family with which he had been staying. There was no way to restrict the reception of the Lord's Supper to Methodists here because Coke was the only one. The incident with Asbury was at the New York Conference on September 2, 1792. Here Asbury, in the context of his sermon, showed "who were proper communicants—true penitents and real believers."[36] Again, this was used by Ruth to show anyone was welcome to receive the sacrament, but the context of the remark is in a Methodist conference, where the majority, if not

34. *1798 Discipline*, 120.
35. Coke, *Journals*, 121.
36. *JLFA*, 1.729.

all, of the attendees would be Methodists. It was not such an open invitation as it would seem.

## THE CAMP MEETING TRANSFORMATION

All of this highlights the fact that, for the MEC at the dawn of the nineteenth century, the closed meeting and a fenced society were seen as essential to the presence of God in the midst of the Methodists and their very success as a movement of God. By the time John Totten had written his apology for camp meetings, this attitude was beginning to change, and thus, Methodist piety was about to undergo a change as well. As the camp meetings grew, the emphasis began to shift to the preaching and praying at those meetings for the particular presence of God in the work of the Church. Whereas the power and presence of God was explicated by Wesley in the sacrament, and subsequently testified to by the MEC in its closed meetings, now it was seen in the mass conversions of the evangelically driven camp meetings. An example of this shift in focus for the work of God can be seen in one of the most famous later accounts of American Methodism, *The Autobiography of Peter Cartwright*. Cartwright's narrative moves from camp meeting to conference, from conference to camp meeting, and there are very few references at all to the Eucharist. This is especially interesting given the origin of the camp meetings in Presbyterian sacramental occasions.

This origin was not unknown to Cartwright. He recounted, "Somewhere between 1800 and 1801, in the upper part of Kentucky, at a memorable place called 'Cane Ridge,' there was appointed a sacramental meeting by some of the Presbyterian ministers, at which meeting, seemingly unexpected by ministers or people, the mighty power of God was displayed in a very extraordinary manner; many were moved to tears, and bitter and loud crying for mercy."[37] The term the Presbyterians used for this meeting and the circumstances surrounding it were known to Cartwright, and not just from reports about this particular meeting. In fact, Cartwright was converted at one such meeting. He further recounted, "In the spring of this year [1801], Mr. M'Grady, a minister of the Presbyterian Church, who had a congregation and meeting-house, as we then called them, about three miles north of my father's house, appointed a sacramental meeting in this congregation and invited the Methodist preachers to attend with them."[38] It was here, during that meeting, that Cartwright experienced salvation. "In the midst of a solemn struggle of soul, an impression was made on my mind, as though

37. Cartwright, *Autobiography*, 30.
38. Ibid., 36.

a voice said to me, 'Thy sins are forgiven thee.' Divine light flashed all round me, unspeakable joy sprung up in my soul. I rose to my feet, opened my eyes, and it really seemed as if I was in heaven; the trees, the leaves on them, and everything seemed, and I really thought were, praising God."[39] Here Cartwright espoused the same language used of the sacramental presence of God in Wesley's Eucharistic theology, and in the language of the closed meetings of the American Methodists of the previous century. While that is a point worth remembering for future reference, another point is that this is one of the last times Cartwright identified these types of meetings as sacramental meetings. There are only two other instances in which Cartwright used the same term, both in 1816 and both on the same circuit.[40] Outside of these two instances, the term camp meeting is used exclusively, and there is no mention of the sacrament ever being at them again. The emphasis had shifted from the sacramental portion of the meeting to the preaching and convicting portion of the meeting.

This transition is also hinted at in Jesse Lee's description of a camp meeting layout at the conclusion of his *Short History*. After giving a description of the layout of the camp, Lee recounted the typical format of a camp meeting. He stated

> We proceed in our religious exercises as follows: soon after the first dawn of day, a person walks all round the ground in front of the tents, blowing a trumpet as he passes; which is to give the people notice to rise; about ten minutes after the trumpet is blown again with only one long blast; upon which, the people in all their tents begin to sing, and then pray, either in their tents, or at the door of them, as is most convenient. At the rising of the sun a sermon is preached, after which we eat breakfast. We have preaching again at 10 o'clock, and dine about one. We preach again at 3 o'clock, eat supper about the setting of the sun, and have preaching again at candle light. We generally begin these meetings on Fridays, and continue them until the Monday following about the middle of the day. I have known these meetings to continue without any intermission for two nights and a day, or longer. The people being continually engaged in singing, praying, preaching, or exhorting without any cessation.[41]

This account was written in 1809, and gone is any reference to the sacrament. It would appear that, as the camp meeting succeeded the quarterly meeting,

---

39. Ibid., 37.
40. Ibid., 176–78.
41. Lee, *A Short History*, 361–62.

the sacrament remained within the context of the quarterly meeting in which it had been placed two decades earlier and references to it become fewer and fewer. This is not surprising, given the fact that the dominant understanding of the Eucharist for the MEC was ecclesiological in nature. The camp meetings did not impinge upon the authority or validity of the MEC as a Church; therefore, there was no need to mention the sacrament at all. In addition, Wesley's soteriological understanding of the Eucharist was moving from the closed meeting to the camp meeting, resulting in a lesser frequency of quarterly meetings as examples of God's presence and a greater frequency of the camp meetings as such. This is also seen in an increased tendency for the quarterly meeting to revert to an almost exclusively business meeting for the MEC as the camp meeting became the locus for revival and God's grace. Ruth has noted, "Unforeseen and unintended was the eventual effect on the role of quarterly meetings. The emergence and promotion of camp meetings as a concentrated form of quarterly meeting helped set the path in the nineteenth century for returning quarterly meetings to an exclusive devotion to administrative business."[42]

This development in post-colonial revivalism, while changing the focus of the MEC's labors from the closed meetings, directed primarily toward Methodists, to the camp meetings, with a broad evangelistic appeal, did not affect their understanding of the Eucharist very much at all. Since the predominant view of the Eucharist was ecclesiological in nature, it was simply a given that they would celebrate it as often as they felt necessary, as "the two sacraments . . . have been allowed to be essential to the formation of a Christian church, by every party and denomination in every age and country of Christendom."[43] Through this understanding, even as the Church's emphasis shifted to revival preaching at the camp meetings, their Eucharistic theology remained the same; it was a sign that demarcated the MEC as a legitimate Church, and as such, was immensely important to the life of the Church, but not in the same manner as it was for Wesley or many of the English Methodists as seen above.

---

42. Ruth, *A Little Heaven Below*, 190.
43. *1798 Discipline*, 6.

# Conclusion

THIS STUDY HAS AS its goal to show the change in the experience of God's grace in American Methodism from the full tables of Wesley to the closed doors of the society meetings to the open fields of the camp meetings. Through this study two factors in this investigation have become apparent and crucial for that understanding. The first factor is that there are two prevailing views within scholarship concerning American Eucharistic practice: either American practice was in continuity with John Wesley and his wishes for his spiritual children, or American practice was in discontinuity with Wesley and his wishes. The second factor is that one's interpretation of the historical record and one's theological understanding of the American Methodist experience hinges upon the Flauvanna Conference of 1779. Theological presuppositions shape how theologians and historians view the reasons leading up to that conference and then, based upon that interpretation, one has a framework of understanding in which to fit the Christmas Conference of 1784, the creation of the Methodist Episcopal Church, and the resultant sacramental piety and understanding that was implemented or reinforced in subsequent years.

Two leading Methodist scholars with opposite positions on this issue summarized these two different understandings well. In arguing that the American Methodists were in continuity with Wesley, Lester Ruth has stated, "While some scholars have recognized the connection between the Eucharist and quarterly meetings, the connection has been portrayed as evidence of a low sacramental piety and of the Eucharist's non-central role in early Methodist worship. In fact, the exact opposite might be the case. Placement of the Eucharist within the rhythm of quarterly meetings might actually reflect the high regard early Methodists had for the Eucharist."[1] For Ruth, the system that was created in 1784 was one that showed a high value

---

1. Ruth, "Reconsideration of the Frequency," 57–58.

of sacramental piety by the American Methodists. In exact opposition to this position is Randy Maddox, who has stated

> In the prefatory letter to this volume [the *Sunday Service*] Wesley had implored the American Methodists to celebrate the Lord's Supper weekly. This request was no passing fancy, nor a mere concern with liturgical etiquette. Wesley had come to value the Lord's Supper as the "grand channel" whereby the empowering grace of the Spirit is conveyed to human souls. He longed for his American followers to be nourished frequently by this grace. But this was not to be, because the American Methodists did not share Wesley's valuation of the Lord's Supper. To be sure, prior to 1784 some American lay preachers had lobbied for sacramental rights, but this had more to do with their tension with—and ridicule by—Anglican priests than a concern for enabling frequent communion. They actually viewed the Lord's Supper more as a duty than as a vital means of grace, and were content to interpret lack of opportunity as suspending the obligation to receive! This helps explain why, even when ordination to sacramental rights came, the celebration of communion remained infrequent—at most usually only at quarterly conference.[2]

These two views are the essence of scholarly debate upon the issue of the sacraments regarding American Methodism and the experience of grace. The bottom line for them is that either the American Methodists followed Wesley or they represented a radical departure from Wesley with respect to the sacraments.

This study has shown that there is a third option to this debate. American Methodists did, in fact, follow Wesley *and* depart from his leading. The reason this statement can be made is because neither Wesley nor the American Methodists were uni-dimensional in their understanding of the Eucharist. As demonstrated above, Wesley had two understandings of the Eucharist. The first was soteriological, in seeing the sacrament as a means of grace. In this respect, Wesley understood it as the means of grace *par excellence*. All of Wesley's admonitions to receive the sacrament as often as possible, his requirement for regular communion for membership in a class and band, his sermon on Constant Communion, must all be seen in this light. Wesley additionally had an ecclesiological understanding of the Eucharist. This is his understanding, in line with the Articles of Religion, that the administration of the sacraments is one of the markers of a true Church. All of Wesley's rhetoric against allowing Methodists to administer

---

2. Maddox, "Social Grace," 136–37.

the sacraments must be seen in this light. When using Wesley to illuminate any Methodist's understanding of the Eucharist, one must delineate which understanding of Wesley's Eucharistic theology is the primary lens through which to view the issue at hand. For Wesley then, the soteriological dimension was always primary and the ecclesiological dimension was secondary. For the American Methodists, the ecclesiological dimension was primary and the soteriological dimension was secondary. This can be most readily seen in the issue of the Flauvanna Conference.

The essence of what happened at the Flauvanna Conference is quite simple to report. In the absence of Francis Asbury's leadership (and the northern preachers' votes) the Annual Conference of 1779 that met in Flauvanna County Virginia decided to take up the topic of administering the sacraments that the previous two years' conferences had tabled. In so doing, the conference voted to create an executive committee to oversee the process, ordain the preachers, and send them out of the conference with the new authority to administer the sacraments. As seen in this study, reporting what happened by scholars has not been difficult; reasoning why it happened has proven much more complex an issue.

One line of reasoning, typified by Lester Ruth in his works, is that early American Methodists had a high sacramental piety and their desire to give themselves the power and authority to administer those sacraments proves the point, seeking the opportunity for the full tables of Methodism. This is the underlying assumption of those scholars who would state that the Flauvanna Conference was the logical outcome of the sacramental issue for American Methodists. Superficially, this seems like a valid point. American Methodists did struggle for access to the sacraments by the hands of their own preachers for several years, yet this conclusion is flawed.

These scholars essentially limit American Methodists' understanding of the Lord's Supper to John Wesley's soteriological dimension alone and read all the debates through that lens. If one only sees the soteriological dimension in Wesley's Eucharistic theology, and transposes Wesley's theology upon American Methodism, then it would only be natural to conclude that the Fluvanna Conference decision was motivated by a desire for greater access to the supreme means of grace. And using Wesley's theology in a uni-dimensional fashion such as this is the primary flaw in the scholarship concerning this Conference, and the one flaw that most directly leads to the flawed conclusion that Flauvanna was about a high sacramental piety in a soteriological sense.

However, when the actual journals and letters of those American Methodists were analyzed, it showed that the motivation for the Flauvanna Schism was to declare the Methodists independent of the Church of England,

and perhaps even John Wesley himself. The debate that occurred over that conference was focused exclusively on the ecclesial concerns raised by the decision. All the preachers were concerned about the unity of Methodism and made their arguments based upon whether they should stay united with one another and the Church of England. There was no mention in their papers of the Eucharist as being the supreme means of grace, or even of it being a means of grace at all. When the Lord's Supper was referred to (even obliquely) as a means of grace by Francis Asbury, he stated that the absence of availability of the sacrament suspended the necessity to receive it.[3] This is because the closed doors of the society meeting already fulfilled that roll. And this is the precise point that Randy Maddox used as the underlying assumption in his position stated above, that the American Methodists had no real sacramental piety and their decision at Flauvanna had more to do with wounded pride on the part of the preachers who had to endure "ridicule" from the Anglican priests. Yet this conclusion, as well, suffers from a unidimensional approach to Wesley and the American Methodists with respect to the Eucharist. Maddox did not find a soteriological understanding of the Eucharist in the American Methodist corpus, and thus concluded that they did not have a high sacramental piety at all.

What this study has demonstrated is that it is necessary to affirm that the American Methodists did have a high Eucharistic piety, but in its ecclesiological dimension. Contrary to Maddox's assessment above, it was not simply because of ridicule that the American Methodists would have risked schism and division between their brothers in their connection. It was precisely because they had such a high understanding of the sacraments as setting apart a true Church, per the definition of a Church in the Thirty-Nine Articles, that they took the momentous and risk-laden step of ordaining themselves to administer the sacraments. While it may seem counterintuitive to say there was a high sacramental piety when the sacrament essentially was used as a tool for separation by the American Methodists, it must be remembered that the only reason the American Methodists sought to cause and justify their separation from the Church of England with the sacramental issue was precisely because they had such a high estimation of the sacraments' place in the life of a Church, specifically demarcating what a true Church is. They understood how powerful a tool for separation the sacraments were, and as such, debated their place within American Methodism for years prior to the Flauvanna Conference. Such was the high value of the sacraments for them in their quest for an independent Church that the

---

3. *JLFA*, 3.31.

decision to ordain themselves and administer the sacraments by themselves was not taken lightly.

In 1784, when Wesley ordained Richard Whatcoat and Thomas Vasey, and consecrated Thomas Coke, a predominantly soteriological dimension of the sacraments informed the explanation he gave for this step. The issue for Wesley was that his Methodists in America no longer had access to the sacraments as a result of the Revolutionary War. To correct this very serious problem in the life of his followers, Wesley separated the American Methodists from the Established Church and gave them sacramental authority. While this seems to be the very same action taken by the Flauvanna Conference, understanding the multi-dimensional facets of Wesley's (and the Methodists') Eucharistic theology and piety make the situation clear. At Flauvanna, the Methodists saw the sacraments as a means of achieving an independent church; in England, Wesley saw an independent church as a means of providing the sacraments. This is the key to understanding the dilemma of early American Eucharistic piety and to seeing how that piety was lived out in the transition from the Eucharist to society meeting to camp meeting.

Because of having a primarily ecclesiological understanding of the Eucharist, the American Methodists saw their newfound sacramental authority as a legitimization of their status as a Church. With this understanding, then, it becomes apparent why the sacrament was relegated mostly to a quarterly meeting. Beyond having authority to administer the sacrament, there was no overriding concern to provide it to the people. This can be seen in Ruth's own admission that the sacrament was not even included in quarterly meetings on many occasions.[4] In addition, as has been demonstrated by this study, there was no further call for access to the sacraments by clergy or laity of the MEC in the subsequent years following its creation at the Christmas Conference. What was Wesley's soteriological dimension of Eucharistic theology, namely that the Lord's Supper was the means of grace *par excellence* and ought to be received as often as one could so do, was not associated with the Eucharist for the American Methodists. Rather, as evidenced by numerous statements in the *1798 Discipline* by Francis Asbury and Thomas Coke, the American Methodists saw the Methodist meeting itself as the supreme means of grace. As time would proceed, and in the post-colonial revival era where camp meetings gained ascendancy over quarterly meetings, that soteriological dimension would be relocated from the Methodist meeting to the revivalistic preaching of the camp meeting. This fell in line with prior Methodist practice to emphasize and replicate

---

4. Ruth, *A Little Heaven Below*, 120.

what practically works in the life of its members. Camp meetings were arenas of great conversion and experiencing of God's grace, therefore they were put forward as the best of all methods for receiving that grace.[5]

It is understandable why, when looking at John Wesley's understanding of the Eucharist and Methodist experiences of grace, that contemporary Wesleyan Methodists have expressed confusion at the state of the sacraments among them today. However, as this study has shown, the incongruence between American Methodists and Wesley significantly preceded the creation of any current denominations. In fact, the present situation occurred precisely because there was both congruence and incongruence between the MEC and Wesley. The MEC, through its ecclesiologically driven understanding of the sacrament, thought it was keeping faith with Wesley and his theology, all the while moving further from implementing his soteriological understanding of the sacrament. Thus, Methodists today do indeed stand well within Wesley's Eucharistic theology, albeit the ecclesiological dimension of it. The soteriological dimension changed from the *full tables* of the Eucharist to the *closed doors* of the society meeting to the *open fields* of the camp meeting.

---

5. *JLFA*, 3.251, 357.

# Appendix A

# Eucharistic References in John Wesley's Works (Jackson)

| Page | Soteriological | Ecclesiological | Other |
|---|---|---|---|
| 1.247–80 | X | | |
| 1.328 | X | | |
| 3.183 | | | X |
| 5.187 | X | | |
| 5.201 | | | X |
| 5.281 | X | | |
| 5.338 | X | | |
| 6.403 | | | X |
| 6.511 | X | | |
| 7.147 | X | | |
| 7.175 | X | | |
| 7.183 | | X | |
| 7.279 | | X | |
| 8.30–2 | | X | |
| 8.149 | | X | |
| 8.224 | | X | |
| 8.280 | | X | |
| 8.320 | | X | |
| 8.323 | X | | |

| Page | Soteriological | Ecclesiological | Other |
| --- | --- | --- | --- |
| 8.376–7 | X | | |
| 8.403–4 | X | | |
| 8.416–7 | X | | |
| 8.434 | X | | |
| 8.442 | | X | |
| 8.444 | | X | |
| 8.486–7 | X | | |
| 9.505 | | X | |
| 10.117–23 | | | X |
| 10.149–58 | | | X |
| 10.184–5 | | X | |
| 10.201–4 | X | | |
| 13.144 | | X | |
| 13.262 | | X | |
| 13.267 | | X | |

This is not meant to be an exhaustive list of every Eucharistic reference Wesley made. Instead, this is for illustrative purposes, showing that Wesley did indeed have two different dimensions to his Eucharistic understanding and theology.

# Appendix B

# American Methodist Membership by Circuit

**1779–1780**

| Circuit | 1779 Membership | 1780 Membership | Change | "Flauvanna Circuit" | Person(s) Appointed |
|---|---|---|---|---|---|
| New Jersey | 140 | 196 | 56 | No | |
| Philadelphia | 89 | 90 | 1 | No | |
| Chester | 90 | 100 | 10 | No | |
| Delaware | 795 | 150 | -645 | No | |
| Sussex | 0 | 260 | 260 | No | |
| Kent | 493 | 725 | 232 | No | |
| Baltimore | 900 | 880 | -20 | No | |
| Frederick | 480 | 524 | 44 | No | |
| North Sub Total | 2987 | 2925 | -62 | | |
| Fairfax | 309 | 361 | 52 | Yes | William Gill, Edward Bailey |
| Berkley | 191 | 205 | 14 | Yes | John Tunnell, John Hagerty |
| Flauvanna | 300 | 342 | 42 | Yes | **Carter Cole, Nelson Reed** |
| Hanover | 281 | 351 | 70 | Yes | **Charles Hopkins, John Major** |
| Amelia | 470 | 506 | 36 | Yes | **Isham Tatum, Samuel Rowe** |

APPENDIX B

| Circuit | 1779 Membership | 1780 Membership | Change | "Flauvanna Circuit" | Person(s) Appointed |
|---|---|---|---|---|---|
| Sussex | 655 | 620 | -35 | Yes | **Francis Poythress**, Stith Parham, John Beck |
| Brunswick | 656 | 454 | -202 | Yes | **Thomas Morris**, Richard Ivy, **James Morris** |
| Mecklenburg | 498 | 455 | -43 | Yes | **Reuben Ellis**, **John Sigman** |
| Pittsylvania | 500 | 634 | 134 | Yes | **Leroy Cole**, Greenberry Green, John Atkins |
| Yadkin | 0 | 21 | 21 | N/A | |
| Roan-Oak | 470 | 480 | 10 | Yes | John Dickins, **Henry Willis** |
| Tar-River | 455 | 455 | 0 | Yes | **Andrew Yeargan**, **William Moore** |
| New-Hope | 542 | 455 | -87 | Yes | **James O'Kelly**, Philip Adams |
| Charlotte | 186 | 0 | -186 | N/A | |
| James-City | 77 | 0 | -77 | N/A | |
| South Sub Total | 5590 | 5339 | -251 | | |
| | | | | | bold indicates approval of Flauvanna in Gatch's Minutes |
| Totals | 8577 | 8264 | -313 | | |

# Appendix C

# Francis Asbury's Eucharistic Celebrations 1785–1800

## As Recorded in His Journal

| Year | Page | Date | Location | Eucharist | Love Feast | Quarterly Meeting |
|---|---|---|---|---|---|---|
| 1785 | | | | | | |
| | 1.480 | Sat Jun 15 | VA | X | | |
| | 1.480 | Tue Jan 18 | VA | X | X | |
| | 1.481 | Thu Feb 3 | NC | X | | |
| | 1.481 | Tue Feb 8 | NC | X | X | |
| | 1.488 | Tue Apr 10 | VA | X | | |
| | 1.490 | Wed Jun 1 | MD | | X | |
| | 1.490 | Sun Jul 3 | VA | X | | |
| | 1.494 | Sun Aug 28 | PA | X | | |
| | 1.494 | Sun Sep 4 | NY | | X | |
| | 1.495 | Sat Sep 24 | NJ | X | | |
| | 1.496 | Mon Oct 3 | DE | X | | |
| | 1.497 | Mon Oct 24 | MD | X | | X |
| | 1.499 | Sun Dec 18 | NC | X | | |

| Year | Page | Date | Location | Eucharist | Love Feast | Quarterly Meeting |
|---|---|---|---|---|---|---|
| 1786 | | | | | | |
| | 1.507 | Mon Jan 23 | SC | X | | |
| | 1.508 | Thu Feb 9 | NC | X | | X |
| | 1.509 | Thu Mar 2 | NC | X | | |
| | 1.516 | Sun Jul 2 | PA | X | | |
| | 1.517 | Mon Jul 10 | VA | X | | |
| | 1.521 | Fri Sep 29 | NJ | X | | |
| | 1.522 | Sat Oct 14 | NJ | X | | |
| | 1.522 | Sun Oct 15 | PA | X | | |
| | 1.523 | Sun Oct 29 | DE | X | | |
| | 1.523 | Fri Nov 10 | MD | | X | |
| | 1.526 | Tue Dec 5 | DE | | X | |
| | 1.526 | Sun Dec 17 | MD | X | | |
| 1787 | | | | | | |
| | 1.531 | Sun Jan 7 | VA | | X | X |
| | 1.532 | Sun Jan 14 | VA | X | | |
| | 1.533 | Wed Jan 31 | VA | X | X | X |
| | 1.534 | Tue Feb 27 | NC | X | X | |
| | 1.536 | Sun Apr 8 | NC | X | | X |
| | 1.543 | Sun Jun 17 | NY | X | X | |
| | 1.543 | Mon Jun 18 | NY | X | | |
| | 1.544 | Wed Jun 20 | NY | X | | |
| | 1.544 | Sat Jun 23 | NJ | X | | |
| | 1.544 | Sun Jun 24 | NJ | X | | |
| | 1.547 | Sun Jul 22 | MD | X | | |
| | 1.548 | Sun Jul 29 | VA | X | X | |
| | 1.549 | Sun Aug 26 | VA | X | X | |
| | 1.550 | Sun Sep 30 | PA | X | | |
| | 1.551 | Fri Oct 5 | PA | | X | |
| | 1.551 | Sun Oct 7 | PA | X | | |
| | 1.552 | Sun Oct 21 | DE | X | | |
| | 1.552 | Mon Oct 29 | VA | X | X | |
| | 1.553 | Fri Nov 2 | MD | X | | |

| Year | Page | Date | Location | Eucharist | Love Feast | Quarterly Meeting |
|---|---|---|---|---|---|---|
| | 1.553 | Sat Nov 3 | MD | | X | |
| | 1.556 | Sun Dec 23 | VA | X | | |
| 1788 | | | | | | |
| | 1.563 | Sat Mar 1 | SC | | X | X |
| | 1.564 | Sun Mar 16 | SC | | X | X |
| | 1.565 | Wed Mar 26 | SC | X | | |
| | 1.573 | Sun May 25 | NC | X | X | |
| | 1.576 | Thu Jul 10 | VA | X | | X |
| | 1.579 | Fri Aug 29 | VA | | X | X |
| | 1.581 | Wed Oct 29 | MD | X | | |
| 1789 | | | | | | |
| | 1.590 | Sun Jan 18 | NC | X | X | |
| | 1.597 | Tue May 12 | MD | X | | |
| | 1.606 | Sat Jul 25 | PA | | X | X |
| | 1.608 | Sun Sep 13 | MD | XX | | |
| | 1.609 | Sun Oct 4 | DE | X | X | |
| | 1.611 | Tue Oct 20 | DE | | X | |
| | 1.612 | Fri Oct 30 | VA | X | X | |
| | 1.612 | Fri Nov 6 | VA | X | X | X |
| | 1.612 | Sat Nov 7 | MD | | X | X |
| | 1.616 | Tue Dec 29 | VA | X | | |
| 1790 | | | | | | |
| | 1.621 | Sat Jan 16 | NC | X | | |
| | 1.623 | Sun Jan 31 | SC | | X | |
| | 1.628 | Thu Mar 11 | GA | | X | |
| | 1.648 | Sun Aug 22 | VA | | X | X |
| | 1.651 | Fri Sep 24 | PA | | X | X |
| | 1.651 | Wed Sep 29 | NJ | | X | X |
| | 1.653 | Sun Oct 17 | DE | | X | |
| | 1.653 | Thu Oct 21 | DE | | X | X |
| | 1.654 | Tue Oct 26 | DE | X | | |
| | 1.655 | Sun Oct 31 | VA | | X | X |
| | 1.655 | Mon Nov 1 | VA | | X | |

## 204 APPENDIX C

| Year | Page | Date | Location | Eucharist | Love Feast | Quarterly Meeting |
|---|---|---|---|---|---|---|
|  | 1.656 | Tue Nov 9 | MD |  | X | X |
|  | 1.656 | Thu Nov 11 | MD |  | X |  |
|  | 1.656 | Sat Nov 13 | MD |  | X |  |
| 1791 |  |  |  |  |  |  |
|  | 1.663 | Sun Jan 7 | VA | X |  |  |
|  | 1.665 | Wed Jan 26 | NC | X |  |  |
|  | 1.665 | Fri Jan 28 | NC | X |  |  |
|  | 1.665 | Tue Feb 1 | NC | X |  |  |
|  | 1.674 | Wed May 20 | PA |  | X | X |
|  | 1.675 | Mon May 30 | NY |  | X | X |
|  | 1.687 | Sat Jul 9 | MA | X |  |  |
|  | 1.687 | Sun Jul 10 | MA | X |  |  |
|  | 1.691 | Sun Aug 7 | NY | X |  |  |
|  | 1.691 | Sat Aug 13 | NY | X | X | X |
|  | 1.692 | Sat Aug 27 | NY | X | X | X |
|  | 1.694 | Fri Sep 16 | NJ | X |  |  |
|  | 1.695 | Wed Sep 28 | PA | X |  |  |
|  | 1.695 | Fri Oct 14 | DE |  | X | X |
|  | 1.696 | Sat Oct 15 | VA |  | X |  |
|  | 1.697 | Wed Nov 2 | MD |  | X | X |
|  | 1.697 | Sun Nov 6 | MD |  | X | X |
| 1792 |  |  |  |  |  |  |
|  | 1.709 | Sun Mar 18 | NC |  | X |  |
|  | 1.714 | Sun May 20 | VA | X |  | X |
|  | 1.717 | Sun Jun 24 | VA |  | X | X |
|  | 1.724 | Sun Aug 5 | MA |  | X | X |
|  | 1.725 | Wed Aug 15 | NY | X |  |  |
|  | 1.728 | Sun Aug 26 | NY | X | X | X |
|  | 1.728 | Fri Aug 31 | NY | X | X | X |
|  | 1.728 | Sun Sep 2 | NY | X | X | X |
|  | 1.729 | Sun Sep 9 | PA |  | X | X |
|  | 1.730 | Mon Sep 10 | DE |  | X | X |

| Year | Page | Date | Location | Eucharist | Love Feast | Quarterly Meeting |
|---|---|---|---|---|---|---|
| | 1.731 | Thu Sep 20 | DE | | X | |
| | 1.731 | Fri Sep 21 | DE | | X | |
| | 1.732 | Thu Sep 27 | VA | | X | X |
| | 1.733 | Sun Oct 14 | MD | | X | X |
| | 1.738 | Wed Dec 26 | SC | X | | X |
| 1793 | | | | | | |
| | 1.744 | Sun Jan 13 | GA | X | X | X |
| | 1.750 | Sun Mar 17 | NC | X | X | X |
| | 1.756 | Sun Apr 21 | KY | X | X | X |
| | 1.756 | Sun Apr 28 | KY | X | X | |
| | 1.758 | Sat May 18 | VA | X | | |
| | 1.765 | Sun Jul 21 | NY | | X | |
| | 1.767 | Sun Aug 4 | MA | X | | X |
| | 1.771 | Sun Sep 15 | DE | | X | X |
| | 1.771 | Sun Sep 22 | VA | | X | X |
| | 1.773 | Sat Oct 19 | MD | | X | X |
| | 1.774 | Sun Nov 10 | VA | X | | |
| 1794 | | | | | | |
| | 2.6 | Tue Feb 25 | SC | | X | |
| | 2.14 | Sun May 18 | VA | X | X | X |
| | 2.16 | Sun Jun 1 | VA | X | | X |
| | 2.16 | Mon Jun 9 | VA | X | | |
| | 2.19 | Sun Jul 5 | NY | X | | |
| | 2.20 | Sun Jul 13 | CT | | X | |
| | 2.21 | Sun Jul 20 | MA | X | X | X |
| | 2.22 | Sun Aug 3 | CT | X | X | |
| | 2.25 | Sun Aug 24 | CT | X | | |
| | 2.26 | Sun Aug 31 | CT | X | | |
| | 2.26 | Sun Sep 7 | MA | X | | X |
| | 2.28 | Sun Sep 14 | NY | X | | X |
| | 2.28 | Fri Sep 26 | NY | | X | X |
| | 2.31 | Sun Oct 26 | MD | | X | X |
| | 2.32 | Sun Nov 9 | VA | X | X | X |

APPENDIX C

| Year | Page | Date | Location | Eucharist | Love Feast | Quarterly Meeting |
|---|---|---|---|---|---|---|
| | 2.32 | Sun Nov 16 | VA | | X | X |
| | 2.34 | Thu Dec 11 | VA | X | | |
| 1795 | | | | | | |
| | 2.43 | Wed Feb 25 | SC | | XX | |
| | 2.44 | Sun Mar 1 | SC | X | | |
| | 2.45 | Sun Mar 22 | SC | | X | |
| | 2.46 | Wed Mar 25 | SC | X | | |
| | 2.47 | Sun Apr 19 | NC | X | | |
| | 2.50 | Sun May 17 | VA | X | X | X |
| | 2.52 | Sat Jun 13 | MD | | X | X |
| | 2.55 | Sun Jul 5 | NY | X | | |
| | 2.57 | Sun Aug 2 | MA | X | | |
| | 2.58 | Sun Aug 9 | MA | X | | |
| | 2.61 | Sun Aug 30 | NY | X | X | X |
| | 2.61 | Sun Sep 6 | NY | X | X | X |
| | 2.65 | Sun Nov 1 | MD | X | | |
| | 2.71 | Thu Dec 31 | SC | | X | |
| 1796 | | | | | | |
| | 2.75 | Sun Jan 3 | SC | X | | X |
| | 2.77 | Wed Feb 3 | SC | | X | |
| | 2.77 | Fri Feb 5 | SC | X | X | |
| | 2.79 | Fri Mar 4 | SC | X | | |
| | 2.82 | Mon Apr 11 | NC | (X)* | | |
| | 2.91 | Fri Jul 22 | DE | | X | |
| | 2.95 | Sun Aug 21 | NY | X | | |
| | 2.96 | Sun Sep 4 | NY | | X | |
| | 2.97 | Sat Sep 10 | CT | X | X | X |
| | 2.98 | Sun Sep 18 | CT | X | X | |
| | 2.105 | Sun Nov 27 | VA | X | | |
| | 2.106 | Thu Dec 1 | VA | X | | |
| | 2.107 | Wed Dec 7 | NC | X | | |
| | 2.110 | Thu Dec 29 | SC | X | | |

# FRANCIS ASBURY'S EUCHARISTIC CELEBRATIONS 1785–1800

| Year | Page | Date | Location | Eucharist | Love Feast | Quarterly Meeting |
|---|---|---|---|---|---|---|
| 1797 | | | | | | |
| | 2.118 | Fri Feb 10 | SC | | X | |
| | 2.118 | Sun Feb 12 | SC | (X)** | | |
| | 2.121 | Sun Feb 26 | SC | X | | |
| | 2.122 | Sun Mar 5 | SC | X | X | |
| | 2.124 | Tue Mar 21 | NC | X | | |
| | 2.139 | Mon Nov 13 | VA | X | | |
| 1798 | | | | | | |
| | 2.156 | Tue Apr 3 | VA | X | | |
| | 2.156 | Thu Apr 5 | VA | X | | |
| | 2.161 | Sun Jun 17 | NY | | X | |
| | 2.177 | Sun Nov 11 | NC | X | | |
| 1799 | | | | | | |
| | 2.184 | Sun Jan 20 | SC | | XX | |
| | 2.187 | Wed Feb 27 | NC | X | | |
| | 2.188 | Sun Mar 10 | NC | X | | |
| | 2.190 | Sun Mar 24 | VA | X | | |
| | 2.192 | Wed May 1 | MD | X | | X |
| | 2.193 | Sun May 12 | MD | X | | |
| | 2.203 | Sun Aug 18 | VA | X | X | |
| | 2.205 | Wed Sep 1 | VA | X | | |
| | 2.212 | Tue Nov 12 | SC | | X | |
| | 2.213 | Sat Nov 16 | SC | X | X | |
| | 2.214 | Sun Nov 24 | GA | X | X | X |
| | 2.215 | Sat Dec 7 | GA | X | X | X |
| 1800 | | | | | | |
| | 2.222 | Sun Jan 5 | SC | X | | |
| | 2.223 | Sun Jan 26 | SC | X | | |
| | 2.224 | Sun Feb 16 | SC | X | | |
| | 2.229 | Fri Apr 4 | VA | X | | |
| | 2.229 | Sun Apr 6 | VA | XX | | |
| | 2.234 | Sun Jun 1 | DE | | X | |
| | 2.238 | Sun Jul 6 | CT | X | | |

| Year | Page | Date | Location | Eucharist | Love Feast | Quarterly Meeting |
|---|---|---|---|---|---|---|
| | 2.243 | Sun Aug 3 | CT | | X | X |
| | 2.243 | Sun Aug 10 | NY | X | | |
| | 2.252 | Sun Sep 28 | TN | X | | |
| | 2.257 | Sun Oct 20 | TN | X | | Camp meeting |
| | 2.266 | Sun Nov 23 | SC | X | | |
| | 2.268 | Sun Dec 7 | GA | X | | X |
| | 2.270 | Sun Dec 14 | GA | X | | |
| | 2.271 | Wed Dec 17 | SC | X | X | X |

\* 2.82—Asbury would have celebrated the sacrament but someone had brought brandy instead of wine; therefore he refused.

\*\* 2.118—Asbury did not record administering the sacrament, but he gave an elaborate (for him) detail of the sermon he preached in which he exhorted those present to utilize all the means of grace including the sacraments.

# Bibliography

Andrews, Dee E. *The Methodists and Revolutionary America, 1760–1800: The Shaping of an Evangelical Culture*. Princeton: Princeton University Press, 2000.
Asbury, Francis. *The Causes, Evils, and Cures of Heart and Church Divisions*. New York: J. Soule and T. Mason, 1817.
———. *The Journal and Letters of Francis Asbury*. Edited by Elmer T. Clark. Nashville: Abingdon, 1958.
———. *The Journal of the Rev. Francis Asbury, Bishop of the Methodist Episcopal Church*. New York: N. Bangs and T. Mason, 1821.
Asbury, Herbert. *A Methodist Saint: The Life of Bishop Asbury*. New York: Alfred A. Knopf, 1927.
Bainton, Roland. *The Reformation of the Sixteenth Century*. Boston: Beacon, 1985.
Baker, Frank. *Methodism and the Love-Feast*. London: Epworth, 1957.
———. *Representative Verse of Charles Wesley*. Nashville: Abingdon, 1962.
Bangs, Nathan. *The History of the Methodist Episcopal Church*. New York: T. Mason and G. Lane, 1836.
Baxter, Richard. *The Cure of Church Divisions*. London: Nevil Symmons, 1670.
Bonhoeffer, Dietrich. *The Cost of Discipleship*. New York: Macmillan, 1959.
Borgen, Ole E. *John Wesley on the Sacraments*. Nashville: Abingdon, 1972.
Bowmer, John C. *The Sacrament of the Lord's Supper in Early Methodism*. Westminster: Dacre, 1951.
Brevint, Daniel. *The Christian Sacrament and Sacrifice by way of discourse, meditation and prayer upon the nature, parts and blessings of the Holy Communion: Thrid* [sic] *Edition*. London: J. Walthoe, R. Wilkin, J. and J. Bonwike, S. Birt, T. Osborne, and E. Wicksteed, 1739.
Burroughes, Jeremiah. *Irenicum to the Lovers of Truth and Peace: Heart-Divisions opened In the causes and evils of them: with Cautions that we many not be hurt by them, And Endeavours to heal them*. London: Robert Dawlman, 1653.
Calvin, John. *Institutes of Christian Religion*. Edited by John T. McNeill. Library of Christian Classics 20–21. Philadelphia: Westminster, 1960.
———. "Short Treatise on the Holy Supper of Our Lord and Only Savior Jesus Christ." In *Calvin: Theological Treatises*, 140–66. The Library of Christian Classics 22. Philadelphia: Westminster, 1954.
Chilcote, Paul W. *Early Methodist Spirituality: Selected Women's Writings*. Nashville: Kingswood, 2007.

Chiles, Robert E. *Theological Transition in American Methodism: 1790–1935*. New York: Abingdon, 1965.
Church, Leslie. *The Early Methodist People*. London: Epworth, 1948.
Coke, Thomas. *The Journals of Dr. Thomas Coke*. Edited by John A. Vickers. Nashville: Kingswood, 2005.
Coke, Thomas, and Henry Moore. *Life of the Rev. John Wesley, A.M. Including an Account of the Great Revival of Religion in Europe and America, of which He was the First and Chief Instrument*. Philadelphia: Parry Hall, 1793.
Coleman, Robert E. *Nothing to Do But to Save Souls*. Grand Rapids: Francis Asbury, 1990.
Cooney, Dudley Levistone. *The Methodists in Ireland: A Short History*. Dublin: Columbia, 2001.
Coxe, A. Cleveland, Alexander Roberts, and James Donaldson, eds. *The Apostolic Fathers with Justin Martyr and Irenaeus*. Ante-Nicene Fathers 1. Peabody, MA: Hendrickson, 1995.
Crowther, Jonathan. *A True and Complete Portraiture of Methodism*. New York: Daniel Hitt and Thomas Ware, 1813.
Daniels, W. H. *The Illustrated History of Methodism*. New York: Methodist Book Concern, 1879.
Davies, Horton. *Worship and Theology in England: From Cranmer to Baxter and Fox, 1534–1690*. Vol. 1. Grand Rapids: Eerdmans, 1996.
———. *Worship and Theology in England: From Watts and Wesley to Martineau, 1860–1900*. Vol. 2. Grand Rapids: Eerdmans, 1996.
———. *Worship and Theology in England: The Ecumenical Century, 1900 to the Present*. Vol. 3. Grand Rapids: Eerdmans, 1996.
Davies, Julian. *The Caroline Captivity of the Church: Charles I and the Remoulding of Anglicanism*. Oxford: Clarendon, 1992.
Dix, Gregory. *The Shape of the Liturgy*. London: Dacre Press, 1945.
Eslinger, Ellen. *Citizens of Zion: The Social Origins of Camp Meeting Revivalism*. Knoxville: University of Tennessee Press, 1999.
Garrettson, Freeborn. *American Methodist Pioneer: The Life and Journals of The Rev. Freeborn Garrettson, 1752–1827*. Edited by Robert Drew Simpson. Rutland, VT: Academy, 1984.
Gatch, George. *Biography of Philip Gatch*. Philip Gatch Papers [microform]. Chicago: University of Chicago Library, 1965.
Gatch, Philip. Papers [microform]. Chicago: University of Chicago Library, 1965.
Grimm, Harold J. *The Reformation Era: 1500–1650*. New York: Macmillan, 1965.
Hatch, Nathan O. *The Democratization of American Christianity*. New Haven: Yale University Press, 1989.
Hatch, Nathan O., and John H. Wigger. *Methodism and the Shaping of American Culture*. Nashville: Kingswood, 2001.
Heitzenrater, Richard P. *Wesley and the People Called Methodists*. Nashville: Abingdon, 1995.
Hillerbrand, Hans J. *The Division of Christendom: Christianity in the Sixteenth Century*. Louisville: Westminster John Knox, 2007.
Hitt, Daniel, and Thomas Ware, eds. *Minutes of the Methodist Conferences Annually Held in America from 1773 to 1813 Inclusive*. New York: Daniel Hitt and Thomas Ware, 1813. Reprint, Swainsboro, GA: Magnolia, 1983.

Hyde, A. B. *The Story of Methodism*. Springfield, MA: Willey, 1888.
Jarratt, Devereux, *Life of the Reverend Devereux Jarratt*. Baltimore: Warner & Hanna, 1806.
*Journals of the General Conference of the Methodist Episcopal Church: Vol. 1, 1796–1836*. New York: Carlton & Lanahan, 1836.
Kidd, Thomas S. *The Great Awakening: The Roots of Evangelical Christianity in Colonial America*. New Haven: Yale University Press, 2007.
Kinghorn, Kenneth *The Heritage of American Methodism*. Strasbourg: Éditions du Signe, 1999.
Knight, Henry H., III. *The Presence of God in the Christian Life: John Wesley and the Means of Grace*. Lanham, MD: Scarecrow, 1992.
Larkins, Jessie Shuman. "John Wesley Among the Colonies: Wesleyan Theology in the Face of the American Revolution." *Methodist History* 45/4 (2007) 232–43.
Lee, Jesse. *A Short History of the Methodists in the United States of America*. Baltimore: Magill and Clime, 1810.
Louth, Andrew. *Greek East and Latin West, AD 681–1071*. Church in History 3. Crestwood, NY: St. Vladimir's Seminary Press, 2007.
Luther, Martin, and Timothy F. Lull, eds. *Martin Luther's Basic Theological Writings*. Minneapolis: Fortress, 1989.
Maddox, Randy. "Social Grace: The Eclipse of the Church as a Means of Grace in American Methodism." In *Methodism in Its Cultural Milieu*, edited by Tim Macquiban, 131–60. Oxford: Applied Theology, 1994.
McEllhenney, John G., ed. *United Methodism in America: A Compact History*. Nashville: Abingdon, 1992.
McTyeire, Holland N. *A History of Methodism*. Nashville: Publishing House of the ME Church South, 1884.
*Methodist Magazine for the Year of our Lord 1823: Volume VI*. New York: N. Bangs and T. Mason, 1823.
*Methodist Review: Volume LXIX*. New York: Phillips & Hurt, 1887.
Noll, Mark A. *A History of Christianity in the United States and Canada*. Grand Rapids: Eerdmans, 1992.
Norwood, Frederick A. *The Story of American Methodism*. Nashville: Abingdon, 1974.
O'Collins, Gerald, and Mario Farrugia. *Catholicism: The Story of Catholic Christianity*. Oxford: Oxford University Press, 2003.
Ormond, William. Papers. Special Collections Library, Duke University Library, Durham, North Carolina.
Outler, Albert. *John Wesley*. Oxford: Oxford University Press, 1964.
Paine, Robert. *Life and Times of William McKendree Bishop of the Methodist Episcopal Church*. Nashville: Publishing House of the ME Church, South, 1869. Digital edition: Holiness Data Ministry, 1998.
Parham, Stith. Papers. Special Collections Library, Duke University Library, Durham, North Carolina.
Phoebus, George A. *Beams of Light: Earl Methodism in America: Chiefly Drawn from the Diary, Letters, Manuscripts, Documents, and Original Tracts of the Rev. Ezekiel Cooper*. New York: Phillips & Hunt, 1887.
Pilmore, Joseph. *The Journal of Joseph Pilmore*. Edited by Frederick E. Maser. Philadelphia: Message, 1969.
Potter, G. R. *Zwingli*. Cambridge: Cambridge University Press, 1976.

*Queen Elizabeth's Prayer Book or The Book of Common Prayer and Administration of the Sacraments.* London: Chiswick, 1863.

Rattenbury, J. Ernest. *The Eucharistic Hymns of John and Charles Wesley.* London: Epworth, 1948.

Richey, Russell E. *Early American Methodism.* Bloomington: Indiana University Press, 1991.

Richey, Russell E., and Kenneth E. Rowe, eds. *Rethinking Methodist History: A Bicentennial Historical Consultation.* Nashville: Kingswood, 1985.

Richey, Russell E., Kenneth E. Rowe, and Jean Miller Schmidt, eds. *The Methodist Experience in America.* Vol. 2, *A Sourcebook.* Nashville: Abingdon, 2000.

———, eds. *Perspectives on American Methodism: Interpretive Essays.* Nashville: Kingswood, 1993.

Rogers, Hester Ann. *Account of the Experiences of Hester Ann Rogers.* New York: T. Mason and G. Lane, 1837.

Ruth, Lester. *Early Methodist Life and Spirituality: A Reader.* Nashville: Kingswood, 2005.

———. "A Little Heaven Below: The Love Feast and Lord's Supper in Early American Methodism." Edited by Michael Mattei. Wesley Center for Applied Theology, 2003.

———. *A Little Heaven Below: Worship at Early Methodist Quarterly Meetings.* Nashville: Kingswood, 2000.

———. "A Reconsideration of the Frequency of the Eucharist in Early American Methodism." *Methodist History* 34/1 (1995) 47–58.

Schmidt, Leigh Eric. *Holy Fairs: Scottish Communions and American Revivals in the Early Modern Period.* Princeton: Princeton University Press, 1989.

Scott, Leland Howard. "Methodist Theology in America in the Nineteenth Century." PhD diss., Yale University, 1954.

Simpson, Matthew, ed. *Cyclopedia of Methodism.* Philadelphia: Everts & Stewart, 1878.

———. *A Hundred Years of Methodism.* New York: Phillips & Hunt, 1881.

Stamps, Robert Julian. "The Sacrament of the Word Made Flesh: The Eucharistic Theology of Thomas F. Torrance." PhD diss., St. John's College, Nottingham/University of Nottingham, 1986.

Stevens, Abel. *A Compendious History of American Methodism.* New York: Hunt and Eaton, 1867.

———. *History of the Methodist Episcopal Church in the United States of America.* 3 vols. New York: Carlton & Lanahan, 1864.

———. *Life and Times of Nathan Bangs.* New York: Carlton & Porter, 1863. Digital edition: Holiness Data Ministry, 1996.

Stevick, Daniel B. *The Altar's Fire: Charles Wesley's Hymns on the Lord's Supper, 1745 Introduction and Exposition.* London: Epworth, 2004.

Sweet, William Warren. *Methodism in American History.* Nashville: Abingdon, 1961.

———. *Religion in the Development of American Culture, 1765–1840.* New York: Scribner's, 1952.

Tigert, John James. *A Constitutional History of American Episcopal Methodism.* Nashville: Publishing House of the ME Church South, 1894.

Tucker, Karen B. Westerfield. *American Methodist Worship.* Oxford: Oxford University Press, 2001.

Tuckniss, Henry, ed. *The Doctrines and Disciplines of the Methodist Episcopal Church in America with Explanatory Notes by Thomas Coke and Francis Asbury.* Philadelphia:

Henry Tuckniss, 1798. Reprint ed., Evanston, IL: Garrett-Evangelical Theological Seminary, 1979.
Tuttle, Robert G., Jr. *John Wesley: His Life and Theology*. Grand Rapids: Zondervan, 1978.
———. *On Giant Shoulders*. Nashville: Discipleship Resources, 1984.
———. *The Story of Evangelism: A History of the Witness to the Gospel*. Nashville: Abingdon, 2006.
Wade, William Nash. "A History of Public Worship in the Methodist Episcopal Church and Methodist Episcopal Church, South, From 1784 to 1905." PhD diss., University of Notre Dame, 1981.
Wakeley, J. B. *Lost Chapters Recovered from the Early History of American Methodism*. New York: Carlton & Porter, 1858.
Walker, Williston, et al. *A History of the Christian Church*. 4th ed. New York: Scribner, 1985.
Ware, Thomas. "The Christmas Conference of 1784." *Methodist Magazine and Quarterly Review* 14 (January 1832) 96–104.
———. *Sketches of the Life and Travels of Rev. Thomas Ware*. New York: T. Mason and G. Lane, 1839.
Ware, Timothy. *The Orthodox Church*. London: Penguin, 1997.
Watson, Richard. *The Life of Rev. John Wesley*. New York: Lane & Scott, 1850.
Watters, William. *A Short Account of the Christian Experience and Ministerial Labors of William Watters*. Alexandria, VA: S. Snowden, 1808. Digital edition: Holiness Data Ministry, 1998.
Webber, Robert E. *Ancient-Future Worship: Proclaiming and Enacting God's Narrative*. Grand Rapids: Baker, 2008.
Wesley, Charles. *Hymns on the Lord's Supper*. Bristol, UK: Felix Farley, 1745. Facsimile. Madison, NJ: Charles Wesley Society, 1995.
Wesley, John. *The Bicentennial Edition of the Works of John Wesley*. Edited by Frank Baker and Richard P. Heitzenrater. Nashville: Abingdon, 1976–.
———. *Explanatory Notes Upon the New Testament*. New York: Carlton & Porter, 1855.
———. *The Journal of the Rev. John Wesley, A.M.* Edited by Nehemiah Curnock. London: Robert Cully, 1909.
———. *Ordination Certificate of Thomas Coke, 1784*. Letters and Manuscripts of the Wesley Family from the Collections of Drew University. Drew University Methodist Library.
———. *The Sunday Service of the Methodists in North America*. London, 1784. Reprint, *John Wesley's Prayer Book: The Sunday Service of the Methodists in North America*. Edited by James F. White. Akron: OSL, 1991.
———. *The Works of John Wesley*. Edited by Thomas Jackson. 14 vols. 3rd ed. London: Wesleyan Methodist Book Room, 1872. Reprinted, Grand Rapids: Baker, 2002.
Whatcoat, Richard. *To Go and Serve the Desolate Sheep in America: The Diary/Journal of Bishop Richard Whatcoat*. Edited by Samuel J. Rogal. Bethesda, MD: Academica, 2001.
Whitaker, Timothy W. "A Sacramental Piety." Edited by Larry Jent. *Virginia United Methodist Advocate*. United Methodist Newsletter for the Virginia Annual Conference. 2003.
White, James F. *The Sacraments in Protestant Practice and Faith*. Nashville: Abingdon, 1999.

Whitehead, John. *The Life of the Rev. John Wesley*. Boston: Hill & Brodhead, 1846.

Wigger, John H. *Taking Heaven by Storm: Methodism and the Rise of Popular Christianity in America*. New York: Oxford University Press, 1998.

Williams, William Henry. *The Garden of American Methodism: The Delmarva Peninsula 1769–1820*. Wilmington, DE: Scholarly Resources, 1984.

Yrigoyen, Charles. *John Wesley: Holiness of Heart and Life*. Nashville: Abingdon, 1999.

www.ingramcontent.com/pod-product-compliance
Lightning Source LLC
Chambersburg PA
CBHW052058230426
43662CB00036B/1436